Y0-BUP-091

The
Sociology
of
Religion

The
Sociology
of
Religion
A Bibliographical Survey

Compiled by
Roger Homan

G. E. Gorman, *Advisory Editor*

Bibliographies and Indexes in Religious Studies, Number 9

Greenwood Press
New York • Westport, Connecticut • London

Library of Congress Cataloging-in-Publication Data

Homan, Roger.
  The sociology of religion.

  (Bibliographies and indexes in religious studies,
ISSN 0742-6836 ; no. 9)
  Includes indexes.
  1. Religion and sociology—Bibliography.
2. Religion and sociology. I. Gorman, G. E.
II. Title. III. Series.
Z7831.H65 1986 [BL60]   016.306'6   86-18471
ISBN 0-313-24710-2 (lib. bdg. : alk. paper)

Library of Congress Catalog Card Number: 86-18471
ISBN: 0-313-24710-2
ISSN: 0742-6836

First published in 1986

Greenwood Press, Inc.
88 Post Road West, Westport, Connecticut 06881

Printed in the United States of America

The paper used in this book complies with the
Permanent Paper Standard issued by the National
Information Standards Organization (Z39.48-1984).

10 9 8 7 6 5 4 3 2 1

Contents

Foreword

As part of the Greenwood Press series entitled Bibliographies and Indexes in Religious Studies, we have developed a subsidiary series of bibliographic surveys dealing with a broad range of topics in religion and theology. The purpose of these surveys is to cover both general disciplines and discrete subjects of interest to the scholarly community which have not received detailed treatment in recent years. Each work is meant to stand as a self-contained unit, and consists of a substantial introduction to the subject, viewed through the literature, plus an annotated guide to serial and monograph literature which the author believes is important for an adequate understanding of the topic. The first part of each volume, the introductory essay or survey chapter, discusses the development of the subject in terms of key concepts and seminal or controversial works; the bibliography which follows this analysis is intended to substantiate and extend the introductory remarks by surveying a widely representative sample of literature from all traditions and viewpoints related to the topic.

Within this framework the Advisory Editor had two ideals in mind: first, to cover all traditions, Western and non-Western, which might fit the most generous definition of "religion"; second, to devise a series of subject-oriented volumes which, within a given discipline, would range from the general to the specific, in order to provide a thorough survey of all areas and segments of a subject. The former ideal is, we believe, approaching realization, with volumes in preparation or under consideration on a wide range of religious and quasi-religious subjects—from monotheistic religions to civil religion and beyond. However, the second ideal is proving more difficult to attain, in part because many specialist scholars today feel unable to tackle with any certainty or authority the broad outlines of their disciplines. More than this, the problem also lies within the very nature of religious studies; disciplinary boundaries are constantly shifting and expanding, and interdisciplinary studies are creating uncertainties—not to mention exciting possibilities—where there was once general agreement about traditional subject parameters. For these and a variety of other reasons, most of us feel comfortable dealing with the narrow fields in which we have particular expertise or interest, but are equally loath to tackle the wider disciplines of which these fields are but a small segment. Important as the narrow fields are, they need to be seen in relation to the wider scholarly enterprise, especially within a series such as the one under discussion.

In other words, any bibliographic series devoted to religious studies needs not only to survey the trees in the forest, but also must chart the forest itself. The volume in hand does precisely that—it charts the forest which we call the sociology of religion. Dr. Roger Homan of Brighton Polytechnic makes a valiant and, we believe, successful attempt to outline the development of the sociology of religion in bibliographic perspective. The key writers, major concepts and important developments in the subject are all discussed in Dr. Homan's volume, which we see as forming a framework upon which more closely focused volumes on the sociology of religion can be built. At this stage we are considering a number of such possibilities, with some volumes in preparation, others planned and one in print. In the last of these categories is Diane Choquette's valuable guide to new religious movements in the United States and Canada, which has obvious links to this general survey.

We hope that Roger Homan's work will be seen in this context—as charting a forest in which others will then describe specific species of interesting or important flora. We are grateful to Dr. Homan for having tackled a subject which others have hesitated to analyze in general terms and are certain that his careful, wide-ranging compilation has established the essential groundwork from which subsequent volumes might be developed. While such related works will stand on their own, we believe that Dr. Homan's survey will provide the necessary background on which a more adequate understanding, especially for the non-expert, needs to be based.

G. E. Gorman
Advisory Editor
Riverina-Murray Institute of Higher Education
Wagga Wagga NSW Australia

Preface

Even as bundles of papers and boxes of cards have lain on the typist's desk, shelves, window sills and floor, waiting to be worked into a presentable form, I have found myself borrowing sequences back to use in teaching and research. It follows first, that I am now rather more convinced of the usefulness of this project than I was when I embarked upon it, and second, that I want to express particular appreciation to the Reverend Gary Gorman who prompted and directed this assignment and to Kathleen Moxon who was unbewildered by the litter with which I encompassed her desk. My comparably long-suffering wife Caroline endured such conditions at home and gave up hours of her evenings to read to me. Every writer's spouse will know the feeling, and every writer will know why a preface must begin with an acknowledgement.

The product of their patience is presented in the following pages. The core of the work is the annotated bibliography which is intended to range across the concerns which engage sociologists of religion; in doing so it touches upon the scope of other titles in this series. The thousand items in the listing are selected by a cluster of criteria that include their significance within the field, date of publication and accessibility. Books and journal articles qualify for inclusion, but conference papers do not. Only in special cases have we included works published more than two decades ago. The details given in the leading reference are normally those of original publication, but entries also include notes of more accessible appearances, such as translations into English, where known.

The compartments of sociology are not mutually exclusive. The problem of knowing in what section of the bibliography to classify particular items has been at times agonizing. Where there is a discrepancy between the emphasis of the title and the preoccupation of the content, classification has been according to the latter. The three comprehensive indices, listing titles, authors and major subjects treated, are intended to facilitate consultation of the bibliography by students with particular needs.

The essay which precedes the bibliography offers an overview of the sociology of religion, but makes no pretense to be a work of vision or to present a new thesis. Indeed, it might be said that the value of this book resides in, of all places, the Subject Index. That index exposes, for example, the enrichment of the sociology of religion that might follow the adoption of a comparative dimension. Such themes as the clerical profession and the liturgical movement have been narrowly observed, yet there are compelling universals to be identified and explained. What is more, sociologists of religion are as guilty as any students in searching the pages of a narrow range of journals for material in their field. It has been possible in the bibliography to bring to their notice many items that might have eluded them by being published in journals on, for example, race, family studies or sociology in non-Anglophone countries. All readers will lament the omission of a cherished work, but it is hoped that as many will be able herein to make new discoveries within their specialized fields.

The
Sociology
of
Religion

The Sociology of Religion: Retrospect and Prospect

FOUNDATIONS OF THE SOCIOLOGY OF RELIGION

As its name implies, the sociology of religion represents the
application of a discipline to a discrete sphere of human experience.
The concerns and categories which occupy sociologists in other fields
occupy sociologists of religion also. Sociologists are broadly
interested in groups within society and the interrelationships between
the two levels. In the sociology of religion the interrelationships
are between the state, the community, the secular domain and the sphere
of everyday life on the one hand and religious organizations,
communities, ideologies and leaders on the other. The division of
society according to caste, social class or some other means of
stratification is a seminal concern of sociology, and it is a major
theme in the sociological study of religion.

The perception of the sociology of religion as a branch of applied
sociology is, however, a recent one. In the classical and formative
years of the discipline religion was the object of study not because
it represented a specialization within the study of society nor even
because it exhibited the range of characteristics that were necessary
for the systematization of the discipline. It was rather because of

the integration of religion within the societies chosen for study.
In the leading work of the French sociologist Emile Durkheim (0064)
sociology was developed with respect to relatively primitive
societies in which, in Durkheim's observation, religion provided
the symbols of cultural integration. Max Weber, too, while
identifying the sociology of religion as a peculiar enterprise
(0069), observed social conditions in which religion was a factor
of such magnitude that no sociological study could proceed without
attention to it. For example, it was the religious sphere that
furnished the model of charisma that features so prominently in
Weber's archetypal analysis of authority.

With the demise of religion as a factor in public life in
Western societies, it has become less compelling a theme of
sociological study. Whereas for Durkheim sociology was the
sociology of religion, today it is as marginal as the sociology
of work, the sociology of art, music and literature, the sociology
of leisure, political sociology, women's studies, the sociology of
education and so on. Sociology has become fragmented and
specialized, and the sociology of religion is but a fragment and a
special application.

Nor has the sociology of religion maintained its formerly high
place in the estimations of the religious organizations themselves.
As is more fully explained below, the faithful and their
intellectuals are inclined to reject sociological approaches on the
grounds that they miss the point of religious behavior or provide
evidence that inhibits procedures authorized at a supernatural

level.   Sociology was formerly deployed in the service of the churches
and in the investigation of its own questions (*sociologie religieuse*)
but is now emancipated from that yoke.

MARX, DURKHEIM AND WEBER

It is, of course, invidious to distinguish the fathers of the
sociology of religion from those of the following generation who
inaugurated identifiable and enduring traditions.   Nevertheless, Marx,
Durkheim and Weber warrant special attention because they are
responsible for the seminal ideas, interpretations, categories and
problems which have occupied so many latter-day practitioners and
which account for the greater part of the material annotated in the
ensuing bibliography.

The contribution of Karl Marx to the sociology of religion is
disproportionate to the attention he gave it.   His examination of
religion was incidental yet deeply insightful.   There are three
themes in Marx's critique which survive as major concerns in present
day sociology of religion.   First, his concern with the social class
structure of Western societies contributes what is arguably the major
variable in the study of religious organizations.   In Western
societies the Christian churches have engaged the middle classes more
effectively than the working classes (Hazelrigg, 0196; MacLaren, 0206)
and the world-rejecting sect-type has traditionally (Dynes, 0308 but
see Beckford, 0305) been identified as the religion of the dispossessed.
In recent years the problematic relationship of social class and
religious activity has been explored in terms of the class composition
of church membership (Mueller, 0210) and attendance of religious

meetings (Clelland, 0186) and the alignment of Church and class in contexts as varied as Victorian sabbatarianism (Homan, 0198) and the politics of Latin America.

Secondly, the expectation of Marx and his followers that religion would wither away together with other apparatuses of the State once socialism had been achieved provides a theme that has at times been exclusive in the sociological study of religion conducted within the Soviet Union and Eastern Europe.   In the Western literature of secularization there is at times a mood of lamentation (Isambert, 0656), while in communist societies the demise of religion is celebrated as proof of marxist theory and of the adequacy of the incumbent political regime (Bokhorova, 0306; De Neve, 0646; Moskalev, 0151).   In the Polish sociology of religion, which is constituted of both atheist and Catholic elements, the evidence of secularization varies according to the instruments used to investigate it: Catholic perceptions include Wierzbicki (0176 and 0637) and Zdaniewicz (0181) while atheist interpretations are evident in the work of Hieronim Kubiak (0659).

Durkheim's influence in the current sociology of religion is not in the contribution of an unassailable model of analysis but in what he places on the agenda and in his normative functionalist approach. The sacred-profane distinction is an important Durkheimian bequest which pervades what is possibly the major concern of the sociology of religion in the postwar years, that of secularization.   The current sociological critique of liturgical reform (0825 - 0850) owes much to the functionalist perspective and is adjacent to the analysis

of ritual in modern anthropology.   The problematic relations of
religion and the State and the pervasive influence of religion in
everyday life (which feature as sections E and H of the ensuing
bibliography) operate and complicate Durkheim's statement with
respect to a more simple society.   The functions of solidarity and
differentiation are widely explored in the sociological study of
sects (0320 - 0466).   Whether directly or indirectly, Emile
Durkheim's insight and his perspective are recognizable across this
broad range of current concerns.   A useful compilation of the work
of Durkheim on religion and of the major contributions to the
ensuing debate, together with a comprehensive bibliography, is
provided by W.S.F.Pickering (0078).

Max Weber deserves a still more enthusiastic testimony than
Durkheim for the sociological character of his work, for the wider
range of its orientations, for its survival in modern sociology and
for the magnitude of recent work which owes its inspiration to Weber.
The recognized persistence of religion in some societies which
claim to be socialist is therefore an embarrassment for marxist
fundamentalists: it is explained in the way that Lenin accounted for
the survival of capitalism by adaptation to changing social
conditions.

Thirdly, Marx criticized religion on the basis of its social
function which was, in his judgment, to dissipate social action by
offering the hope of a better and eternal life to those who endure a
miserable existence in this world.   In Marx's phrase, religion was
the "opiate of the people", in Lenin's it was the "intoxicant".

This penetrating critique was based on evidence from a wide range of religions in Asia, of Islam and of the Christian church in the mid-nineteenth century.   It is an insight that features in the sociological study of religious sects as rejected and dispossessed communities.   But more important, it has been taken on board by many of the mainstream churches, and Marx's thought is predominant in the posture and "liberation theology" of sections of the Roman Catholic Church in central America (0168, 0199).   Durkheim and Weber belong to the classical period of sociology which is reckoned to have run from about 1890 until about 1920.

In common with the opium theme of Marx's critique, Emile Durkheim's work is occupied not with the veracity or otherwise of religious belief but with what it does in a given society.   But whereas Marx's interpretation leads to a rejection of religous belief, Durkheim's constitutes a demonstration of its necessity or expedience.   Durkheim's sociology of religion is developed in *Les Formes Élémentaires de la Vie Religieuse* (0064), first published in 1912.   The major reference of Durkheim's work is Australian aboriginal religion, which he calls totemism.   The totem is the emblem in which each aboriginal clan celebrates its own identity in the fashion of the national flag in the United States and other countries the world over.   Worship, in Durkheim's analysis, is directed at the society, community or clan, but because this is too complex and abstract a phenomenon to engage, it is expressed in an adherence to symbols.   It follows that the social function of religion most noticed in Durkheim's account is that of integration, solidarity or cohesion.   Insofar as solidarity is achieved within a discrete community such as a clan, totemism also performs the function of social differentiation: it has exclusive as well as inclusive dimensions.   The appreciation of primitive societies or tribes as independent communities unified in the rehearsal of religious ritual has proven very appealing to social anthropologists, and the influence of Durkheim may be seen in the work of Bronislaw Malinowski and others.

Within sociology, however, there are certain problems in Durkheim's account.   It is arguable whether the totem is a religious symbol or, at least, whether one should regard as religious its counterparts in more complex societies.   Durkheim's classification of sacred and profane domains of human experience is applied by him to aboriginal society by the criteria of access or prohibition with respect to commonly recognized symbols; in more advanced societies there are prohibitions within the secular domain, while explicitly religious symbols are openly accessible.   Furthermore, Durkheim is regarded as excessive in his suggestion that religion is ultimately the workship of society and the legitimation of its norms: quite the opposite is true in the highly differentiated societies of the modern world in which sectarian religion is associated with a rejection of the prevailing values in a given society.

Like Marx, Weber was interested in the relationship of religion to economic conditions; but whereas Marx considered economic conditions as the variable upon which religion was dependent,   Weber developed the theory that these were themselves the product of religious belief and practice.   Furthermore, whereas Durkheim had observed religious practice in a comparatively static social formation,

Weber was much concerned with religion in conditions of social change.

Weber's most celebrated and compelling work in these respects is that which appears in English as *The Protestant Ethic and the Spirit of Capitalism.* Weber's method is historical, and he takes account of the social and individual values enshrined in ascetic protestantism, most notably in the form of Calvinism, and of the extension of such values in the religious beliefs lending support to the industrial revolution. The personal values he identifies in religious principles include such values as honesty, conscientiousness, frugality, thrift, avoidance of extravagance and wordly pleasure, plain taste, humility and modesty. These values are sanctified in the Beatitudes of the Christian tradition and operationalized by the protestant sects as taboos upon indulgence, entertainment, pleasure, theater, sport, cosmetics, ostentatious dress, sexual licence and all other expensive habits. These constitute the protestant ethic which for Marx and Kautsky reflects the spirit of capitalism but which for Weber has capitalism as its function. The plain life of ascetic protestantism yields a surplus value. Indeed, sociologists have been much occupied with the tendency of world-rejecting sects of the dispossessed to accrue wealth and then change their social and ideological orientation, a tendency known as "denominationalization".

Both among sociologists and historians, such as R.H.Tawney and Hugh Trevor-Roper, Weber's protestant ethic thesis has enjoyed wide appeal and has experienced periodic revision. The relationship between religion and everyday life has been researched at a more general level than that which has the economic dimension as its focus. So generalized has this element of the Weberian tradition become that in the ensuing bibliography it has not been practical to distinguish work on the protestant ethic from more global research on religion and everyday life. Among the leading and most widely noticed investigations is that of Gerhard Lenski (OO68), conducted in Detroit, Michigan. In confirmation of Weber, Lenski finds a significant difference between the economic and achievement aspirations of Protestants and those of Catholics. Achievement orientations have in recent years been frequently investigated by sociologists of religion (Fox, O244), not least because of the accessibility of suitable subjects in undergraduate communities: and among these Andrew M.Greeley's work is to be noted for his finding that there is no significant differential (O247).

Among Weber's other enduring contributions to the sociology of religion, his elaboration of ideal-types of religious organization deserves mention here, although it will be explored later as a concern of current research. The church-sect distinction corresponds in the work of early sociologists of religion to a system of social stratification. The church-type is the religion of the dominant classes and exists in harmony with prevailing secular values. The sect-type is by contrast the religion of the dispossessed and it expresses a rejection of the secular sphere which it designates as "the world". Although most sects have developed within particular historical periods, the sociologist attaches significance not so much to their historical background as to their orientation toward contemporary society.

More extensive discussion of Marx, Durkheim and Weber than is either possible or appropriate here will be found in Towler (0057), Robertson (0049) and Sharf (0051).

SECONDARY TRADITIONS

The second and subsequent generations of sociologists have produced a number of leading figures who have opened up new fields of inquiry or offered new perspectives. In particular, the theoretical work of Marx, Durkheim and Weber has been subjected to empirical testing of various kinds. Though less creative an enterprise, this has been a necessary element in the emancipation of the new discipline.

The distinction of church-type and sect-type was picked up by Ernst Troeltsch, who explored these contrasting forms with regard to a number of related variables. In his analysis the church was distinguished by open membership rather than recruitment on the basis of personal piety or religious experience; its relationship with state and government was even manipulative. Membership of a church is by birthright, and of a sect by conversion. Participation in the life of a sect is characterized by enthusiasm and emotional satisfaction, and it is in this connection that Troeltsch portrays sectarian religion as the faith of the lower classes in Western societies. The typical sectarian posture towards "the world" is one of disengagement. The coexistence of these organizational and doctrinal characteristics was in its day an important discovery and the types which Troeltsch elaborated with respect to particular historical conditions have survived and are of considerable utility. On the other hand he offered little explanatory account of the relationship in dynamic terms between the tendencies he identified; and inevitably there have emerged since Troeltsch case studies of religious sects which do not conform to his stereotype.   For example, James Beckford has questioned Troeltschian models with reference to Jehovah's Witnesses (0305).

Richard Niebuhr's *The Social Sources of Denominationalism* (0331) not only elaborated the characteristics of the intermediate type but also introduced a dynamic perspective to the study of religious organizations and the changing relationships of these to their respective societies.   One of the most illuminating works on sect development is the collection of studies assembled by Bryan R.Wilson under the title, *Patterns of Sectarianism* (0344), several of which are annotated in this bibliography.   Both the study of sect development and the relationship of theology to society, each of which corresponds to a section in the ensuing bibliography, derive much from Richard Niebuhr's seminal work.

John Milton Yinger's subsequent *Religion, Society and the Individual* (0070) sustained the study of religious organizations in dynamic relationships both with the wider society and with each other. Furthermore, Yinger offered a systematic typology from which are derived a number of the categories in current sociological use.   The six types which Yinger distinguished were differentiated not on the basis of socioeconomic status but on the basis of social inclusiveness and the significance attached to social integration.   The "universal church" was independent of political and national boundaries and powers and thereto manifested characteristics of both the church-type and the

sect-type; the "ecclesia" is a national church which is less
effective than the universal church in reconciling itself with secular
powers and also at accommodating the needs of its members; the
"denomination" is of selective membership; the "sect" is as received
from Troeltsch and is therefore still less comprehensive; and
Yinger's peculiar type, the "established sect", represents a
stabilization and assimilation of the pure type under such strains
as that of a second generation.

In recent years the revision of typologies and the delineation of
types have been afforded by some detailed studies of particular cases:
Bryan R.Wilson's *Sects and Society* (0461) and James Beckford's *The
Trumpet of Prophecy* (0356) are worthwhile examples.   During and since
the 1960s a number of "new religious movements" have emerged which
correspond to Yinger's sixth category, the "cult", in that they
attach greatest significance to individual needs and have a tendency
in some cases to disintegrate.   However, unlike Yinger's cult-type
some of these, such as Scientology and the Unification Church, are
highly organized.   Notable recent scientific studies include those of
Roy Wallis (0448), James Beckford (0357) and Eileen Barker (0355;
0779).

The predominantly empirical character of the sociology of religion
in the United States has brought to the foreground certain
methodological and procedural problems, notably the dimensions of
religiosity and the forms of religion that elude the formal
organizations.   The seminal work on dimensions is that of Charles Y.
Glock and Rodney Stark (0122) while Peter L.Berger (0640), and
Robert N.Bellah (0883) have respectively promoted the study of religion
in its variant and noninstitutional forms.

The measurement of religiosity is an important but problematic area
of sociological endeavor.   Some estimation of changes in the level of
religious activity is important in the consideration of secularization,
both in Western and communist societies.   However, there is a
difficulty in finding indicators that are satisfactory in comparative
study.   Some of the mainstream churches have for their own purposes

collected numbers of communicants on Easter Day, a measure that is not
only dependent on accidents such as the weather but which provides no
basis for comparison with less sacramental organizations.   Furthermore, attendance is only one dimension of religious activity, albeit
the easiest to quantify.   Glock and Stark (O122) have set out a
cluster of five dimensions of religiosity which afford a clearer
definition than was previously achieved and a more balanced basis for
the assessment of changes.   These are the experiential, the
ritualistic, the theological, the intellectual and the consequential.
The last of these has to do with the implications of religious belief
and practice in everyday life while the first four explain themselves.
The utility of these five dimensions has been widely appreciated.
Both in secularization studies and also in the typification of
religious organizations they constitute a reference for the analysis
of commitment, exclusivity, the delineation of sacred and profane
and the pervasiveness of the organization in the lives of its members.
With some modifications, such as the specification of an ethical
dimension in place of the consequential and the addition of the
mythological dimension, they provide the model for the academic
pursuit of religious studies in universities and religious education
in British schools.   Furthermore, the work of Glock and Stark has
been the starting point for a great deal of research on the
relationships between the dimensions and the salience of religion in
the life of the believer.   Numerous examples are annotated within
this volume and will be found indexed under "religiosity".

The dimensions of Glock and Stark are useful, too, in indicating
the manifestations of religion that occur outside the formal

organizations such as churches and sects.   The persistence of religion
in private and public life has attracted much recent attention by some
of the most notable of modern sociologists.   Among the more noticed
and illuminating accounts are Thomas Luckmann's *The Invisible Religion*
and Peter L.Berger's *A Rumour of Angels* (0640).   Folk beliefs, myths,
superstition, primitive forms of religious belief endure outside the
official sphere and penetrate private life.   As the official
doctrines of the churches progress and evolve, traditional beliefs
survive among outsiders.   Even within the churches great discrepancies
have been discerned between official and actual beliefs.

The reality of religion in the private sphere has its counterpart
in public life.   The contexts of the two phenomena are opposite,
but their characteristics have much in common, both being insulated
in some measure from the formal agencies of contemporary religion.
The character of "civil religion" has been elaborated by Robert N.
Bellah, a scholar whose sensibilities are anthropological.   In a
celebrated article (0883) Bellah characterizes civil religion in the
context of the United States.   Civil religion is spatially
coextensive with national religion but is independent of it.   It is
as organized as conventional religions but is unified rather than
denominational in its structure.   It performs the functions of
integration and cohesion accorded by Durkheim to more primitive forms.
It has its own prophets, religious language, festivals and solemn
rituals.   The notion of civil religion which Bellah has done much to
expose is currently enjoying exploration in and application to other
societies (Gehrig, 0885;   Hughey, 0889;   Seneviratne, 0896;   Stauffer,
0898).

PROBLEMS OF PURPOSE AND METHOD

It is said to be of the essence of a sociological statement that, once uttered, its truth seems obvious. Certainly one of the hazards of sociology arises from the proximity of its evidence and analysis to common sense, from which sociologists have attempted to become aloof by the practice of esoteric scientific methods. The second hazard which we shall treat here is peculiar to the sociology of religion and concerns the erstwhile dependence of sociologists upon the religious organizations which were also their subjects. This has been largely overcome, and emancipation from the client relationship has been necessary for the academic respectability of the discipline.

We use the more cumbersome name "sociology of religion" in preference to "religious sociology" for **very good reasons.** So does the Conference Internationale de Sociologie des Religions and so do the *Archives de Sciences Sociales des Religions,* each of which formerly used the description, *"sociologie religieuse".* Such is the sense of release from the yoke that modern sociologists in the anglophone world refer to the former relationship and practice by its French name, as though to distance themselves still further from it.

There are two characteristics by which *sociologie religieuse* was distinguished and for which it is now universally disapproved. Firstly, it was a highly mechanical, sociographic and nonanalytical pursuit. Its normative method was the census. It offered measures of religiosity, then crudely defined, within particular geographical regions, by gender, age, occupational grouping and so on.   Thereby the church knew whether its strength was rural or urban.   Gabriel Le Bras (0033), F.Boulard (0044) and others adduced evidence which was useful to the religious organizations, not least because it had pastoral implications and gave some indication of effective strategies.   The early years of the journal *Sociaal Kompass* (0099), as *Social Compass* was then called, are filled with research reports in this tradition.

The second characteristic was the relationship of sociologists to the Church, which took its most extreme form in a country like France in which many practitioners of sociology were themselves Catholic priests, where the hierarchy prevailed and there was no radical tradition within the clergy.   In such conditions the ecclesiastical authorities dictated what was appropriate to research.   The Church set the agenda of sociological inquiry, prescribed the methods to be deployed, controlled the publication of results.   It was appropriate to investigate fluctuations in sacred vocations, but the relationship would not have suffered market researches on liturgical changes of the kind that the Church in the 1980s is finding so uncomfortable (0837; 0842).

It is not suggested that the practice of consultancy has been succeeded by the sociology of religion, for there are still those who are faithful to their church and who are commissioned to conduct scientific investigations within the social dimension (0494).   But over the last thirty years the churches have conceded more of their activities as fit for sociological study and to claim sanctuary less frequently in defending territory from persons with clipboards.

The mechanical tradition is alive and well in the American sociology of religion. Articles in major journals such as *Social Forces*, *Sociological Analysis* (0101) and the *Journal for the Scientific Study of Religion* (0096) show a preoccupation with quantitative methods and statistical analysis. One is left with a clear picture of the aspiring professor of the sociology of religion who must keep publishing, if only to achieve tenure. He or she is to be seen on the first day of semester with a class full of captive freshmen, obediently supplying the data that will yield a paper on the comparative career orientations of Presbyterians and Methodists or the courtship behavior of black and white pentecostals in Midwestern urban high schools (0242; 0262; 0292; 0300; 0304). This is a world of correlations, scales and rarefied statistical techniques, but the theoretical analysis is invariably weak; often the writers offer no more of a conclusion than that there is a need for further research. In Poland, too, sociological data are served raw; the major debate there concerns whether or not religiosity is in the ascendancy or decline, a matter of great consequence for the legitimacy of the government, and assiduous sociography is appropriate in the investigation of this problem.

On the other hand there is a body of theoretical work which, at its most extreme point, is innocent of the social realities documented in the descriptive literature. Close reference to this literature is not in the habits of, say, a Berger or a Luckmann. Whereas in the classical period sociologists of religion synthesized empirical and theoretical elements, these have in recent years become separated and are practised by different persons in different places.

At the risk of chauvinism one might suggest that it is among British
scholars that examples of balance are to be found.   In Bryan R.Wilson's
sociological studies of sectarianism (0461, 0462) and in David Martin's
work on, say, secularization (0665) there is throughout the closest
attention to detail, achieved for the most part in the field in the
former case and by the most meticulous reading of the literature in the
latter.   However, these scholars and their peers are not enslaved by
data; their insights are penetrating, their interpretation creative and,
by way of a bonus, their language use exemplary.

That said almost by way of a statement of personal taste, there
remains a problem which has loomed large in the selection of material
for the ensuing bibliography: when is a particular work not
sociological?   Some items will be found annotated in this volume which
inform sociological themes but which, strictly speaking, might be
considered as anthropology or social psychology.   This is a matter in
which licence has been exercised, but it is not the problem; the question
is not of boundaries but of quality.   It is rather, in the terms with
which this section opened, that of designating some publications as
sociological and others merely as common sense.   In the majority of
cases there is no difficulty; sociologists have laid claim to certain
categories such as organization and social class, and certain methods
such as the questionnaire survey: the appearance of these spells
sociology.   But what of a work like Calley's *God's People* (0554)?
This is a descriptive account of West Indian pentecostals, illustrated
with photographs - which is a very unscholarly practice!   The work is
innocent of sociological jargon, specialist methodology, "discipline"
and cross-references to the sociological literature.   As sociological

interpretation, it falls far short of work in the field such as Wilson's

study of Elim (0461).   It is very raw: Calley has done a research and

reporting job on a little known fellowship.   Nevertheless, it was

decided to include this and all comparable work, such as Hollenweger's

(0384), because the range of the sociology of religion as signified by

its journals encompasses not only the analytical but also the purely

documentary.   A systematic, documentary style passes often with respect

to subjects that are being introduced for sociological consideration and

in offering local or national data for attention by an international

readership.   Furthermore, while the study of religious organizations

is normally conducted with clear reference to existing paradigms and

literature, material on the relationship between religion and politics

is often presented as straightforward historiography.

PREOCCUPATIONS

   The agenda which evolved in the classical period of sociology and

was developed by the subsequent generation continues to command the

attention of sociologists in the modern period.   The functionalist

perspective was to become unfashionable as an approach to the study of

religious organizations and beliefs in society but is favored in the

analysis of elements of religious behavior such as ritual and religious

language (0385, 0386).   The interest of Marx, Durkheim and Weber in

non-Christian religions unfortunately was not sustained, and until

recently sociologists have been inclined to observe and interpret the

most accessible manifestations of religion and to leave those further

afield for the attention of anthropologists.   A renewal of interest in

non-Christian religions and the societies of the underdeveloped world

is signified by special issues of the relevant journals; *Social Compass*

(0099), for example, featured Sri Lanka in 1973 and Central America in

1983.   Sociologists applying the discipline to the conditions of the

underdeveloped world include François Houtart, Geneviève Lemercinier,

Giancarlo Milanesi (0955) and H.L.Seneviratne   (0896).

The Singhalese context has proven most compelling from a

sociological point of view. The native religion is Buddhism; the

missionary confession is Catholicism.   The coexistence of the two

faiths provides an interesting case of religious tension in which the

control of schools is a certain advantage.   The situation in Central

America is again a compelling field, one in which the political

alignment of Catholic clergy has widely detached them from the

hierarchy.   Some sociologists have suggested that the adaptation of the

Catholic Church to political and social change and its support for such

change is necessary for its legitimacy.   The cases of Sri Lanka and

Central America, then, have manifested problems of their own kind, and

it is suggested that more area studies will serve only to enhance the

sociology of religion.

The division of clergy and hierarchy which studies of Central America

have revealed is a phenomenon that is general in the Catholic Church and

relates to a role conflict that is common among clergy of many churches.

The taboo upon political activism constrains a tendency to legitimize

the priestly or ministerial role in the secular world (Leat, 0724).

The crisis for clergy is one of prestige, and historical accounts of

the clerical profession make it clear that the modern clergy are less

educated and less respected (0696, 0739, 0747); the corresponding decline

in sacred vocations is a matter that concerns the churches and upon which sociologists have offered a comment (O736; O759).

The ubiquitous problems of the clerical profession are but a
manifestation of a more general trend, the decline of organized religion
both in the measure of active support it enjoys and in the influence it
exerts.   Religion is to be found less and less in the intermediate
sphere of organizations and more in the private domain in the form of
folk religion and on state occasions in the form of civil religion.
The declining influence of religious organizations and beliefs and,
related to it, the increasing independence of political from religious
life are aspects of "secularization" which is studied as a problem by
Western sociologists and as the confirmation of a millennial hope by
atheist sociologists in communist societies (Orsolic, O225).
Secularization is studied in historical perspective and found to be a
concomitant of industrialization and urbanization; the more complex a
society becomes, the less adequate is the capacity of the churches to
permeate social, cultural, economic and personal life and to imbue
these sectors with religious values.   Studies of migrants from countryside to town bring into focus the complexity of urban communities in
which religious organizations are often isolated.

The most recent major work on secularization is David Martin's
General Theory (O665), which offers not an explanatory account but a
typology of the kinds of political formation in which secularization
has a particular character.   He distinguishes basic patterns according
to the degree of monopoly enjoyed by church or secular government;
Eastern Europe, for example, provides several instances of secular
monopoly, while the United States exemplifies protestant pluralism.

Within the confines of postwar Christendom, Martin's work is
encyclopaedic, and the basic patterns he elaborates commend their
application to non-Christian cases of religious monopoly and the
Islamic antidote to secularization in such societies as Iran,
Pakistan and Saudi Arabia.

In another important sociological field, however, religious values
are found more often to prevail and to serve an important integrative
function.   The religious organizations serving the minority
communities are important agencies of culture maintenance and also
offer, in certain conditions, refuges for the disprivileged and
inspiration and organization at the political level.   Hunt and Hunt
(0253) have usefully studied the relationship of black religion in the
United States and civil rights militancy, but there is scope for much
more sociological study of the religious organizations of ethnic
minority communities and their bearing upon political orientations,
economic, educational and occupational aspirations, the cohesion of
the community in the first generation of migration and the resistance
of assimilation in the second and subsequent generations.   While
black and white pentecostals in North America and Great Britain have
organized themselves separately, the conditions of segregation and
integration have been studied in an exploratory way (Hill, 0582)
but warrant more analysis than has yet been achieved.

Nothing can be more exciting and rejuvenating for a discipline
than the emergence of new phenomena which do not match available
stereotypes.   There has been considerable interest, therefore, in
the modern cults or "new religious movements" which have been as

widely noticed in the popular press as in the sociological literature.

The Hippies of the late 1960s had their Christian counterparts in the

Jesus People and the Children of God; though fundamentalist in belief

and sectarian in organization, these movements were comparatively

youthful, middle class and composed of the better educated (Fichter,

0481). It was predicted that these movements would stabilize in due

course and that their members would assimilate within more conventional

organizations; and these expectations have been confirmed. The

"alternative culture" from which these purely Christian forms emerged

fostered a sympathetic interest in Indian philosophy, and this

resulted in the proliferation of syncretic cults such as Divine Light

(0373) and Krishna Consciousness. A further group of cults sought

to harmonize forms of religious doctrine with elements of psychology

and business acumen. These are the organizations most commonly

denoted by the term "new religious movements" and the best known

examples of which are the Church of Scientology and the Unification

Church. As Divine Light deferred to its young guru, so the new

religious movements give prominence to the writings and insights of

their respective cult heroes, Lafayette Ron Hubbard in the case of

Scientology and Sun Myung Moon in the case of the Unification Church.

The sensational tenor of popular interest in the new religious

movements has presented a difficulty for those having a more

scientific purpose. Whether for good reasons or otherwise, the Moonies

and Scientologists stand accused of kidnapping and brainwashing in the

recruitment and induction of members. Bona fide sociological

researchers such as Roy Wallis (0448) and Eileen Barker (0355) find

that the public looks to them for evidence of guilt, and the cults hope for acquittal.   An interest in techniques of conversion and

socialization has always been on the agenda of the sociology of

sectarianism, and it cannot easily be avoided.   Complicating the

situation still further is the consideration that the new religious

movements are known to be litigious as at least one practitioner

has found to his cost (Wallis, 0449); this is bound to inhibit all

but the most courageous explorer of the field.   The conflict between

politicians and legislators on the one hand and the new religious

movements on the other is expressed in anti-cult campaigns, the

lively interest of the press, litigation and legislation; and it is

the subject of a crossnational study recently produced by James

Beckford (0357).   The social response to the new religious movements

is interpreted by him as a manifestation of the centralization of

moral concern in the "therapeutic state" exemplified in West Germany,

France and Great Britain.

This enumeration of some recent departures in the sociological

study of religion is of necessity selective.   Other themes, such as

the sociology of ecumenism, the sociological analysis of the liturgy,

Jewish sociology, religious communities, the sociology of mission

and studies of attitudes, are well represented in the bibliography

and approachable through the subject index.

There remains, however, one conspicuous area of neglect in the

sociology of religion.   Whereas sociology in general has developed

a concern for the role of women, and even though there is within the

Christian churches a lively movement for the recognition of women by,

for example, ordination, the subject of women has barely been examined

within the sociology of religion.   A major factor in this situation
is the evacuation of women from the branches of applied sociology to
women's studies, leaving the branches to be dominated by men.   The
notion that the place for women sociologists is in women's studies
has been counterproductive to the development of the women's
dimension in the sociology of religion.   Happily there are several
women sociologists of religion, but they have not applied themselves
to the study of women in religion.

SOCIOLOGY AND RELIGION : RETROSPECT AND PROSPECT

   Sociologists frequently distinguish between two types of expression,
the priestly and the prophetic.   The models of priest and prophet are,
of course, drawn from the Old Testament in which the archetypal priest
defended the status quo, while the prophet drew attention to short-
comings, abuses, injustice and exploitation.   The expressions of
sociologists are inevitably perceived by the religious organizations
as belonging to one or other of these postures.   The compliant
tradition of *sociologie religieuse* seldom caused offence; but some
sociological work has been bitterly resented by its religious subjects,
and sociologists cannot depend upon a cordial welcome in religious
fields.   Further, sociological wisdom is often defined as irrelevant
and as an intrusion upon a domain of experience by those who lack an
appropriate understanding.   In the introduction to the 1960 English
edition of Ferdinand Boulard's *Introduction to Religious Sociology*
Jackson warned that

   There are aspects of the Church's life which sociology
   cannot penetrate.   The Church is more than a social,
   historical institution; it is the Body of Christ.
   This ambiguity of the Church's nature sets certain
   limits upon religious sociology (p.xi).

The problem is to determine what part if any of the activities of the

church is appropriate for sociological investigation. In practice

the measure of Jackson's caution has been exceeded, and church

authorities have rejected sociological evidence on even the most social

and organizational aspects of church life.   For example, the Paul

Report on the deployment and payment of the clergy (0739) was perempt-

orily discarded by the Bishop of Pontefract:

> Whilst not denying the need for clear heads and a recognition
> of facts in ordering the life of the Church, we must ever
> have in mind that the Spirit bloweth where it listeth, and
> that the Spirit can make nonsense of statistical and
> sociological surveys (Gill, 0862:p.18).

The problem is one of situation definition and the delineation

of boundaries.   The model of the sacred domain inhabited and

territorially guarded by the professionals of the church is the

shekinah, the cloud which veiled Mount Sinai as Moses reportedly

communed with God prior to the promulgation of the Ten Commandments.

Its bounds, beyond which the laity must not trespass, are symbolized

by the screen or *ikonostasis* in Orthodox usage.   Whatever happens

in the cloud or beyond the screen must not be knowable to the laity.

The possibility of demystification is threatening, not least to the

clerical profession which in any case has lost much of the transcend-

ance by which it was formerly distinguished.   Once the only experts

in theology, pastoralia, education, architecture, economics and all

the skills appropriate to the management of a church and parish,

the clergy now frequently find themselves surrounded by graduates

and professionals in each of these fields (0837).   Theology, formerly

a clerical prerogative, is widely available in universities to those

not electing the Church as a profession, so lay members of churches may have a greater dose than the part of a course of ministerial

training taken by their clergy.   Furthermore, modern theologians

recognize the place of sociological research and accommodate it

within their own discipline.   The Catholic theologian, Karl Rahner,

warns that the authorities of the Church indulge in "epistemological

imperialism" when they venture into sociological speculation:

> The first step to be taken is the recognition in all
> honesty that we do not know the situation in which
> we ourselves stand in terms of sociology and human
> ideas. (1)

Likewise, Professor Hans Küng recognizes the hazards of intellectual

complacency in the conduct of theology and warns his fellow theologians

against it:

> Serious theology does not claim any elitist privileged
> access to the truth.   It claims only to be a scholarly
> reflection on its object with the aid of a method
> appropriate to this object, a method whose usefulness -
> as in other sciences - is to be proved by results.
> Theology can never be content to be graciously tolerated
> within a field where conclusions are notably inexact
> and lacking in binding force, as if religious truth
> were similar to 'poetic truth' (2)

The Bishop of Pontefract in response to the Paul Report represented

an enduring tension among the clergy about withholding the affairs of

the Church for evaluation and direction by its professionals, un-

inhibited by experts of secular disciplines.   Pontefract and at

least one interpretation of Jackson contradict the basic assumption

of the sociology of religion, which is that sociology has some purchase

on major institutions and transactions in the religious domain, both

in theology and in the life of the Church; upon the structure and

stability of the hierarchy; upon the effectiveness of strategies for

pastoral oversight; upon such provisions for the maintenance of decency and order as Calvin developed; upon the cohesion of religious

organizations in respect of beliefs; upon the conformity or otherwise

of marginal contingents such as younger generations; upon the

political postures of churches and the effects of these upon their

legitimacy; upon the social, economic and political consequences of

religious doctrines; upon the effects on membership of liturgical

change and ecumenical schemes.   These problems and many more of

their kind are aspects of the Body of Christ in its social dimension,

and it is contended that they are most appropriately assessed by

sociological methods.

The tension between the Church and sociology is most visible and

perhaps most revealing in the course of structural or practical

change and in the context of a crisis in the clerical profession.

As a case of this tension, it is illuminating to observe the case

of liturgical change in the Roman Catholic, Episcopal and Anglican

Communions.   In the period of the last ten or fifteen years this

change has involved a modernization of liturgical language, an

adjustment of theological emphases from a supposed obsession with

sin to a stress upon the role of the Holy Spirit, and the greater

participation of the laity.   In general terms church attendance

has declined over the period but the authorities of the church

assert that, for example, "It is significant that the churches

where there is real life and growth are the ones where [the new

forms of] service is used" (Homan, 0867: p.429).

To the extent that the concept of "growth" includes a quantif-

iable element it may be verified by conventional sociological methods.

More dangerous still, it can be falsified.   The privileged authority
of the hierarchy is undermined by the practice of sociology.   As
Canon Ian Dunlop recognizes, "the clergy have been conditioned to be
loners" and "the presence of an informed laity is seen as a threat
to their position" (0867 : p.429).   One of the options available to
clergy is the strategy of withdrawal, either into a purely spiritual
role in a cloud or behind a screen or in a privatized therapeutic
activity such as counseling (Leat, 0724).   The last public strong-
hold of the clergy is the liturgy and even here sociologists have
haunted the Church with their menacing surveys.

The unpopularity of liturgical change was attested by the 1976
poll of Dr George Gallup in the United States, by the 1976 Allensbach
survey among German Catholics and by a Gallup poll conducted in
Britain in 1980 (0866).   In a study of over one hundred parishes in
the south of England there was found to be a correlation between the
introduction of modern services and losses of church membership
(0836); this finding was rejected by the church authorities on the
grounds that the data had not been collected from incumbents and were
therefore "unreliable" and "irresponsible" (0836   : p.433).
Nostalgia, perhaps, for the privileged role of gatekeeper enjoyed in
the days of *sociologie religieuse.*

Similarly, the new religious movements have not been indifferent
to the publication of sociological insight and the infringement of
outsiders upon their own territories.   For the Church of
Scientology and the Unification Church a favorable public image is
critical, and an adverse reputation is likely to incur anti-cult

legislation, the withdrawal of charitable status or religious
privilege and economic sanctions through the tax system.   Roy Wallis,
an erstwhile defendant against cult litigation, has analyzed the
sectarian fear of publicity in a study of Christian Science and
Scientology (0449).   In his judgment both of these sects are highly
authoritarian, so that inquiry by outsiders is likely to subvert the
authority that the hierarchy enjoys.   Furthermore, each of the two
sects claims a privileged access to the truth, which in their view
might be corrupted by the wisdom of outsiders.   The analysis of
Roy Wallis of the sensitivity of cult leaders is a compelling one
and it is to be remarked that it corresponds closely to the
commentary offered in the above pages to the responses of clergy
and hierarchy in the mainstream churches.

CONCLUSIONS

It is now possible, by way of a conclusion, to make some general
observations or desiderata in consideration of which the future of
the relationship between religious organizations and sociology should
be negotiated.   The checklist, like the commentary above which leads
to it, is offered from a position of vested interest in the enterprise of sociology but also in an endeavor to engage, understand and
accommodate the principles of the sacred domain.

Firstly, the sociology of religion contends for recognition as a
respected branch of applied sociology in a climate of academic
freedom.   This aspiration is not achievable if its agenda, methods
and publications are controlled by its subjects or the data at its
disposal are available only from gatekeepers.

Second, major elements of religious organizations and transactions are palpably "social" and thereby fit for sociological investigation. The discipline of theology has its place but, as certain of its enlightened practitioners have recognized, can claim no monopoly in an understanding of religious affairs.   Further, many of the statements and concerns of those who defer to theology as the queen of disciplines are themselves sociological in character.

Third, the antagonism between theology and sociology relates to the ambiguity of the notion that the Church is the Body of Christ. The defense of the sacred domain takes the forms of isolation and mystification: that which the faithful cannot see they will not understand, and that which they will not understand they cannot challenge.   The demystification of the sacred by sociological analysis is therefore perceived as a subversive activity threatening the legitimacy of church leaders.   However, sociologists are not alone in lifting the veil; the intellectual prowess of the clerical profession is declining relative to a number of secular professions, and the comprehension of the religious is a multidisciplinary and polymethodic enterprise.

Fourth, the public and political responses to marginal groups such as the new religious movements have serious implications for the professional conduct of sociologists who find themselves treading in the footsteps of investigative journalists, with their reports awaited and packaged by publishers in a more excited atmosphere than that to which sober researchers are accustomed.   On the one hand, they should not be intimidated by the probability of litigation if their accounts do not endear them to their subjects; on the other, it is not the place of sociologists to adjudicate on matters of ethical principle.   It is incumbent upon any responsible professional to be mindful of the implications and probable consequences of his or her own conduct and report.   This principle is commonly established in ethical guidelines given by the professional bodies in sociology, and its observance is particularly difficult in the study of some religious subjects.

Fifth, sociology belongs to a critical tradition.   The penetrating critique of Marx, with which we opened this account, was as indicative of religious belief and practice as any current studies on the clergy or the liturgy; but it is demonstrable that in the course of time it was taken to heart by the Catholic Church, whose liberation theology is arguably the basis of its continuity in Latin America.

Notes:

1.   Karl Rahner.   *Theological Investigations 14: Ecclesiology, Questions in the Church, The Church in the World*   (London: Darton, Longman and Todd, 1970), p.105.

2.   Hans Küng.   *On Being a Christian* (London: Collins, 1977), p.87.

Annotated Bibliography

A. GENERAL WORKS

0001 Banton, Michael, ed. *Anthropological Approaches to the Study of Religion.* London: Tavistock, 1966.

A collection of readings on the relationship between religion and social structure with contributions from some important scholars. Melford E. Spiro is sensitive to psychological perspectives in his general review of the field. Clifford Geertz comprehensively explores the cultural features of religion. Victor W.Turner examines color symbolism in an African tribe. There are further essays by R.E.Bradbury and Edward H.Winter.

0002 Beidelman, T.O. *W.Robertson Smith and the Sociology of Religion.* Chicago: University of Chicago Press, 1974.

William Robertson Smith was born in Scotland in 1846 and had a distinguished academic career. However, he is little remembered as a sociologist and this essay is an endeavor to rediscover his work on totemism, evolutionism and the historical-functionalist method of which he was an early exponent. In 1878 Smith commenced field work in the Middle East and his *Lectures on the Religion of the Semites* is acclaimed by Beidelman as a classic in the sociology of religion.

0003 Bellah, Robert N. *Beyond Belief: Essays on Religion in a Post-traditional World.* New York: Harper and Row, 1970.

This is a valuable collection of essays which has been widely recognized as an outstanding contribution to the sociology of religion. Bellah offers authoritative accounts of the sociology of religion, of religious evolution, of religion and social and economic development. There surface here the issues which appear in any comprehensive sociology of religion, such as the protestant ethic and the collection includes Bellah's essay "Civil Religion in America" (0883). But Bellah carries the sociology of religion as developed in western scholarship beyond the parish of Christendom. The protestant ethic is made analogous to Asia. There are instructive case studies and applications of China, Japan and Islam through which Bellah pursues consistent themes of religion, tradition, change and modernization.

0004   Bellah, Robert N.   "Religious Evolution." *American
Sociological Review* 29 (1964): 358-374.

After the fashion of Marx's account of the evolution of societies,
Bellah traces the evolution of religion through primitive, archaic,
historic, early modern and modern phases.   He argues that world-
acceptance at the primitive and archaic levels is to be
interpreted as the only possible response to a reality that
invades the self to such an extent that the symbolizations of the
self and the world are only partially separate.   The great wave
of world-rejection of the historic religions, he suggests, is a
major advance in the differentiation between experience of the
self and the world which acts upon it.   Reprinted in Bellah
(0003) and in Robertson (0049) and criticized by Pruett (0045).

0005   Bellah, Robert N.   "Sociology of Religion." *International
Encyclopaedia of the Social Sciences* 3, edited by David L.Sills,
pp.406-414. New York: Macmillan and Free Press, 1968.

As its location suggests this article is a very general overview.
Bellah's procedure is to identify and distinguish three kinds of
enterprize undertaken by sociologists of religion.   First, they
have apprehended religion as a central problem in social action.
Second, they have related the religious factor to other variables
such as the State, the economy, political life and the class
system.   And third, religion has provided them with a system of
institutions, organizations and roles which have been the subject
of extensive sociological research.

0006   Benson, J.Kenneth, and Dorsett, James H.   "Toward a Theory of
Religious Organizations." *Journal for the Scientific Study of
Religion* 10 (1971): 138-151.

The authors propose and explore a conceptual scheme of four
dimensions, bureaucratization, professionalization, secularization and integration.   This serves to promote a theory of
structural change through the analysis of structural conflict
and the sources of developments within each of the four dimensions.

0007   Berger, Peter L.   *The Sacred Canopy: Elements of a Sociological
Theory of Religion.* New York: Doubleday, 1967.

This work has been universally recognized as a major contribution
to the field and is widely cited.   It provides a classified agenda
for the sociology of religion that is comprehensive and
applicable to a broad field.   Berger distinguishes between
systematic and historical elements.   By way of the first group,
he explores religion first in the construction and second in
the maintenance of "the world".   In the dialectic of externaliz-
ation, objectivation and internalization that occupies Berger in
his consideration of systematic elements, a major problem is that
of religion and alienation.   Within his treatment of historical
elements the preoccupation is with secularization which he studies
in respect of the problems of plausibility and legitimation.
Appendices address the common ground of sociology and theology
and focus upon problems of sociological definition.

0008 Berger, Peter L. and Luckmann, Thomas. "Sociology of Religion and Sociology of Knowledge." *Sociology and Social Research* 47 (1963): 417-427.

It is argued that the sociology of religion has been too much preoccupied with religion in the institutional context of churches and denominations and that the focus of the sociology of religion should be broadened to encompass new forms of belief and commitment which serve to maintain the sense of reality and consistency necessary for the maintenance of everyday life. In proposing a theoretically and philosophically more ambitious agenda for the sociology of religion, they commend the pertinence and usefulness of the sociology of knowledge for the exploration of the conditions of social life. Reprinted often, and included in *Sociology of Religion: Selected Readings*, edited by Roland Robertson. Harmondsworth: Penguin, 1969 (0049).

0009 Birnbaum, Norman and Lenzer, Gertrude, eds. *Sociology and Religion: A Book of Readings*. Englewood Cliffs: Prentice-Hall, 1969.

This collection gives pride of place to classical contributions and major writers in the field.   Readings are grouped on a thematic basis; the themes include the origins of religion (Hume, Hegel, Comte, Spencer, Wundt, Freud, Bellah), religion as an historical expression (Feuerbach, Marx, Mill, Nietzsche), religion in transformation (Troeltsch, Weber, T.W.Adorno, Herberg, Lenski). Many items in this anthology adopt psychological, historical and anthropological perspectives.   See also Morioka (0957).

0010 Bouma, Gary D. "Beyond Lenski: A Critical Review of Recent 'Protestant Ethic' Research." *Journal for the Scientific Study of Religion* 12 (1973): 141-155.

Bouma examines post-1960 research in the Weber-Lenski tradition. His review takes account of a full range of books and journals and he finds researchers guilty of too simplistic a representation of the Weber thesis, poor operationalization of the independent variable of religious belief; further none of the studies surveyed was adequate for causal influence as implied in the Weber thesis.

0011 Budd, Susan. *Sociologists and Religion.* London: Collier-Macmillan, 1973.

An introductory work which gives ample attention to the Durkheimian tradition of anthropological and evolutionary theories and to the work of Weber.   The survey of evidence addresses empirical problems such as the relationship of religion and belief; there are overviews of the study of secularization and of types of religious organization; and the book carries an extensive bibliography with brief annotations.

0012 Charnay, Jean-Paul. "Préalables Épistémologiques à une Sociologie Religieuse de l'Islam." *Archives de Sciences Sociales des Religions* 37 (1974): 79-86.

Sociology has been slower than other disciplines in being taken
to the study of Islam.   Charnay's purpose is to set out the
agenda of preparations for the development of a sociology of
religion appropriate to the ontology of Islam, as opposed to one
that is developed for a western Christian model of religion.

0013 Davis, J., ed. *Religious Organization and Religious
Experience*. London: Academic Press, 1982.

Davis collects conference papers approaching the subject with the
benefit of the insights of sociology, theology, history and
anthropology.   Universes studied include the Israeli kibbutz,
Zulu Zionist churches, village Buddhism and Shona Spirit mediums.
Contributions noted in this bibliography are those of Alison Bowes
(0991), Godfrey Lienhardt (0726), Martin Southwold (0897), Jim
Kiernan (0399) and M.F.C.Bourdillon (0690).

0014 Demerath, N.J. and Roof, Wade Clark. "Religion - Recent Strands
in Research." *Annual Review of Religion* 2 (1976): 19-33.

The authors present a necessarily selective account of live and
continuing issues in the sociology of religion.   These include
the dimension of social protest that is evident in the postures
of the world-rejecting sects.   They pursue the Weberian theme of
a connection   between religion, education and status attainment.
There is a discussion of civil religion and the neo-Durkheimian
view of cultural meaning and integration which has been put on
the agenda by Robert N.Bellah (0883).

0015 Demerath, N.J. and Hammond, Phillip E. *Religion in Social
Context: Tradition and Transition*. New York: Random House, 1969.

The work of Demerath and Hammond is useful both as an introductory
textbook and as a clarification of persistent problems in the
sociology of religion.   It gives a treatment of conceptual development, revives Weber on early Christianity and protestantism in
capitalist society and deals with the complexity of the religious
factor in contemporary society.

0016 Desroche, Henri. *Sociologies Religieuses*. Paris: Presses
Universitaires de France, 1968.

This is a general work by a celebrated exponent of the now
unfashionable science of *sociologie religieuse*. By a systematic
examination of alternative perspectives and tasks such as
functionalism, the morphology and typology of religious groups,
Desroche traces and accelerates the evolution of religious
sociology and speculates about a new dimension and a new relationship between sociology and theology.

0017 Desroche, Henri. "Sociologies Religieuses et Discours Franco-
phones." *Archives de Sciences Sociales des Religions* 35 (1973):
113-138.

This is the summary report of a colloquium of Francophone
sociologists of religion and provides an overview of the research
projects of participants. Major concerns emerging as themes in
current sociology included the relationship of religion and
development, the production of the religious speech, the
succession of literary genres in religion and the assessment of
the sociology of religion as a profession.

0018 Dobbelaere, Karel. "Trend Report of the State of the Sociology
of Religion, 1965-1966." *Social Compass* 15 (1968): 329-365.

This is a two-year survey of activities in the sociology of religion,
the most important themes being the problem of dimensions of
religiosity, sect and church, the hierarchy, religion and the
integration of society, religion and the economy, the family, race
and prejudice, and catholic education.   In conclusion, Dobbelaere
appeals for a sound theoretical and methodological foundation to
the subject, possibly by reference back to the classical studies
of Weber and Durkheim, and in this connection he welcomes Berger's
The Sacred Canopy (0007).

0019 Dobbelaere, Karel and Lauwers, Jan. "Definitions of Religion:
A Sociological Critique." *Social Compass* 20 (1973): 535-551.

Definitions of religion are shown to have a fundamental impact upon
the outcome of any endeavors to study it.   So too with the
functions ascribed to religion.   The authors examine the
implications of choosing one definition or another set of functions.
Ideological bias is inherent in the sociological study of religion
and investigators must ever be critical of the starting points
they adopt.

0020 Eister, Allan W. "Religious Institutions in Complex Societies:
Identities in the Theoretic Specification of Functions." *American
Sociological Review* 22 (1957): 387-391.

Eister demonstrates the magnitude of difficulties confronting the
theoretic specification of the functions of religious institutions
and suggests from a survey of the literature that these had not
been appreciated.

0021 Fallding, Harold. *The Sociology of Religion: An Explanation of
Unity and Diversity in Religion.* New York: McGraw-Hill, 1974.

Fallding identifies religion both as the desire to express unity
of experience and as the belief in an ideal society in relation to
religious affirmation in myth, ritual and dogma.   These
manifestations are exemplified not only in conventional religious
organizations but in various totalitarian movements, psycho-
analysis, drugs and "hippyism".

In the second half of his book Fallding discusses the development
processes of religious movements and identifies a religious
dynamic: social change, involving disaffection and alienation
among individuals, creates minority groups who find a unifying

purpose in religious dissent.   Such groups have a tendency to
stabilize and seek responsibility in institutional forms as new
official religions.

0022   Freytag, Justus.   *Die Kirchengemeinde in Soziologischer Sicht.*
Hamburg: Furche-Verlag, 1959.

Freytag presents a meticulous German analysis of the institutional
structure and social system within which religion is organized.
The book is a short essay much occupied with the social functions
of religious forms which characterized the sociology of religion in
Europe in its early period.

0023   Glock, Charles Y. and Hammond, Philip E., eds.   *Beyond the
Classics: Essays in the Scientific Study of Religion.*   New York: Harper
and Row, 1973.

This collection of papers reflects and demonstrates a recent
enhancement and expansion of the sociology of religion.   Its subject
matter is no longer confined to conventional concerns with organized
forms.   Its methods and techniques have been refined to deserve its
parity with other branches of applied sociology.   Further, it relates
much more to cognate disciplines such as psychology, anthropology
and history.

0024   Greeley, Andrew M.   *Religion: A Secular Theory.*   New York: Free
Press, 1982.

Greeley's procedure is to develop a coherent theory by the
accumulation of ninety-nine distinct propositions; these concern,
for example, the need for the periodic validation of religious hope
and religious heritages as systems of symbols articulating intense
experience.   The theory is based in the human personality and
proceeds from there rather than from social structures.   See also
0927.

0025   Haralambos, Michael.   *Sociology: Themes and Perspectives.*   Slough,
England: University Tutorial Press, 1980.

This is a standard introductory and comprehensive textbook on the
discipline of sociology.   Chapter 11 is entirely devoted to
religion and introduces the classical theoretical perspectives of
Durkheim, Malinowski, Parsons, Marx and Weber, the study of
secularization and of religion in its institutional context.

0026   Hill, Michael.   *A Sociology of Religion.*   London: Heinemann,
1973.

A comprehensive introduction to the sociology of religion which
offers the standard accounts of the development of the subject, the
contributions of Durkheim and Weber, typologies of religious
organization, the protestant ethic debate and the theory of
secularization.   In addition, Michael Hill pursues special interests
in the Weber thesis, contemporary applications of "classical"
sociology, charismatic leadership and in Halevy's account of

religious ideology as an antidote to political revolution in
Britain in the wake of that in France.

0027 Hoult, Thomas Ford. *The Sociology of Religion.* New York: Holt,
Rinehart and Winston, 1958.

This was a substantial textbook in its day which opens up the subject
with an exploration of theoretical considerations and goes on to
treat of religion in its institutional forms, with studies of
organization and leadership and comparisons with other Social
Institutions from the family to the economic and political orders.
The appendix offers a concentrated survey of world religions such
as no sociological scholar would now undertake in a few pages.

0028 Isambert, François-André. "Métamorphose Contemporaine des
Phénomènes Religieux?" *Archives de Sciences Sociales des Religions* 36
(1973): 119-123.

Isambert offers a discussion of contemporary transformations within
the religious domain in western societies with particular reference
to religious groups.

0029 Johnstone, Ronald L. *Religion and Society in Interaction: The
Sociology of Religion.* Englewood Cliffs: Prentice-Hall, 1975.

This is a comprehensive introductory text-book which ranges over
sociological perspectives, societal and individual variables of
religiosity, quantitative measures and projections. A special
account is given of religion in America.

0030 Kehrer, Günter. *Religionssoziologie.* Berlin: Walter de Gruyter,
1968.

Kehrer contributes a slim volume on religious sociology German-
style. He treats of the origins of the discipline and examines its
theoretical foundations before pursuing the study of specific
problems relating to religion, such as politics and the family.
The style and content are introductory, albeit precise.

0031 Knudten, Richard D., ed. *The Sociology of Religion: An
Anthology.* New York: Appleton-Century-Crofts, 1967.

This is a prudent collection of key readings in the sociology of
religion.   Charles Glock, Liston Pope, J.Milton Yinger and other
old favorites are represented but the purpose of the collection is
not so much to be encyclopaedic as to answer some urgent questions
concerning the state of the art and the relationship of contemporary
religion to minority life and social change.   Readings are
organized around these and other problems.

0032 Köpping, Klaus-Peter. "Bewusstseinszustände und Stufen der
Wirklichkeit, eine Kritische Bestandsaufnahme zur Neueren Literatur
auf dem Gebiete der Religionssoziologie." *Kölner Zeitschrift für
Soziologie und Sozial-psychologie* 24 (1972): 821-835.

The development of the sociology of religion is critically reviewed by Köpping who suggests that the discipline has stagnated at the theoretical and methodological levels after a promising start by Durkheim and Weber.   The early concerns of sociologists with forms and functions were important but, in the author's estimation, they need to have been succeeded.   The article points to the importance of the experiential dimension which is a prominent feature of new generationally-oriented religious forms and which can be illuminated as well by psychological as by sociological method.

0033 Le Bras, Gabriel. *Etudes de Sociologie Religieuse.* Paris: Presses Universitaires de France, 1956.

This is the seminal two-volume work of a major exponent of religious sociology.   His geographical focus is Europe in general and France in particular and his denomination preoccupation is Catholicism. His thematic range, however, is great; examples of topics treated include religious typologies and morphology, the historical development of Catholicism, the Catholic Church in Germany and religious orders.

0034 Martin, David. "The Sociology of Religion: A Case of Status Deprivation." *British Journal of Sociology* 17 (1966): 353-359.

Although Weber and Durkheim devoted their most strenuous efforts to religion, there is current what David Martin calls "vulgar sociologism" which directs the discipline to so-called "reality" and away from the supposedly unreal world of religion.   In consequence, the sociology of religion suffers progressive marginalization.   In response, Martin recognizes the limitations of the empiricist tradition of *sociologie religieuse* and challenges sociologists of religion to look critically at their own faith and insularity.   Reprinted as "Secularization Among the Sociologists" in Martin (0664): 61-9.

0035 Martin, David. *The Dilemmas of Contemporary Religion.* Oxford: Blackwell, 1978.

A collection of six essays, all sociological in character, which together provide a perspective on Christianity and Judaism as examples of what the author calls two "closely related kinds of sociologic".   There are investigations of various manifestations of civic religion in western societies, of tradition in religion seen in terms of the modern discipline of sociology, the fear of institutionalization in religion and the nostalgia for community, and the collapse of puritanism and humanism.   There is also a provocative interpretation of marxism as the functional equivalent of religion: this paper was originally written for a conference of east European professors.

0036 Martin, David. "The Prospects for Non-scientific Belief and Ideology." In *Les Terreurs de l'An Deux Milles.* Paris: Hachette, 1976.

This paper speculates on the likely course of religion and political dogma over a future period of twenty-five years.   The author notices the eclipse of Marx by the burgeoning of marxism, leaving Weber and Durkheim as the only survivors in the field of prophetic sociology. While pluralism of ideologies is allowed in western liberalism, one of these, at least, strives to prevail and eliminate the basis of its toleration. Christianity, nationalism, liberalism and political dogma are observed in various permutations in different societies, Albania providing the clearest example of the pursuit of a truly atheist state. Professor Martin supposes that the tensions might be resolved by the domination of one creed and the subordination of another but expects that Christianity will survive to usher in the third millennium. Reprinted in *The Dilemmas of Contemporary Religion*, by David Martin. Oxford: Blackwell, 1978 (0035).

0037 Mehl, Roger. *Traité de Sociologie du Protestantisme.* Neuchâtel, Switzerland: Delachaux & Niestlé, 1965.

Much sociology of religion happens to be the sociology of protestantism; and in bringing together a range of researches in order to identify governing trends, Mehl deals with familiar problems such as secularization, religious practice and the evolution of religious structures. Particular interests include the ociology of ecumenism and of missions, sociology and pastoralia, and the involvement of protestants with politics. This work is published in English as *The Sociology of Protestantism.* London: SCM Press, 1970.

0038 Moberg, David O. "Some Trends in the Sociology of Religion in the U.S.A." *Social Compass* 13 (1966): 237-243.

Moberg reports a rapid expansion in the sociology of religion since 1945 and draws from Charles Y.Glock five core dimensions of religiosity in which commitment may be manifested - the ritualistic, ideological, intellectual, experiential and consequential. While this agenda is useful for promoting empirical sophistication, it does not satisfy the Christian theologian or devout believer. Moberg therefore proposes a sixth, the "transcendental" or "spiritual", albeit recognizing the problems of observing it scientifically.

0039 Moberg, David O. "Presidential Address: Virtues for the Sociology of Religion." *Sociological Analysis* 39 (1978): 1-18.

This is not a content analysis of statements from the White House but the address delivered in 1977 by Professor Moberg in his capacity as president of the Association for the Sociology of Religion. He welcomes the emergence within sociology of various groups characterized by the pursuit of ideological objectives. Sociology, in Moberg's view, cannot be value-free. He perceives as virtues the values he endorses and the list of these includes justice, love, humility, integrity, vision and detachment.

0040 Newman, William M. *The Social Meanings of Religion.* Chicago: Rand McNally, 1974.

Newman brings together work within a variety of perspectives and
from a wide range of cultural contexts to inform the problems which
occupy modern sociologists of religion such as dimensions of
religiosity, religious organization, the religious structure of
contemporary America and patterns of religious change, notably
secularization. He has, for example, Bellah's famous paper on
civil religion in America (0883), Martin Marty on the occult
establishment (0410), Fukuyama on major dimensions of church membership (0790) and Berger and Luckmann's widely used "The Sociology
of Religion and the Sociology of Knowledge" (0008).

0041 O'Dea, Thomas F. and O'Dea, Janet K. *Readings on the Sociology
of Religion.* Englewood Cliffs: Prentice-Hall, 1973.

This is a useful collection of sociological extracts from a range
of books, many of which would not otherwise be noticed by the
sociologist but which have important sociological content. Alongside readings from Durkheim are to be found more psychological
interpretations, such as that of Erik H.Erikson on the religious
development of the young man Luther. Problem areas across which
the selected readings range include religion and social
stratification, secularization, mysticism and the youthful quest
for new religion.

0042 Piwowarski, Wladyslaw. "Les Orientations, Les Méthodes et la
Problématique dans la Sociologie de la Religion en Pologne." In
Religiousness in the Polish Society State, edited by Witold
Zdaniewicz, pp. 5-35. Warsaw: Pallotinum, 1981 (0181).

A retrospective view of the concerns and orientations of sociology
of religion in Poland from 1957 to 1977. Piwowarski pays
particular attention to studies of the influences upon religion of
social and cultural change, of interaction between religion and
other dimensions of human life, and of religious communities,
the latter being one characteristic concern of Catholic
sociologists in Poland.

0043 Poloma, Margaret M. "Toward a Christian Sociological Perspective:
Religious Values, Theory and Methodology." *Sociological Analysis* 43
(1982): 95-108.

A contribution to the discussion pursuing a value-free sociology
of religion which suggests that the values with which sociology
is laden are themselves anti-religious. The author argues that the
positivistic basis of sociology precludes a sufficient understanding
of belief and believer. The illuminative potential of the
Christian perspective is explored in the study of the world view
of a charismatic Christian.

0044 Poulat, Émile: Gaudemet, Jean; Boulard, Ferdinand; and
Maître, Jacques. "La Sociologie Religieuse de Gabriel Le Bras."
Année Sociologique 20 (1969): 301-334.

Gabriel Le Bras is acknowledged as one of the principal exponents of
the now unfashionable tradition of *Sociologie Religieuse.* This is a

collection of notes written on the occasion of his death which typify the quality, character and assiduity of his work and distinguish the vein in which he and his collaborators pioneered sociology as a contributory discipline to the study of religion.

0045 Pruett, Gordon E. "A Note on Robert Bellah's Theory of Religious Evolution: The Early Modern Period." *Sociological Analysis* 34 (1973): 50-55.

Bellah's much noticed paper on "Religious Evolution" (0004) is appreciatively treated by Pruett who picks up only Bellah's delineation of the early modern stage of development. According to Bellah this centers on the Protestant Reformation. Pruett inclines to the view that Bellah attaches disproportionate significance to the dimension of religious belief in the displacement of the Eucharist and suggests that concern over the place of the sacrament arose not from the problem of the real presence but from the social activity of communion with the faithful.

0046 Reed, Myer S. "An Alliance for Progress: The Early Years of the Sociology of Religion in the United States." *Sociological Analysis* 42 (1981): 27-46.

This is a content analysis of articles on religion published in American sociology journals between 1895 and 1929. It is found that most authors had religious ideals of their own and were intent upon furthering these through the social gospel. Curiously they had allies among secular sociologists who joined them in the struggle against conservative forces both within academia and outside. See also Reed (0047) for an account of a later period.

0047 Reed, Myer S. "After the Alliance: The Sociology of Religion in the United States from 1925 to 1949." *Sociological Analysis* 43 (1982): 189-204.

This essay follows Reed's earlier paper (0046) dealing with a period of alliance between religious and secular sociologists. After 1925 the social gospel movement declined, and so did the sociology of religion, which reached an all time low in the 1930s. Religionists retreated from the sociological journals. The establishment in the 1940s of the *American Catholic Sociological Review* brought to notice the work of Catholic sociologists, only to confirm the old image of "religious sociology".

0048 Robertson, Roland. "A Sociological Portrait: Religion." *New Society* 19, 434 (1972): 8-10.

Robertson conducts a discussion from previous published research of the salience of religion and its relationship to a familiar set of demographic variables. Being written for a general but enlightened readership, the scope of the article is wide. It covers findings on the strength of racial prejudice in different religious groups, the social characteristics of religious participants and an indication of neglected areas, such as the interrelationship of religious activity and sexual behavior.

0049   Robertson, Roland, ed.   *Sociology of Religion: Selected Readings.*
Harmondsworth: Penguin, 1969.

A collection of seminal readings which represents the contributions
of the grand masters Weber, Durkheim and Parsons, Berger, Luckmann,
Troeltsch and others.   There are anthropological comments on
aspects of primitive religion and Luckmann, Wilson, Geertz and
Willems are extracted on religion in industrial society.   The
perennial themes of religion, social change and social
stratification are addressed in key readings and Stark and Glock,
Bellah, Worsley and Swanson are used to raise problems of analysis
and interpretation.

0050   Russell, Dora.   *The Religion of the Machine Age.* London:
Routledge and Kegan Paul, 1983.

Aside from some disturbing contrivances and an apparent endeavor to
assimilate too much of the history of Christianization, there is in
this volume a useful survey of intellectual and organized religious
responses to economic and social change.   The sensitivity of one
to the impact of the other is clearly reviewed and the work
complements studies on popular movements.

0051   Scharf, Betty R.   *The Sociological Study of Religion.*   London:
Hutchinson, 1970.

This textbook is outstandingly successful in its aims of rendering
the sociology of religion accessible, interesting and lively.
There are the obligatory presentations of Durkheim, Weber, church,
sect and denomination; there is a section on religion in industrial
societies which addresses problems of secularization and a treatment of church and state that makes comparative reference to
Buddhist and Islamic society.   The book is written in a succinct
and elegant style.

0052   Schreuder, Osmund.   "Die strukturell-funcktionale Theorie und
die Religionssoziologie."   *Internationales Jahrbuck für
Religionssoziologie*   2 (1966): 99-132.

The author considers criticisms that sociologists of religion rely
too heavily on measures emanating from the main religious
institutions and neglect   non-institutional religiosity.   He
elaborates a number of points in defence of structural-functionalism
which he commends as being capable of systematizing the sociology
of religion.

0053   Seneviratne, H.L.   "A Critique of Religion and Power in the
Sociological Sciences."   *Social Compass*   32 (1985): 31-44.

An examination of the problematic relation of religion to politics
in which the author finds it expedient to distinguish between
modern and pre-modern societies.   Those of the pre-modern type
exhibit an integration of the two dimensions.   He studies the
particular case of Sri Lanka in which traditionally integrated
ideologies have been succeeded and now survive only in fragmented
form.

0054 Simmel, Georg. "A Contribution to the Sociology of Religion."
American Journal of Sociology 60 (1955): supplement pp. 1-18.

A sensitive treatment of the credal and social manifestations of
religion which has implications for the positivistic and sometimes
dismissive analysis of religious behavior.   His "most important"
concern is to demonstrate that scientific interpretations of
religion, including explanatory accounts, in no way diminish the
validity - he even says "dignity" - of religious ideals.
Reprinted in an abridged form in Yinger (0070): 332-344.

0055 Stark, Werner. *The Sociology of Religion: A Study of
Christendom   1. Established Religion.* London: Routledge and Kegan
Paul, 1966.

Stark's procedure is to distinguish between primary and secondary
forms, in the former treating of the sacred leader, the sacred
nation and the sacred mission and in each case studying the
examples of Byzantium, Russia, France and England.   He
differentiates secondary forms by polity and class structure and
studies the additional cases of Poland and the United States.
Durkheim and Weber get passing references but no more.

0056 Stark, Werner. *The Sociology of Religion: A Study of
Christendom 5.* London: Routledge and Kegan Paul, 1972.

The fifth volume of Stark's great work deals with types of
religious culture.   Stark's study commences with the historical
period of *Gemeinschaft*-type social organizations and the
religious cultures associated with these.   Community evolves
into "association" and thence to secular civilizations.   He is
principally occupied with the Catholic and Calvinist traditions
and offers in appendix a study of the culture of the sect.

0057 Towler, Robert. *Homo Religiosus: Sociological Problems in
the Study of Religion.* London: Constable, 1974.

Towler studies Weber's ideas on the relationship of economic to
religious aspects of society and discusses the association of
religious and social change in medieval and Reformation Europe
and in Northern Ireland.   The examination of contemporary
American and British religiosity ranges from the mainstream to
the crypto-religious.   The study raises perennial questions
about the definition of religion, the role of religion in
society and of the sociology of religion in sociology.

0058 Wach, Joachim. *Types of Religious Experience: Christian and
Non-Christian.* London: Routledge and Kegan Paul, 1951.

The focus is not upon religious experience as understood by
psychologists of religion but upon what marks a phenomenon as
religious.   To this end Wach traces the historical development
of non-Christian and Christian religions, deploys the church-
denomination-sect typology and draws from Rudolf Otto's idea of
"the holy".   Originally published in German.

0059 Whaling, Frank, ed. *Contemporary Approaches to the Study of Religion 2. The Social Sciences.* Berlin: De Gruyter, 1985.

A collection of papers on the study of religion in the social sciences, following volume one which is concerned with the humanities.   There is a focus upon recent developments, recent trends and issues and future prospects.

0060 Zadra, Dario, ed. *Sociologia della Religione: Testi e Documenti.* Milan: Ulrico Hoepli, 1969.

Zadra draws together a substantial collection of seminal readings in the sociology of religion and presents these in Italian translation.   Texts include excerpts from Bellah, Durkheim, Fitchter, Geertz, Lenski, Malinowski, Marx, Robert K.Merton, Parsons, Liston Pope, Georg Simmel, Troeltsch, Wach, Weber and Bryan R.Wilson.

B. CLASSICS

0061 Durkheim, Emile. *De la Division du Travail Social: Étude sur l'Organisation des Sociétés Supérieures.* Paris: Alcan, 1893.

This is Durkheim's doctoral thesis and his first book.   In it he establishes the religious character of the origins of penal law and examines the demands of religion upon the individual.   In the primitive societies that engage him there are no functional divisions between religion, morality, the law and political activity.   The eclipse of religious criminality is a phenomenon distinctive of developed Christianity.

0062 Durkheim, Emile. *Les Règles de la Méthode Sociologique.* Paris: Alcan, 1895.

In this celebrated essay on sociological method Durkheim establishes religion as a social factor and lays the ground for the scientific study of it.   In particular he disapproves the requirement of religious commitment among students of the history of religion and warns against emotional involvement.   His counsel is to that extent a timepiece in the sociology of religion.   Published in English as *The Rules of Sociological Method.*   Chicago: University Press, 1938 and Free Press, 1950.

0063 Durkheim, Emile. *La Suicide: Étude de Sociologie.* Paris: Alcan, 1897.

This sociological classic includes many useful studies of religious phenomena, including in chapter 2 of Book II a study of the incidence of suicides within various religions.   There are also notes on the high incidence of insanity in Judaism, the relationship of religion to capitalism and a speculation that Catholicism is more potent than Protestantism to check suicidal tendencies.   Published in English by Chicago: Free Press, 1951.

0064   Durkheim, Emile. *Les Formes Élémentaires de la Vie Religieuse.*
Paris: Alcan, 1912.

One of the major works in the sociology of religion. Durkheim's
concern was the evolution of primitive religions, his observations
upon which have ylelded seminal categories and distinctions,
notably that between the domains of the sacred and the profane.
His discovery in primitive religious forms of the symbols of
cultural integration initiated the persistent interests of
sociologists in the social consequences of conformity in belief
and practice, in the nature of attitudes toward the sacred, in the
sacred as a normative factor in daily life and in the sacred
community as a discrete social entity.   Well known and widely
accessible in English as *The Elementary Forms of the Religious
Life.*

0065   Durkheim, Emile. *L'Éducation Morale.* Paris: Alcan, 1925.

Durkheim argues for a rational morality in education that is
independent of religious legitimation: but the expurgation of
religious contents is not the course by which such a morality can
be achieved, for it needs to be rethought more radically and
there is a danger that essential moral elements might also be
expelled thereby. Durkheim insists on the necessity of a
discipline derived not from religion but from the expedient of
nature.   Published in English as *Moral Education.* New York:
Free Press, 1961.

0066   Halévy, Elie. *A History of the English People in 1815.*
London: T.Fisher Unwin, 1924.

Halévy's thesis is a corollary of Weber's and pays particular
attention to the social and political functions of religious
ideology.   In his view of the history of England in the 18th
and 19th centuries, he attributes its extraordinary stability
through an age of revolutions to the distinctive character of
English piety.   Central to the argument is the role of
Methodism which occupied an intermediate social location and
proposed a corresponding ideology, thereby averting the
polarization of English society.   Marx's view of religion as
an "opiate" which dissipates revolutionary fervor provides a
subordinate theme to Halévy's argument.   Originally published
in French in 1906.

0067   Herberg, Will. *Protestant-Catholic-Jew: An Essay in American
Religious Sociology.* New York: Doubleday, 1955.

This is a classic, first because it was a pioneer work in its day
and second because it continues to provide an analytical framework
for the sociological study of the three religious traditions of
its title.   The background to what Herberg calls "the triple
melting pot" is migration, predominantly from Europe; in the
process of migration and settlement religious identies and value
systems variously fossilize and dissolve.   The three religious
communities are here studied separately in historical and
sociological perspective, differentiated, and observed both in

tension and in unity. Herberg's propositions have been widely
picked up and investigated and to that extent this book has
provided the agenda of much recent sociology of American religion.
See for example Ward (0088).

0068 Lenski, Gerhard. *The Religious Factor: A Sociological Study
of Religion's Impact on Politics, Economics and Family Life.* New
York: Doubleday, 1961.

A classical empirical study in the Weberian tradition conducted in
Detroit, Michigan, and designed to assess the extent to which
religion affects everyday life. The operational definition of
religion conventionally includes belief and attendance (in
Lenski's terminology the "orthodoxy" and "associational"
dimensions); Lenski usefully adds to these other indicators, the
"devotional" which relates to prayer habits and the "communal"
which concerns identity with a particular religious community.
The work is saturated with statistical data which in Lenski's
interpretation attest to the rigor, influence and increasing
vitality of contemporary religion in America and confirm Weber's
hypotheses on the differential economic behavior of Catholics
and Protestants.   Later investigators, however, have found
little or no such difference: of these, reference should be
made to the criticisms advanced in Andrew M.Greeley's *Religion
and Career* (see 0484).

0069 Weber, Max. *Religionssoziologie.* Tübingen: Mohr, 1922.

Reckoned by Talcott Parsons to be the supreme contribution to the
discipline of sociology, this work comprehends Judaism, Taoism,
Hinduism, Buddhism and Confucianism as well as Christianity and
demonstrates in respect of each the relationships of religion to
economics and politics which are particularly studied in his
better known *Die Protestantische Ethik.* He studies the
accommodation of the great religions to the world and their flights
from it and provides thereby a basis for the characterization of
sect-types.   This work is significant not only for its seminal
insight and encyclopaedic content but for setting out an agenda
that has occupied sociologists of religion for sixty years.
Religionssoziologie was a self-contained part of Weber's unfinished
magnum opus *Wirtsthaft und Gesellschaft* and appears in English as
The Sociology of Religion.

0070 Yinger, J.Milton. *Religion, Society and the Individual: An
Introduction to the Sociology of Religion.* New York: Macmillan, 1957.

This is a massive and seminal work in the sociology of religion
that reasserts the principle of the founding fathers that the study
of religion is the essence of the scientific study of society.
To that end, over half the volume is taken up with classic
readings from Durkheim, Malinowski, Talcott Parsons, Troeltsch,
Weber, Niebuhr and others.

Yinger's own essay centers upon such conventional concerns as
religion and social status, religion and economics, religions and
social change and the sociological theory of religion.   Among

his more widely noticed contributions is his typology of
religious organizations on the two criteria of inclusiveness/
exclusiveness and attention to social integration/personal need.
On this basis he distinguishes six types: universal church,
ecclesia, denomination, established sect, sect and cult.

C. COMMENTARIES

0071 Bankston, William B.; Allen, H.David; and Cunningham, David S.
"Religion and Suicide: A Research Note on Sociology's 'One Law'."
Social Forces 62 (1983): 521-528.

In *La Suicide* (0063) Durkheim indicated suicide rates in different
religious groups and showed that the rate among Roman Catholics
was relatively low.   The authors of this article report their
study of the situation in Louisiana, the findings of which
contradict Durkheim's point about Catholics but accord with
suicide theory in a more general way.

0072 Beltser, L.L. "Problema Religioznosti Sotsial'nykh Grupp v
Sotsiologii Maksa Vebera." *Vestnik Moskovskogo Universiteta
Filosofiya* 29 (1974): 84-93.

Beltser conducts a discussion on the theory of religious groups in
Max Weber's sociology of religion.   Weber is taken to task for
his inadequate knowledge in certain areas such as the relationship
of the Russian Orthodox Church and it is suggested that a theory
constructed upon a base of such fragmentary understanding is at
best tenuous.   Marxist theory of the relation of religion and
society is commended as superior.

0073 Buchignani, Norman L. "The Weberian Thesis in India."
Archives de Sciences Sociales des Religions 42 (1976): 17-33.

The author recognizes the importance of Max Weber's *Hinduismus
und Buddhismus* and endeavors here to remedy the neglect which he
feels that work to have suffered.   He addresses questions of
historical religion and modernization and assesses the
applications of Weberian rationalism to the religious system of
India.

0074 Bühler, Antoine. "Production de Sens et Légitimation Sociale:
Karl Marx et Max Weber." *Social Compass* 23 (1976): 317-344.

Bühler offers a comparison of Marx's critique with Weber's
sociology of religion.   Marx regards religion as a necessary
inversion of social reality and as a projection beyond the real
world.   Weber also treats religion as legitimization or as the
provider of sense or meaning, but develops his theory in a
comparative historical perspective.   Both interpretations
anticipate a society without religion and the author of this
article compares their views of the emancipation of secularism.

0075 Freund, Julien. "Le Charisme selon Max Weber." *Social Compass*
23 (1976): 383-396.

The author undertakes a close study of all Weber's references and
elaborations of the concept of charisma.   It transpires that
Weber used the concept in his political sociology to explain
social movements of an explosive kind rather than the leadership
of those that persisted in the long term.   The perpetuation of
the force of such a movement is invariably by its systematization.

0076 Isambert, François-André. "L'Élaboration de la Notion de
Sacré dans l'École Durkheimiennne." *Archives de Sciences Sociales
des Religions* 42 (1976): 35-56.

Isambert refers to the work of Robertson Smith and others in tracing
a development of the significance of the holy in Durkheim's work,
which reaches its zenith in *Les Formes Élémentaires de la Vie
Religieuse* (0064). See also Isambert (0890).

0077 Ling, Trevor. *Karl Marx and Religion in Europe and India.*
London: Macmillan, 1980.

Ling writes essays on Marx's critique of state religion, mysticism
and the case of state religion in England.   English religion
conveyed to India engages both Marx and Weber.   The author
addresses some abiding problems for marxist interpretation such as
the persistence of religion, modes of religious counterculture such
as Krishna Consciousness and the analysis of marxism as a religious
form.

0078 Pickering, William S.F. *Durkheim's Sociology of Religion.*
London: Routledge and Kegan Paul, 1984.

Though itself formidable this volume encourages the reader to come
to terms with Durkheim by taking him in biographical stages
corresponding to phases in the great man's thought.   The emphasis
is upon Durkheim's sociology as opposed to his anthropology and
Pickering contributes useful discussions on, for example, the
pretences of *sociologie religieuse.*

0079 Pickering, William S.F. "Abraham Hume (1818-1884): A Forgotten
Pioneer in Religious Sociology." *Archives de Sciences Sociales des
Religions*.33 (1972): 33-48.

Though unremembered, Hume was an assiduous stocktaker, collector
of statistics and applied sociologist, doing the work in the 19th
century that the modern Church of England appoints departments to
undertake.   Pickering provides a list of Hume's publications
and appreciates the scope of his work and the energy and
resourcefulness with which he undertook it.

0080 Pickering, William S.F., ed. *Durkheim on Religion.* London:
Routledge and Kegan Paul, 1975.

Pickering makes a selection of key excerpts from Durkheim's works
together with reviews and reflections by Van Gennep, Goldenweiser,

Richard and Stanner, and a comprehensive bibliography.

0081   Poggi, Gianfranco. *Calvinism and the Capitalist Spirit: Max Weber's Protestant Ethic.* London: Macmillan, 1983. 121pp.

Poggi is much concerned with identifying the true character of Weber's *Protestant Ethic* (see 0069). He submits that it should not be read as a causal historical study but as an essay in the methodology of social science and in the theory of social development.

0082   Prades, J.A. *La Sociologie de la Religion chez Max Weber.* Louvain: Nauwelaerts, 1966.

This exposition of Max Weber's sociology of religion is described as an analytical and critical essay on Weber's methodology. Sociology is compared with other sciences applied to the study of religion.   In the author's appraisal Weber is unique as a sociologist and his seminal work provides a focus for many of the methodological problems which attend sociological practice, such as conceptual elaboration and causal analysis.   The book carries as an appendix a chronological list of Weber's works.

0083   Raphael, Freddy. "Les Juifs en tant que Peuple Paria dans l'Oeuvre de Max Weber." *Social Compass* 26 (1976): 397-426.

In Weber's work the Jews are classified as a pariah or outcast people, surviving in a foreign environment only by the adoption and enactment of prescriptive rituals which reduce the frustration at being dislocated from the historical goal of restoration in Palestine.   Jewish self-perceptions, nourished by the testimony of the prophets, do not however accord with the pariah complex. Weber's concepts of "pariah capitalism" and "dual morality" are here challenged as being inadequate assessments of the complexities of Jewish economy.

0084   Roth, Guenther. "Religion and Revolutionary Beliefs: Sociological and Historical Dimensions in Max Weber's Work." *Social Forces* 55 (1976): 257-272.

The burgeoning in recent years of many politico-religious movements and ideologies is the context for a stocktaking and assessment of Weber's *Sociology of Religion* (0069).   That work is approved for its conceptual adequacy and the author considers the model of a revolutionary religion in the political and religious conditions of the United States.

0085   Seyfarth, Constans. "The West German Discussion of Max Weber's Sociology of Religion since the 1960s." *Social Compass* 27 (1980): 9-25.

Seyfarth conducts a lucid examination of the main themes of the discussion, with special reference to the problem of secularization in Weber's sociology.   The participants in this debate are German but the applications of their contributions are more general.

0086   Stanner, W.E.H.   "Reflections on Durkheim and Aboriginal
Religion."   In *Social Organization: Essays Presented to Raymond Firth*,
edited by M.Freedman.   pp.217-40.   London: Cass, 1967.

As editor of *L'année sociologique* Durkheim emerged as the first
serious student of aboriginal society.   In Stanner's paper there is
an assessment of his contribution to the study of this field
together with an appraisal of those who followed him.   Stanner
feels that the categories that constitute Durkheim's principal
bequest are strained and static and their utility has long been
exhausted.

0087   Waddell, R.G.   "Charisma and Reason: Paradoxes and Tactics of
Originality."   *A Sociological Yearbook of Religion in Britain* 5
(1972): 1-10.

Waddell addresses himself to some of the ambiguities and confusions
inherent in Weber's concept of charisma: he suggests that some of
these are imagined while others stem from the paradoxical nature
of the phenomenon.   "It is," he reckons, "a striking peculiarity of
Weber's followers (many disciples and critics alike) that they have
busied themselves hewing and chipping at his theory in order to
reinstate (the) old dichotomy between personality and society -
some, it would seem, out of a sense of ancestor-worship, but most
for purposes of target practice."

0088   Ward, W.R.   "Will Herberg: An American Hypothesis Seen from
Europe."   *Durham University Journal* 65 (1973): 260-270.

One of many intriguing hypotheses offered by Herberg (0067) was the
suggestion that migration from Europe to the United States involved
adaptation and assimilation and these processes effected a
compromise in religious behavior and affiliation.   This was in
Herberg's view the explanation of the characteristic quality of
American religiosity, marked by high degrees of profession and low
degrees of devotion.   Ward explores beyond Herberg's account,
looks at conflict and differentiation between migrant groups and
complements Herberg's Protestant, Catholic and Jew dimensions with
that of Black.

0089   Winter, J.Alan.   *Continuities in the Sociology of Religion:
Creed, Congregation and Community.*   New York: Harper and Row, 1977.

There is much in Winter's essay that is little more than an updating of Weber, Herberg, Troeltsch and conventional wisdom.
But even this mechanical operation is worthwhile in the light of
latter-day political activism among the clergy and the emergence
of religious communes.   Of these and other contemporary manifestations of religion the author treats in a lucid way, without
making the student reject time-honored theories.

0090   Zeitlin, Irving M.   *Ancient Judaism: Biblical Criticism from
Max Weber to the Present.*   Oxford: Polity Press, 1984.

Beginning from the classic work of Max Weber, the author analyzes
the origins of Judaism in the light of more recent scholarship.

Zeitlin sets out to criticize both those modern scholars who have
cast doubts on the scriptural account of the history of Israel, and
those who hold that the religion of Israel originated either as
polytheism or as a fusion of Baal and Yahweh.   He finds unconvinc-
ing the non-sociological modes of approaching these questions.
Following Max Weber's interpretative method, Zeitlin strives to
grasp the subjective meanings which the actors themselves
attributed to their conduct.   Drawing on biblical and extra-
biblical evidence, he addresses the question of how the actors
concerned - whether they were patriarchs, prophets, judges, kings
or the people - understood themselves, their world and their faith.
Weber pioneered the application of this method throughout his
writings on the sociology of religion and most notably in his own
work *Ancient Judaism*.

D.   JOURNALS

0091 *Actes de Conférence Internationale de Sociologie des Religions*.
Biennial. 1948-   .

The International Conference for the Sociology of Religion
(C.I.S.R.) meets in alternate years and publishes in a single
volume the *Actes*, all papers presented at the plenary sessions
of each conference.   The Conference meets in different cities in
the countries of its members and the Actes are published from
Paris (formerly from Lille).   Each congress, and therefore each
volume, is devoted to a broad theme which is broken down into sub-
themes in the French manner.   In 1983 the seventeenth congress
met in London and the theme was "Religion and the Public Domain".
Papers appear in English or French, according to the preference
of the authors.

0092 *Archives de Sciences Sociales des Religions*. Paris, 1956-   .

Formerly *Archives de Sociologie des Religions*, this is a quarterly
journal almost exclusively devoted to the sociology of religion,
carrying occasional articles in related disciplines such as
history and politics.   Articles are published in English or
French, according to authorship, with abstracts in the alternative
language.   Two issues per year are given to descriptive
periodical reviews *(bulletin des périodiques)* and book reviews in
the field *(bulletin des ouvrages)*.   Subjects include methodology
and epistemology, reflections on classical works, area studies,
messianic movements, charisma, the sociology of sects, world
religions, new religious movements, religious participation and
affiliation, attitudes and the relation of religion to everyday
life, the religious factor in economic development and political
society.

0093 Brunkow, Robert de V. ed. *Religion and Society in North
America : A Bibliography*. Santa Barbara : ABC Clio, 1983.

This bibliography provides more than 4,000 abstracts of recent
journal articles on religion in US and Canadian history from the

17th century to the present.   It is extensively indexed for ease of reference.

0094 *Internationales Jahrbuch für Religionssoziologie.* Köln and Opladen: Westdeutscher Verlag, 1965-   .

The journal published articles in German and English and bore the English title *International Yearbook for the Sociology of Religion.* Successive volumes adopted special themes such as "Religious pluralism and social structure" (1,1965) and "Theoretical perspectives" (2,1966). Major contributions are annotated in this bibliography under author.

0095 *Jewish Journal of Sociology, The.* London: Heinemann, 1959-   .

Contributions range across the themes of religion, race and ethnicity and there is a special interest in the sociology of Israel including settlement, integration, social class and political alignments. Published twice yearly.

0096 *Journal for the Scientific Study of Religion.* Storrs, Ct.: Society for the Scientific Study of Religion, 1961-   .

The quarterly journal of the Society for the Scientific Study of Religion (founded 1949) consisting of articles and research notes. Its principal disciplines are social psychology and sociology. It is almost exclusively a North American house journal and overseas contributions are very rare.   Most work reported is narrowly empirical, most typically comprising analyses of survey data with particular interest in statistical relationships between critical variables.

0097 *Religion: A Journal of Religion and Religions.* Newcastle-upon-Tyne: Oriel, 1971-   .

The journal has ranged widely over world religions and the major part of its material has related to Asian religions.   Articles are commonly theological, philosophical and historical in perspective but the occasional sociological treatment is featured here.   Latterly *Religion* has been published by Academic Press.

0098 *Review of Religious Research.* Storrs, Ct.: Religious Research Association, 1959-   .

This a quarterly journal of the Religious Research Association which is published from the University of Connecticut.   The review has carried scholarly work in sociology and cognate disciplines; many of its articles are annotated in this bibliography, with which the range of its interests are coextensive.

0099 *Sociaal Kompass:Tijdschrift Voor Sociologie, Sociografie, Sociale Psychologie en Statistick.* 1953-   .

A bi-monthly review of scientific studies of religion, issued under the International Catholic Institute for Social-Ecclesiastical

Research.   The name was changed to *Social Compass* in 1955.   In early years work was exclusively sociographic.   Latterly the journal has attracted a wider range of scholars and it has become established as a major resource.   A case of sect to denomination.

0100 *Social Forces.* University of North Carolina, 1922-   .

A journal of substantial articles, principally but not exclusively of aspects of the social structure of North America and tending to be empirical in approach.   First concerns are with macro-factors such as class, the economy, labor, politics, race and demographic variables and the correlates of these.   Religious concerns are featured frequently and the occasional issue, such as that for March 1983, has religion as its major theme.

0101 *Sociological Analysis.* University of Connecticut, 1940-   .

A quarterly journal published by the Association for the Sociology of Religion, University of Connecticut, offering a good range of articles, comments and reviews, all at a good critical level. Now called *SA*.

0102 *Sociological Yearbook of Religion in Britain, A.* London: S.C.M. Press, 1968-1975.

A series of eight volumes variously edited by David Martin and Michael Hill which served to bring together and stimulate new work in the sociology of religion and - by the inclusion of comprehensive bibliographies of research published and in process (volumes 3 ff.) - to provide a current system of reference that was all too short-lived.

Each volume carried about eight articles, the quality and sociological style of which varied greatly.   Perhaps the greatest contribution of the *Yearbook* was its imaginative broadening of an agenda that was in danger of being preoccupied with studies of sects and denominations and of religious attitudes to the world. The series featured papers on various missions, humanism and unbelief, religious functionaries, Sunday observance and the religious dimension of football support.

E.   RELIGION AND THE STATE; RELIGION AND POLITICS

0103 Andrews, Stuart. *Methodism and Society.* London: Longman, 1970.

The perspective is historical and the organization of material is chronological.   The subject matter, however, is sociological in significance if not in insight.   The author deals with the development of English Methodism from the Holy Club period and gives thorough treatment of educational and philanthropic work, of organization and of the impact of Methodism upon social and political change.   The book is presented as a student text.

0104   Aubert, Roger.   "L'Église Catholique et la Vie Politique en Belgique depuis la Seconde Guerre Mondiale." *Rex Publica* 15 (1973): 183-203.

An examination of the extensive influence of the Roman Catholic Church upon social and political life in Belgium since the Second World War.   The principal agent of such influence is the Catholic party, electoral support for which is urged by the bishops.   A campaign to deconfessionalize Belgian politics was not sustained and the anticlericalism promoted by the political left only engendered a resolute stand by the Catholics.   The decade preceding this analysis, however, witnessed a formaliz-ation of the Church's place in Belgian political life and the autonomy of the political domain is now regulated.

0105   Avila, Raphael.   "Religion et Société Politique au Nicaragua après la Révolution Sandiniste." *Social Compass* 30 (1983): 233-259.

This paper observes the distinction between the private and public sectors of the Nicaraguan economy.   It offers an analysis of the religious position, whether of support or of opposition, to the Sandinista regime as it is evidenced among bishops, groups of priests, Catholic and ecumenical organizations.   This affords a functionalist account of religion in the social conditions of a revolution.

0106   Bauman, Zygmunt.   "Social Dissent in East European Politics." *Archives Européennes de Sociologie* 12 (1971).

This is a much noticed paper in which Bauman develops a typology of social dissent that has since proven illuminative in the analysis of the role of the Church in, inter alia, Poland.   He distinguishes among his types forms of dissent discernible among uprooted peasants, those from whom status has been with-drawn, and those for whom upward mobility is obstructed; he views nationalist resistance against Soviet supremacy and modern intellectual currents.   The paper shows an insight ahead of its time.

0107   Beckford, James A.   "The State and Control of New Religious Movements." *Actes de C.I.S.R.* 17 (1983): 115-130.

The State control of religious movements is not new, as Beckford shows, but the tension of State and the new religious movements deserves the close sociological analysis which Beckford gives it.   He points to characteristics of State control in the modern period; it is directed at those religious groups which offer the most comprehensive service for their members; there is a discrepancy between official policy on the freedom of the cults and the actions of administrators; and the State is quite ready to sponsor research on the new religious movements and public hearings concerning them.   Beckford extends these observations with a discussion of the tensions of the State, capitalist ideology, liberal philosophy and religion.

0108 Brothers, Joan. *Church and School: A Study of the Impact of Education on Religion.* Liverpool: Liverpool University Press, 1964.

This is the report of an empirical investigation of Roman Catholicism in Liverpool; on the basis of interviews of priests, teachers and young people. It is found that ideas communicated in selective schools have implications for the traditional relationships of priest and people. The community studied is transformed by educational policy and there arise new networks of relationships centered upon the schools.

0109 Cano, José Sánchez. "La Nacionalidad y la Consagración Conciliar en la Iglesia Ortodoxa Ucraniana." *Revista Española de la Opinion Publica* 31 (1973): 239-311.

The Ukrainian Orthodox Church is introduced in historical perspective and in respect of its relation to nationalism. After its succession by Catholicism the Russian Revolution had the effect of reactivating the Ukrainian national spirit and the Orthodox Church was revived as the "Ukrainian Autocephalous Orthodox Church". The relation of this Church to the State is intended by its Council to be cooperative but resistant to manipulation.

0110 Carey, Michael J. "Catholicism and Irish National Identity." In *Religion and Politics in the Modern World,* edited by Peter H. Merkl and Ninian Smart, pp. 104-120. New York: New York University Press, 1983 (0148).

The identity of the Roman Catholic Church with national identity in the Republic of Ireland is perhaps as proximate as any case in Christendom. Catholics constitute 95% of the population and mass attendance is the norm. Irish Catholicism is described as austere, puritanical and authoritarian; and its conjunction with Irish cultural identity predates the modern Republic. Carey treats of the early history of the alignment and traces the development of this in modern nationalist politics.

0111 Carré, Olivier. "Notes sur l'Islam Politique Aujourd'hui." *Actes de C.I.S.R.* 17 (1983): 57-73.

This is a close analysis of the politics of Islam with special reference to its militant and violent expressions. The author examines the activity of the Muslim Brotherhood and considers the idea that in the Islamic context violence begets violence.

0112 *Church and State: Report of the Archbishops' Commission.* London: Church Information Office, 1970.

The church in question is the Church of England. This is a most useful volume for raw data, for it condenses the perceptions of the hierarchy and lay élite on their Church's privileged establishment, the entanglements of which include the relative autonomy of synodical government, the system of patronage, the parliamentary right of veto and an allocation to bishops of seats in the House of Lords.

0113 Cipriani, Roberto. "Religious Influence on Politics in Italy:
Diffused Religion." *Actes de C.I.S.R.* 17 (1983): 75-95.

The Catholic religion persists in Italy as a force prevailing in
national politics and this is attested by Cipriani.   However
that influence is not a simple and direct relationship between
centers; Catholicism has rather devolved in recent years and it
has become appropriate to use more global and multivariate
conceptions such as "the Catholic world". Cipriani explores the
range of the meaning of being Catholic vis-à-vis Italian
political life.

0114 Colonna, Fanny. "Cultural Resistance and Religious Legitimacy
in Colonial Algeria." *Economy and Society* 3 (1974): 233-252.

This is a case study which has general applications to the
relationship of religious movements and the political life of
colonial or developing countries.   The author considers variables
in the relationship and warns against the notion prevailing in
Islam that religion and the State are inextricably related; this
view, it is suggested, precludes an effective study of the
respective spheres.

0115 Deiner, John T. "Radicalism in the Argentine Catholic Church."
Government and Opposition 10 (1975): 70-89.

Deiner analyzes the relationships of the Argentine State and the
Catholic Church at levels of clergy and episcopacy, as respecting
political problems of violence, rioting, the suppression of
opposition and development issues.   Political opposition is
constituted by the Movement of Priests for the   Third World but
this movement, inaugurated in 1967, has itself been checked by
the Catholic hierarchy.   Political orientations and involvements
thus divide sections of the Catholic Church.

0116 Djalili, Mohammed-Reza. *Religion et Revolution: L'Islam
Shi'ite et l'État.* Paris: Economica, 1981.

Djalili presents a sympathetic account of Shi'ite Islam, its
origins, evolution and political significance in relation to the
modern state of Iran.   The Shi'ite conception of political power
and the organizational apparatus of Shi'ia are explained in
application to the demise of the Pahlavi dynasty and the
revolution of 1978 and 1979 which introduced an Islamic
dispensation.

0117 Francis, Leslie J. *Assessing the Partnership 1944-1984.*
Abingdon, Oxfordshire: Culham College Institute Occasional Paper 5
(1984).

This is chiefly notable as an example of the deployment of
sociological methods in program evaluation, as in the assessment
of ecumenical projects.   In this case the scheme concerned is
the partnership of churches and state in the provision of
religious education and parochial schools in the county of
Gloucestershire.   There is provision for religious education and

worship in schools under the terms of the 1944 Education Act and this
is the report of surveys among elementary schools, some 83% of which
responded to one of the surveys. Data range widely within the
problem area and include the frequency of church attendance by headteachers, participation and refusal rates at school worship and the
extent to which religious worship in school relies upon the 1944
Act for its legitimacy; in the event, over 90% of all headteachers
would want the pattern of worship to remain unchanged if the legal
requirement were removed and the figure is higher still, 98%, among
headteachers of Church of England aided schools.

0118 François, Martha Ellis. "Reformation and Society: An Analysis of
Guy Swanson's *Religion and Regime.*" *Comparative Studies in Society
and History* 14 (1972): 287-305.

The author picks up Swanson's thesis concerning social and political
factors relating to the succession of Calvinism in national states
of Catholic monopoly (0163). She utilizes the five-point typology
of governments elaborated by Swanson and applies his thesis to the
development of non-official religions with special reference to
Poland, France, England and Bohemia.

0119 Fridel, Wilbur M. "Modern Japanese Nationalism: State Shinto,
the Religion that was 'Not a Religion'." *Religion and Politics in the
Modern World,* edited by Peter H.Merkl and Ninian Smart, pp.155-169.
New York: New York University Press, 1983 (0148).

Japan opened its doors to the west during the 1860s and the
following eight decades are regarded as the critical period of
Japanese modernization. Throughout the period Shinto was brought
increasingly forward as a unifying force in national identity and
"the great energizer" for the national effort.

0120 Gellner, Ernest. "A Pendulum Swing Theory of Islam." *Annales
de Sociologie* (1968): 5-14.

A discussion of the dynamics of Islam and its relation to "the world"
compared with Christianity, with particular reference to the
religious factor in the establishment of a dominant ideology. The
title of the essay refers to the work of David Hume's theory (in
The Natural History of Religion, 1956) concerning a perpetual
oscillation in religious phenomena between polytheistic and
monotheistic views. Reprinted in the collection of readings edited
by Robertson (0049).

0121 Gilbert, Alan D. *Religion and Society in Industrial England.*
London: Longman, 1976.

The perspective of Gilbert's work is historical and the period
studied is 1740 to 1914. But his insight and findings belong in
the sociology of religion, for he traces the growing apart and
conflict of church and sect ("chapel") in terms of their respective
functions. Religious practice is quantified and analyzed in a
social context, on the one hand by an examination of the
metamorphosis of the religious establishment and on the other by
a study of the rejection of "the world".

0122   Glock, Charles Y. and Stark, Rodney. *Religion and Society in Tension*. Chicago: Rand McNally, 1965.

A widely regarded contribution to the sociology of religion which is valuable not least in delineating a comprehensive set of five "dimensions of religiosity": the experiential, the ritualistic, the ideological, the intellectual and the consequential. Of these, the last encompasses the secular effects of religious belief. Glock and Stark provide an interpretive survey of selected cases of social and religious tension, including the religious revival in America said to have followed World War Two, the new denominationalism and the dilemmas of the parish church. In the sections devoted to religion and social change, the authors observe a religious ambivalence to the status quo in social policies, sometimes promoting social integration and harmony and other times fostering conflict.

0123   Greene, Evarts B. *Religion and the State: The Making and Testing of an American Tradition*. New York: New York University Press, 1941.

This is in part a longitudinal documentary study but the dimension of time is by no means exclusive of other perspectives and the work offers details and interpretations of the complex and changing role of the State in religious activity and of the Americanization of religious values. Cases studied include the current tension of the relation of churches and State in the field of education and formulations of Church-State relations are traced through migration from Europe.

0124   Hadj-Sadok, Mohammed. "De la Théorie à la Pratique des Prescriptions de l'Islam en Algérie Contemporaine." *Social Compass* 25 (1978): 433-443.

The majority following of Algeria regulates itself according to the Shari'a, the Islamic social law compiled by Malik, a great teacher from Medina. The colonization of Algeria by France challenged the Shari'a with western codes in law, politics, economics and ethics. The French formally ceased to influence social life in Algeria in 1962 but the Shari'a has not been reinstated and Algeria has not forsaken the western road to modernization.

0125   Hammond, John I. "Revival Religion and Antislavery Politics." *American Sociological Review* 39 (1974): 175-186.

Associations of religious and political orientations receive various explanations in the literature; commonly the commitment of a particular organization to a respective political or secular movement is said to be accidental rather than credal, or at least explicable as the self-interest of the socioeconomic group within which the religious organization operates. Hammond tests for a more direct relationship of theology and politics in respect of the role of revivalism transformed religious orientations which were then pertinent to the slavery issue.

0126   Hartmann, Karl. "Stagnation in den Beziehungen zwischen Kirche und Staat in Polen." *Ost-europa* 27 (1977): 20-30.

Church-State relations in Poland entered a period of "normalization" after the accession of Edward Gierek to the leadership
at Christmas 1970. Both sides were committed to achieve a
satisfactory relationship but this was not resolved in a
decisive way. The State conceded to the Church a quasi-
official status in return for a low profile on the Church's
part. However, the period is described by the authors of this
article as one of stagnation.

0127 Hedges, Tony. *Jehovah's Witnesses in Central Africa*. London:
Minority Rights Group, 1976.

An investigative study principally concerned with religious
freedom and its denial. The work details numbers of Jehovah's
Witnesses in central Africa, the largest contingents being in
Nigeria, South Africa, Zambia, Mozambique and Ghana. The
political upheavals of southern and central Africa have seen
the involvement of Witnesses in several periods and the current
legacy is a chain of relationships of confrontation between
Jehovah's Witnesses and the state authorities in Malawi, Zambia,
Mozambique and elsewhere. The report takes the form of short
nationally focused case studies.

0128 Hellberg, Carl-Johan. *Voice of the Voiceless: The Involvement
of the Lutheran World Federation in Southern Africa 1947-1977*.
Lund, Sweden: Skeab Verbum, 1979.

The period studied was one of active engagement of Church and
State on a variety of social issues. The author is interested
to document the official stances of the Lutheran churches on
relationships between themselves and on social issues such as
race. The acts of commissions and conferences provide the base
of Hellberg's data.

0129 Heper, Metin and Israeli, Raphael. *Islam and Politics in the
Modern Middle East*. Dover, N.H. : Croom Helm, 1984.

The recent resurgence of Islam in the Middle East is a far more
complex phenomenon than is often suggested by those analyses
which reduce recent developments in the area to no more than an
intensification of religiosity. This book challenges that
perception of the contemporary Middle East. It explores the
nature of the Islamic revival. It tries to establish what was
the original impulse behind particular instances of Islamic
resurgence. It also explores the degree to which religious
institutions have served as a mechanism of expressing secular
demands and frustrations, and investigates to what extent
politics is a functional alternative to religion.

0130 Israel, Herman. "A Religious Basis for Solidarity in
Industrial Society." *Social Forces* 45 (1966): 84-95.

After Durkheim, Israel explores the integrative function of a
religious system, in this case nationalism within an industrial
society; unlike peasant nationalism, that of industrial society

fosters social integration in accordance with a scheme of
universal and visible symbols.

0131   Jukić, Jakov.   "Le Religion et les Sécularismes dans les
Sociétés Socialistes." *Social Compass* 28 (1981): 5-24.

The concern of this paper is the problematic relationship of
marxism, socialism and religion and the recognition of the
religious factor paradoxically signified in the rejection of it
within socialist societies.   The author identifies three kinds
of secularism, the ideological, the political and consumer
secularism.   Ideological secularism is a recognition of the
rationality of religion, political secularism of spirituality
and consumer secularism evidences religious poverty.

0132   Kaufmann, Franz-Xaver.   "The Churches and the Emergent
Welfare State in Germany." *Actes de C.I.S.R.* 17 (1983): 227-241.

The rise of the welfare state in the 20th century has been a
factor of widespread consequence for the churches whose former
social roles it has in various measures usurped.   Kaufmann's
study of the German case gives attention to the German
Socialpolitik and analyzes the relationship of the churches to
the State.   Social policy is separately examined in respect of
Catholicism and Protestantism, the influence of the former
proving to be the more powerful.

0133   Kennedy, Michael D.   Simon, Maurice D.   "Church and Nation
in Socialist Poland."   In *Religion and Politics in the Modern World,*
edited by Peter H.Merkl and Ninian Smart, pp. 121-134.   New York:
New York University Press, 1983 (0148).

In its time Poland has been infringed from all directions and
practically obliterated as a political entity.   The maintenance
of a national identity and the rehabitation of the nation-state
have implied a persistent spiritual and political role for the
Roman Catholic Church.   The identity of Catholicism with Polish
nationalism survives the political supremacy of the Communist
Party.   At the time of writing the Church was threatened by
the introduction of martial law; but "as the historical
protector of Polish nationhood, the Catholic Church remains a
key institution for assuring its continued existence."

0134   Klüber, Franz.   *Katholische Soziallehre und Demokratischer
Sozialismus.*   Bonn: Verlag Neve Gesellschaft, 1974.

The relationship of the Christian religion to politics and the
State is in the Anglophone world an occupation of psephologists;
on the continent of Europe, however, there are clear associations
of political parties and particular churches.   Klüber studies
the case of Catholicism and the Social Democratic tradition in
West Germany and he addresses the question of a "Christian
politic" in the German context.

0135   Krusche, Günther.   "L'Église dans la Société Socialiste."
Social Compass   28 (1981): 79-91.

The protestant churches of East Germany have suffered relegation
from the role and status of State religion to that of minority
churches.   Krusche documents the major themes and phases of this
transition including postwar denazification, anticlericalism,
the challenge of marxist ideology and the foundation in East
Germany of a Federation of Protestant Churches.   The article
concludes with an investigation of the self-perception of the
protestant churches and the roles they assign themselves in
socialist Germany.

0136   Lekachman, Robert; Miller, William Lee; Cohen, Arthur; Clancy,
William; and Howe, Mark de Wolfe.   *The Churches and the Public.*
Santa Barbara: Center for the Study of Democratic Institutions,
1960.

The four authors present reflective essays on the religious factor,
the presence of the Church in society, its intervention in public
life and the perils of enjoying a position of power.   There is a
strong ethical tone in the discussion of whether religious groups
should take positions on political issues, on pressure-group
activities and lobbying by religious bodies and on the right of
religious liberty in relation to other constitutional rights and
guarantees.

0137   Lemercinier, Geneviève.   "Aspects Sociologiques de la Genèse
de l'Islam."   *Social Compass*   25 (1978): 359-369.

The temporal focus of this paper is the first century or so of the
hijrah.   The author identifies the following of Mohammed as a
protest movement reacting against the higher social groups of
contemporary Medina, the Christians and Jews, against whom they
were subsequently engaged in armed conflict.   In due course the
Moslems themselves gained political power and the ideology that
served the protest movement underwent a transformation in order to
justify the exercise of authority.

0138   Lienard, Georges and Rousseau, André.   "Conflict Symbolique
et Conflit Social dans le Champ Religieux: Propositions Théoriques
et Analyse d'un Conflit Suscité l'Action Catholique Ouvrière dans
le Nord de la France."   *Social Compass*   19 (1972): 263-290.

The analysis of this article is based on activities and religious
involvements following the political action of Catholic workers in
the mining district of Lille, north-east France, in 1970.   Their
initiative attracted the support of numbers of Catholic priests
and nuns.   While the religious field offered an open stage for
the rehearsal of symbolic conflicts, the sphere of politics was
entered by Catholic professionals in celebration of a social
dimension in their role and mission.   Each field is invaded by
functionaries of the other in pursuit of specific interests, whether
initially religious or political.

0139 Lourie, Richard. "The Prophet and the Marrano: Two Ways of
Religious Being in the Soviet Union." *Social Research* 41 (1974):
328-339.

The "prophet" and the "Marrano" represent two styles of religious
being that are functions of a sociopolitical system that insists
upon the control of religious phenomena and has driven religion
underground.   Lourie analyzes religious expression in literature,
classifying Solzhenitsyn as an extravert prophet and Andrei
Sinyavsky as the Marrano.

0140 MacDonald, A.L. and Kruijt, D.A.N.M.   "Ontzuiling en Stemgedrag
bij Katholieken: Enkele Resultoden van een Onderzoek bij Nijmeegse
Kiesgerechtigden." *Sociologische Gids* 15 (1968): 98-105.

A study of Catholic voting behavior in Nijmwegen reveals that
Catholics following the church line support the traditional
Catholic party, the KVP.   Some parties were formerly proscibed
by the Church and Catholics now supporting these do so against the
norm of their Church; these are the so-called "interest parties".
Youth and male gender are the characteristics of the Catholic
behaving independently in political elections.

0141 Markoff, John, and Regan, Daniel.   "The Rise and Fall of Civil
Religion: Comparative Perspectives." *Sociological Analysis* 42 (1981):
333-352.

The study is based on the cases of post-revolutionary France and
contemporary Malaysia: in the first case civil religion was
participatory and ecstatic, in the second it is passive and
controlled.   The question arises: why is civil religion so visible
at particular historical junctures?   It is suggested that in
periods of political disequilibrium, civil religion becomes
manifest in the state's assault upon parochialism.

0142 Martin, David. *A Sociology of English Religion.*   London:
Heinemann, 1967.

This was a timepiece in its subject of which it treats historically,
empirically and theoretically.   It was intended as an introductory
work at a time when the sociology of religion needed systematic
development in Britain; this purpose it has served, not least in
the prescription of a number of perspectives for further research.

0143 Martin, David. *Tracts Against the Times.* Guildford:
Lutterworth, 1973.

This is a collection of essays concerned principally with the role
and character of the university in the ferment of the late 1960s.
The last essay asks the speculative question "Can the church
survive?" and develops an answer that challenges the current mood
of resignation to inevitable secularization.

O144 Martin, David. "Religion in Bulgaria." *Theology*. (1967):
495-503 and 539-542.

This essay is a case study of planned secularization. Whereas
Ochavkov has explained the decline of religious practice in
Bulgaria as a function of social structures which no longer
alienate man from himself, David Martin draws attention to a state
system of rewards and sanctions, and the conditions in which 45,000
Jews departed from Israel in the late 1940s, leaving a remnant of
5,000 who are reported by a government official to be secularized
and content with the regime. Reprinted in Martin (O143):137-152.

O145 Martin, David. "The State, Res Publica and the Church of
England." *Actes de C.I.S.R.* 17 (1983): 325-342.

The author brings the advantage of comparative oversight to this
examination of the function of the Church of England, a religious
organization which he finds to be more traditional than the churches
of other societies with a long experience of social change by
industrialization. However, the established Church of England has
undergone a transformation in recent years and now enacts a
critical role in respect of the State comparable with that
historically associated with the "nonconformist" churches.

O146 Martin, David. "Ethical Commentary and Political Decision."
Theology 76 (1973): 525-531.

Martin provides a comment on the morality of corporate bodies -
in particular Church and State - insofar as they affect the ethical
aspects of political decisions and a study of the tension between
corporate morality and individual decision-maker. David Martin
demonstrates the importance of empirical consequences for both
commentary and decision and differentiates respective modes of
activity.

O147 Matthes, Joachim. *Kirche und Gesellschaft: Einführung in die
Religionssoziologie II*. Munich: Rowohlt, 1969.

This offers a systematic study of church and society, of religion
and the social structure, religion and the social system, society
and the religious system, church and sect and so on. The subject
is approached from all angles in true German style.

O148 Merkl, Peter H. and Smart, Ninian. eds. *Religion and Politics
in the Modern World*. New York: New York University Press, 1983.

The approach adopted is historical and comparative and the work
includes several cases of relationships between religion and
nationalism in the modern world. Those studied in detail include
Catholicism and Irish national identity, German nationalism in
the Weimar era, church and nation in Socialist Poland, "State
Shinto" in modern Japan, mysticism and politics in Israel and
the Islamization of Pakistan. Papers annotated in this
bibliography are those by Carey (O110), Fridel (O119), Kennedy
and Simon (O133) and Metcalf (O149).

0149 Metcalf, Barbara. "The Case of Pakistan." In *Religion and Politics in the Modern World,* edited by Peter H.Merkl and Ninian Smart, pp.170-190. New York: New York University Press, 1983 (0148).

The volume in which this paper appears as a chapter treats of the variable relations of religion to politics, in most cases to some form of nationalism. The dichotomy of religion and politics is denied in orthodox Islam; and Pakistan represents the case of a national development according to strict Islamic ideals. The author rejects the notion that there has been a "rebirth" of Islam and recognizes a passionate adherence to Islam as a constant factor in Pakistani national identity.

0150 Moore, Robert. "The Political Effects of Village Methodism." *A Sociological Yearbook of Religion in Britain* 6 (1973): 156-182.

Moore revisits the Halevy thesis (0066) but finds the working class more astute and less easily beguiled than Halévy supposed. In an empirical study of Methodism in Durham mining villages, Methodist revivalism is affirmed to be largely non-revolutionary. Whereas the leadership of the working class by the middle class cannot be assumed, Halévy's view of the intermediary role of an élite within the working class is more convincing.

0151 Moskalev, Y.L. "Mesto Tserkvi v Politicheskoi Organizatsii Burzhuaznogo Obschchestva." *Vestnik Moskovskogo Universiteta* 28 (1973): 41-45.

A study of the place of the Russian Orthodox Church and politics in bourgeois society, historically introduced. The Church is held to account in this article for its perceived opposition to the people's struggle in Czarist Russia. The Church was controlled after the Revolution because of its support for the displaced monarchy, but in any case, the author believes, the masses defected from organized religion in large numbers.

0152 Nottingham, Elizabeth K. *Religion and Society*. New York: Random House, 1954.

This is a short study which comprehends a range of the classical sources of the early development of the sociology of religion, including history and anthropology. The *Leitmotiv* of this presentation, however, is functional theory and its contribution is to trace the manifest and latent functions of religion in society including system maintenance, the reinforcement and integration of values and socialization of the individual. The work represents early application to the phenomenon of religion of the ideas of Talcott Parsons.

0153 Pratt, Henry J. "Organizational Stress and Adaptation to Changing Political Status: The Case of the National Council of Churches of Christ in the United States." *American Behavioral Scientist* 17 (1974): 865-883.

This article points to the recently increased involvement of the National Council of Churches in the United States in the formulation and execution of national policy issues and the author interprets this as an attempt on the part of the churches to recover lost prestige and visibility.   This political involvement, however, has had the effect of disaffection among some of the more conservative denominations associated in the National Council, whose members regard social and political programs as inappropriate.   Their continued association with NCC has only been secured by the purchasing power of the Council's servicing, a benefit not else-where available.

0154 Prendes, Jorge-Caceres.   "Revolutionary Struggle and Church Commitment: The Case of El Salvador." *Social Compass* 30 (1983): 261-298.

This provides a general socioeconomic account of the background to the war between El Salvador and Honduras, views the pattern of political commitment, assesses religious participation as "the option for the poor" and so moves to an account of the emergence and organizational development of basic Christian communities.

0155 Rivière, Claude. "A Quoi Servent les Rites Séculiers?" *Social Compass* 29 (1982):   369-387.

Functionalist perspectives on secular rites have tended to emphasize their integrative role and to neglect the ways in which they strengthen the structure of power and neutralize hostility. The legitimation of the sacred and of relationships of power have been much observed in the study of religious rituals and Rivière explores these concerns in respect of the functions of secular rituals.

0156 Saurma, Adalbert. "Quelques Formes de 'Piete Politique' en Suisse." *Social Compass* 18 (1981): 341-355.

In the author's view there has been an over-simplification of Church and State as dichotomous and his purpose in this article is to revive the study of the complexity of the relationship.   This he does by a survey, in part historical, of some examples of "political piety" in Switzerland.   He characterizes a type of territorial devotion which prevailed in primitive Switzerland, then a more developed patriotic form of piety, and lastly civil theologies in the modern period.

0157 Schoultz, Lars. "The Roman Catholic Church in Columbia: Revolution, Reform and Reaction." *America Latina* 14 (1971): 90-108.

The Roman Catholic Church in Latin America exercises its influence in the spheres of labor, education and politics; in the latter respect it has traditionally been conservative and the author suggests that it has a limited capacity to accommodate change. In recent years it has adopted a more progressive political orientation but continues to express limits upon the magnitude of tolerable social change; in short, the author regards the Catholic

Church as liberal rather than radical.   This is exemplified with
reference to the Church's stand on certain social programs.
Schoultz suggests that the Catholic Church must adapt to more
radical policies if it is to maintain its legitimacy as a
political voice.

0158 Seneviratne, H.L.   "L'Ordination Boudhiste à Ceylon."
Social Compass 20 (1973): 251-256.

This is an interpretation of the 18th century Buddhist ordination
rite used in Ceylon in terms of two symbolic meanings, each
expressed in such elements of the rite as the dress of the
ordinand.   The first has to do with the renunciation of worldly
ways in favor of the path that leads to Ultimate Release or
Nirvana: this is of course a celebration of the sacred-profane
dichotomy.   The second meaning, for which the ordinand is dressed
in princely apparel, is a rehearsal of the political relationship
between the individual citizen represented by the ordinand and
authority personalized in the King; the function of this element
in the ordination rite is to legitimize royal power.

0159 Simon, Gerhard.   "Das Neue Sowjetische Religionsgesetz."
Ost-europa 27 (1977): 3-19.

Church-State relations in the Soviet Union are regulated by a
number of measures including the 1975 Religion Act which is
closely analyzed here.   The Act specifies situations in which
state interference in religious activity is appropriate.   The Act
enshrines a number of principles which had for some time been
evident in practice if not in law.   It provides for the control of
religious worship in private accommodation and constrains fund-
raising for religious organizations.

0160 Smith, Donald Eugene. *Religion and Political Development*.
Boston: Little Brown, 1970.

This is an important study of social formations in the Third World
which recognizes as central to their development the respective
dominant religions; invariably these are functional in the
resistance to modernization and Eugene Smith's purpose is to study
the various transformations from religious to secular society.
He provides a systematic analysis of the legitimation of political
change in Islam, Hinduism, Buddhism and Catholicism.

0161 Smith, Donald Eugene, ed. *Religion and Political Modernization*.
New Haven: Yale University Press, 1974.

This is a substantial comparative work that draws on many cases of
the changing relationship of religion and politics in the developing world.   The secularization of politics is evident in various
ways in Nepal, Burma, Thailand, modern Egypt, Israel, Latin
America.   Mass politicization is studied both in Asia and in Latin
American contexts, as is the religious legitimation of political
change in Hinduism, Islam and Catholicism.

0162   Suksamran, Somboon.   *Political Buddhism in Southeast Asia.*
London: Hurst, 1977.

Suksamran studies the role of the Sangha in the modernization of
Thailand.   This is analyzed with particular reference to the
structural interrelationship of the Sangha and the State and its
erstwhile promotion by the secular establishment.   The author
asks whether the Sangha is the best possible apparatus for
political modernization and the effects upon its position which
stemmed from its endorsement of the government's programs.

0163   Swanson, Guy E.   *Religion and Regime.*   Ann Arbor: University
of Michigan Press, 1970.

Swanson's study of the Protestant Reformation in Europe yields a
thesis that has been much noticed and explored in the sociology
of religion.   His argument is that in such matters as the maintenance of sovereignty and peace the impact of external factors
and interests upon a particular government was directly related
to the supplanting of Catholic monopoly by Calvinism.   Swanson
brings this idea from the study of primitive tribes and sociological assessments of the thesis include that by Martha Ellis
François (0118).   Swanson's typology of governments according
to degrees of religious monopoly inspires a line of thought that
runs through David Martin's *General Theory* (0665).

0164   Sweet, Douglas H.   "Church Vitality and the American
Revolution: Historiographical Consensus and Thoughts Towards a New
Perspective."   *Church History*   45 (1976): 341-357.

This provides a good general survey of the scholarly literature
concerned with the relationship of religion to the State in
American history.   The importance of religion in the colonial
period is universally recognized, as is the decline of religion
thereafter.   But the author suggests that the measure of
religious decline has been exaggerated.

0165   Talmon, Yonina.   "Pursuit of the Millennium: The Relation
between Religious and Social Change."   *European Journal of
Sociology*   3 (1962): 125-148.

Talmon's paper follows Norman Cohn's *The Pursuit of the
Millennium,* Bryan Wilson's *Sects and Society* (0461) and Eric J.
Hobsbawm's *Primitive Rebels* (0197).   Talmon takes stock of the
comparative study of different types of millenarian movements
and of millenarian and non-millenarian movements and suggests
that further progress in this field will be achieved primarily
by means of theoretically oriented yet very detailed case studies.
He offers hypotheses for elaboration in the course of further
research.

0166   Tennekes, Johannes.   "Le Mouvement Pentecotiste Chilien et
la Politique."   *Social Compass*   25   (1978): 55-80.

An analysis of 1971 and 1973 survey data on the attitudes toward
political life expressed by Chilean pentecostals.   It transpires

that during the Allende period there was a contrast of political
orientation between pentecostal leaders who tended to the right
and the mass of pentecostal followers whose sympathies were with
the left.   This constitutes a caution against assuming that what
pentecostals believe is signified by the statements of their
leaders.   However, both leaders and ordinary members were united
in disapproving the active participation of believers in political
life.

0167 Tomka, Miklos. "Problems in the Identity-formation of the
Catholic Church in Second and Third World Societies." *Actes de
C.I.S.R.* 17 (1983): 151-176.

Tomka treats of the effects of modernization as they relate to the
religious domain, particular features of unicentric and multicentric
models of the Church and theoretical problems in the acquisition of
identity.

0168 Turner, Frederick C. "Catholicism and Nationalism in Latin
America." *Social Compass* 18 (1971): 593-607.

At the level both of empirical (statistical) evidence and
theoretical analysis a variable relationship is established between
different types of nationalism on the one hand and the posture of
the Roman Catholic Church on the other, the latter being measured
as the support expressed at clerical and hierarchical levels.
Interview methods are used and pastoral letters are cited to
indicate manners in which nationalism is recognized and evaluated.

0169 Underhill, Ralph. "Economic and Political Antecedents of
Monotheism: A Cross-cultural Study." *American Journal of Sociology*
80 (1975): 841-861.

The author explores the economic and political correlates of
monotheism through a cross-cultural study.   Belief in a single
and transcendant deity, he finds, correlates with complexity in
both economic and political spheres.   The effect upon monotheistic religion of economic structure is greater than that of
the political and the effects of each are independent of the
other's.   There follows (pp. 862-869) an analysis of Underhill's
correlations by Guy E.Swanson.

0170 Van der Mehden, Fred R. *Religion and Nationalism in Southeast
Asia.* Madison: University of Wisconsin Press, 1963.

The author surveys the many tensions active between forms of
religion and variants of nationalism in Indonesia and the
Philippines.   Alongside the development of religio-nationalist
movements there are spheres of conflict such as anticlericalism,
secularism and non-political Islamic movements.   Alignments of
religious and political ideologies serve the adherents of both
and the author gives a chapter to the use of religion for
political ends.

0171 Vasquez, Rodrigo Fernando. "Essai d'Interprétation Historique de la Reforme Sociale et de l'Action Ecclésiale au Costa Rica." *Social Compass* 30 (1983): 299-316.

The article is concerned with the impact of social, economic and political processes on the activities of the Church in Costa Rica between 1940 and 1982. The Church is presented as ideologically independent and as supportive of social and democratic reforms.

0172 Vatikiotis, P.J. *Islam and the Nation State*. Dover, N.H.: Croom Helm, 1985.

This book examines the theoretical problems which arose when the modern European ideology of nationalism was adopted by Muslim societies organized into formally modern states. It also deals with the practical difficulties arising from the doctrinal incompatibility between Islam itself, as a political ideology, and the alien, non-Muslim concept of the territorial nation-state. It illustrates this conflict with a consideration of the record of several states in the Islamic world. It suggests that whereas the State, as an organization of power, has been a most durable institution in Islamic history, the legitimacy of the nation-state has always been challenged, in favor of the wider Islamic Nation, the *umma*, which comprises all the faithful without reference to territorial boundaries. To this extent too, the more recent conception of, say, Arab Nationalism projects a far larger nation-state than the existing territorial state in the Arab world today.

0173 Vidal, Claudine. "De la Religion Subie au Modernisme Refusé." *Archives de Sciences Sociales des Religions* 38 (1975): 63-90.

This paper is concerned with the deculturation of the peasantry which in Europe was effected by economic necessities, by the educational systems and the elimination of minority languages. In Africa, however, the strategy has been to erode native religions. The author takes the example of Rwanda in which Catholicism enjoyed considerable success under Belgian colonialism, but far from being extinguished the traditional religious practices such as ancestor worship were merely driven underground. In the early years of independence Catholicism was observed as an official religion and ancestor worship remained covert but dormant. In recent years political opposition to the new regime has been manifested in an overt rejection of Catholicism and the more open practice of traditional religions.

0174 Wallis, Roy. "Societal Reaction to Scientology: A Study in the Sociology of Deviant Religion." In *Sectarianism*, edited by Roy Wallis, pp.86-116. London: Peter Owen, 1975.

The model of development supported by the evidence adduced by Wallis is that of deviance-amplification; that is, initial deviation by Scientology led to hostile societal reaction which forced it into various defensive and aggressive positions. But Wallis argues that amplification in such cases is not inevitable and he notes the occurrence of de-escalation of

societal reactions to Scientology, following the severity of
government action and a decline in its growth rate.

0175 Whythe, John. "Patterns of Catholic Politics: Europe and the
English-speaking World." *Actes de C.I.S.R.* 17 (1983): 97-114.

Catholic behavior in the two constituencies in the title provides
a marked contrast which Whythe sets out to investigate and analyze.
In seeking explanations, he considers the proportionate strength
of a Catholic population as a relevant factor; this factor is
pertinent to the development of a Catholic subculture but not a
sufficient condition for the phenomenon being examined.   The
author looks too at differences in antecedent political culture
and finds this again insufficient for explanatory purposes.   In
the end, he suggests that the crucial factor affecting the political
behavior of Catholics in Europe against those in the Anglophone
world is the character of political alliance made by Catholics in
the 19th century.

0176 Wierzbicki, Zbigniew T.   "On a Certain Stereotype of Sociology
of Religion in Poland." In *Religiousness in the Polish Society Life*,
edited by Witold Zdaniewicz, pp.53-66. Warsaw: Pallottinum, 1981 (0181).

Wierzbicki examines critically the stereotypes of popular Polish
religion before 1939 which are variously developed by Czarnowski and
Piwowarczyk. In particular, he questions the direct lineage assumed
between feudalism and rural religion. Originally published in Polish.

0177 Wilson, Bryan R. *Religion in a Secular Society: A Sociological
Comment.* London: Watts, 1966.

This book documents the process of secularization in England from
statistical evidence on church membership and religious participation
to the demise of the churches as agencies of social control and the
loss of status in the clerical profession. The principal religious
response to this process, it is argued, is ecumenicalism, which is
seen as a stratagem to revive the intensity of distinctive belief
and commitment and the sense of superiority and apartness.

0178 Wimberley, Ronald C. and Christenson, James A.   "Civil Religion
and Other Religious Identities." *Sociological Analysis* 42 (1981):
91-100.

Civil religion is normally conceived - though not tested - as an
integrative belief system that transcends denominational allegiances.
The authors find that civil religious beliefs are shared by all
churched respondents, while Jews, Unitarians and those claiming
no religious identity do not signify such beliefs.   See also 0903
and 0904.

0179 Yule, George. *Puritans in Politics.* Abingdon, Oxon.: Sutton
Courtenay Press, 1981.

This volume typifies many which, being historical in perspective,
provide essential data for the sociology of sect development and

of relations between religious organizations and the State.   The
case of national authority studied is the English Long Parliament
of 1640-1647.   It deals with government involvement in Church
reform and various cases of conflict between parliament and
religious groups.

0180   Zdaniewicz, Witold.   *The Catholic Church in Poland 1945-1978*.
Poznan-Warsaw: Pallottinum, 1979.

A mine of statistical information from surveys of the Catholic Church
in Poland, including numbers of clergy by diocese, ages of priests,
numbers and sizes of religious communities and their schools, and
details of the principal non-Catholic denominations in Poland.

0181   Zdaniewicz, Witold, ed.   *Religiousness in the Polish Society
Life*.   Warsaw: Pallottinum, 1981.

A collection of papers by Catholic sociologists in Poland which
present the facts and figures of Polish religiosity in recent years
and identify problems for the sociology of religion in Poland.
Contributors include Zdaniawicz (0180), Wladyslaw Piwowarski (0042),
Zbigniew Wierzbicki (0176) and Andrzej Swiecicki (0281).
Originally published in Polish.

0182   Zubaida, Sami.   "Economic and Political Activism in Islam."
Economy and Society   1   (1972): 308-338.

The author is concerned with the assumption widely held that the
major world religions carry inherent orientations toward political
activism.   This view he challenges with a particular analysis of
the case of Islam of which he traces the historical development
through three stages, each being characterized by different levels
of politicization.   Further, he relates levels of political activism
not to inherent beliefs but to the accidents of social relations
between religion, class and state.

F.   RELIGION AND SOCIAL CLASS

0183   Aoude, Ibrahim.   *The Lebanese Conflict: Class or Confessionalism*.
London: Zed Press, 1984.

Since its independence in 1943 Lebanon has experienced an escalation
of conflicts.   Aoude traces the class factors in these and
dismisses as a simplistic myth the notion of a mere confrontation of
Moslem and Christian communities.

0184   Benington, John.   *Culture, Class and Christian Beliefs*.   London:
Scripture Union, 1973.

Benington explores the tensions that can arise in industrial inner-
city areas between cultural background and Christian tradition.
The book is written on the basis of community development experience
in the English city of Coventry.

0185 Burton, Lewis. "Social Class in the Local Church: A Study of Two Methodist Churches in the Midlands." *A Sociological Yearbook of Religion in Britain* 8 (1975): 15-29.

On the basis of studies of two Methodist churches of different character, the one an estate church, the other serving a suburb, evidence is collected with which to question the general view of Weber and others that religious organizations are effective only within the middle class. Further, it is suggested that success should be measured not only on the basis of numerical response but also in terms of the penetration of teaching; by this criterion Burton's estate church is relatively "successful".

0186 Clelland, Donald A.; Hood, Thomas C.; Lipsey, C.M., and Wimberley, Ronald C. "In the Company of the Converted: Characteristics of a Billy Graham Crusade Audience." *Sociological Analysis* 35 (1974): 45-56.

A battery of survey questionnaires was administered to the attenders of a Billy Graham crusade at Knoxville, Tennessee and the audience assessed against a non-attending sample for demographic and religious variables. Findings support the conventional typific- ation of the Billy Graham crusade as middle-class and respectable. Crusade attenders were of comparatively high socioeconomic status and occupational prestige and were more frequent in church attendance. In the authors' interpretation crusades of this kind persist as assertions in favor of a morality and lifestyle perceived by the sponsors as jeopardized by the secular age. See also 0773.

0187 Cipriani, Roberto. "Tendances Actuelles dans les Recherches Sociologiques sur le Thème 'Religion et Classe Ouvrière'." *Social Compass* 27 (1980): 287-305.

The author surveys a number of studies which bear upon the relation- ship of the working class to religious institutions and lays stress upon the importance of the cultural dimension in such research. He points to the study of the religious dimension of work ethics as a research enterprise hitherto lacking a cultural perspective.

0188 Dassetto, Felice. "Pratique Idéologique, Pratique Social et Intérêts de Classe." *Recherches Sociologiques* 6 (1975): 222-238.

A discourse analysis of the products of left-oriented political elements.in the contemporary Church in Europe, principally the Catholic Church. The author is interested in the reformulation of secular ideologies according to Christian ethical principles and of traditional religious positions in the context of current political movements. In particular, the classical leftist class analysis of society is expressed in religio-ethical terms as the division of rich and poor; in this familiar language there is an established response to the problem. In the development of this position the Church, epitomized in the Vatican, represents material wealth and so the function of leftist discourse is a radical posture within the Church itself.

0189   Davidson, James D. "Socio-economic Status and Ten Dimensions of Religious Commitment." *Sociology and Social Research* 61 (1977): 452-485.

Middle-class and working-class Baptist and Methodist congregations constitute a sample of four congregations yielding 570 responses. High socioeconomic status is associated with lower levels of belief in transcendance and private devotions and a more critical view of official religious teachings.   The author does not find a significant difference in public religious practice relating to social class, but this factor was in any case equalized in his sampling procedure.

0190   Demerath, N.J. *Social Class in American Protestantism.* Chicago: Rand McNally, 1965.

Demerath offers a useful review of previous research on religion and social class in America and he collates statistical evidence from a range of sources.   The measurement of religiosity is itself problematic and he approaches this critically, in the end favoring the dimensions elaborated by Glock.   With statistical tables throughout Demerath relates religiosity to socioeconomic status, the former being variable along the church-sect continuum and the latter being subjected to sub-stratification.   He finds both sectlike and churchlike parishioners within particular protestant churches. But for those of low status who look to organized religious participation as a respite from the secular world that judges them, Demerath points out that there are other agencies offering consolation and opportunity such as the military, the university and extremist political groupings.   On the whole Demerath stays close to his data.

0191   Fay, Leo F.   "Catholics, Parochial Schools and Social Stratification." *Social Science Quarterly* 55 (1974): 520-527.

Faye provides an investigation of the factors that incline parents to send their children to Catholic schools.   Findings vary according to social class.   In the upper ranges of the classes examined parents tend to show higher levels of religiosity and to choose schools for religious reasons.   The basis of choice among lower middle-class and working-class parents, however, is not principally religious: these parents show low levels of religious commitment but seek in Catholic schooling the opportunity of upward social mobility.

0192   Gilley, Sheridan.   "Catholics and Socialists in Glasgow 1906-1912."   In *Hosts, Immigrants and Minorities,* edited by Kenneth Lunn, pp. 160-200.   Folkestone, Kent: Dawson, 1980.

Irish settlement in Glasgow occurred during the nineteenth century following but not exclusively related to potato famine in Ireland. In the years covered by this paper Catholic thought was dominated by the peasant conservatism of Pius X which struck cords that were tuneful upon the ears of Irish Catholics.   Glasgow, however, is an industrial city and the labor movement there was strong. This paper is a study of the tensions between settlers and host community at the religious and political levels.

0193 Goldschmidt, Walter R. "Class Denominationalism in Rural
California Churches." *American Journal of Sociology* 49 (1944):
348-355.

Class segregation in a rural community under an industrialized
agricultural economy pervades all social institutions. The
protestant churches serve the upper class, the evangelical sects
an ostracized laboring group, not least in a psychological way
by asserting another value system in a putative heavenly
society. Denominationalism is viewable as a dimension of class
discrimination, it is argued.

0194 Goode, Erich. "Class Styles and Religious Sociation."
British Journal of Sociology 19 (1968): 1-16.

An empirical study of the reciprocal relationships of selected
secular and religious variables, based on a 1957 survey of the
Congregational Christian Church in the United States. Findings
attest to the relative independence of the various dimensions of
religion (such as ritual and psychological), and to the weakening
of religiosity in the routinization of religious practice. By
way of indicating methodological implications, Goode warns against
the use of religious participation as a reliable indication of
religious involvement.

0195 Guzman Garcia, Luis and Puente de Guzman, Maria. "Formation
des Classes, Luttes Populaires et Discours Religieux au Nicaragua."
Social Compass 30 (1983): 211-231.

This provides a study of the structure of social classes in
Nicaragua in historical perspective and sets out the pattern of
American involvement in the context of the Samozist dictatorship.
The Catholic Church supported Samoza until the degree of oppression
became intolerable. The authors analyze the bishops' position
as "bourgeois reformist" and go on to examine the Christian
support or opposition toward the subsequent Sandinist regime.

0196 Hazelrigg, Lawrence E. "Occupation and Religious Practice in
Italy: The Thesis of 'Working-class Alienation'." *Journal for the
Scientific Study of Religion* 11 (1972): 335-346.

Sophisticated statistical methods and analysis are deployed to
test the assumption that alienation from the (Roman Catholic, in
this case) Church is a phenomenon peculiar to the urban working
class. In the case of Italy the hypothesis is not in simple terms
verified and the author considers intervening factors such as
political orientation; further, he draws attention to manifestations of alienation from the Church within other social strata.

0197 Hobsbawm, Eric J. *Primitive Rebels: Studies in Archaic Forms
of Social Movements in the 19th and 20th Centuries*. Manchester
University Press, 1959.

This is the classic study of outlawry and social banditry, cases of which treated by Hobsbawm include Robin Hoodism and the Mafia. The cases of most interest to sociologists of religion include millennarian movements, notably the Lazzarettists, a group which in the 1870s followed the Savior of Monte Amati, David Lazzaretti.

0198   Homan, Roger.   "Sunday Observance and Social Class." *A Sociological Yearbook of Religion in Britain*   3 (1970): 78-92.

A study of mid-Victorian sabbatarianism in Britain as a manifest-ation of inter-class conflict, perceived as such by the conflicting parties.   It is argued that norms governing the use of Sunday were largely determined by elements within the bourgeoisie and that the institutions and structures which these supported were either contrary to the interests of the working class or else were not within reach of its members.   The article's focus is upon the Sunday Trading Bill of 1855 and of the reactions of the Chartists and of Marx; the responses of the working class are studied in terms of norm-acceptance and norm-rejection.   This article and its subject matter are further studied in Pickering's "The Secularized Sabbath" (0673).

0199   Houtart, François.   "Religion et Lutte des Classes en Amérique Latine."   *Social Compass*   26 (1979): 195-236.

This article looks at the Catholic religion in Latin America in the formation of its social class system.   Houtart recognizes Catholicism as an instrument of metropolitan hegemony operating as much through ideology as through its own institutional forms. The author delineates class religions within Catholicism, which respectively legitimize domination and support the revolt of the oppressed classes.   While on the whole the Church as an institution reacts against political powers, those powers are able to draw upon religious expressions to justify the fact of their own domination.

0200   Isambert, François A.   "Les Ouvriers et l'Église   Catholique." *Revue Française de Sociologie*   15 (1974): 529-551.

Despite the efforts of the Catholic Church in France to engage workers by approving what it perceives to be their political cause, the workers remain the marginal or excluded group which they have represented since 1945.   The Church in France does not suffer from the anticlericalism of its neighbor Spain, but the interventions of the Church in public life are no more appreciated by the workers.   Workers welcome the Church's involvement in political affairs no more than other social groups within its membership.

0201   Kahane, Reuben.   "Priesthood and Social Change: The Case of the Brahmins."   *Religion*   11 (1981): 353-366.

The priestly caste is constituted by the culture bearers in a given society who have at their command such effects as value commitments, prestige and influence: these are less flexible than economic factors such as wealth.   Kahane analyzes the role of the *brahmins* in conditions of social change and suggests the

factors that will affect their support and capacity to adjust.
The analysis of this paper has a usefulness well beyond the
particular case it examines.

0202 Kelley, Jonathan and McAllister, Ian. "The Genesis of Conflict:
Religion and Status Attainment in Ulster, 1968." *Sociology* 18
(1984): 171-187.

The writers use 1968 survey data to identify disparities in
social status between Ulster Catholics and Protestants at the
beginning of the period of intensified civil disturbances.
While differences in occupational status are attributable to
educational background, the more marked disparities in economic
status cannot be so explained.   Detailed analysis suggests that
discrimination is most acute among élite Catholic families.

0203 Lanternari, Vittorio. *Movimenti Religiosi di Liberté e di
Salvezza dei Popoli Oppressi.* Milan: Giangiacomo Feltrinelli, 1960.

A wide-ranging study of modern messianic movements throughout the
world.   Cases scrutinized include various such movements in the
continent of Africa, the Peyote cult, the prophet Handsome Lake,
the Ghost Dance, the Earth Lodge Cult, and other phenomena among
the North American Indians, the Cargo and Taro cults and other
messianic movements in Melanesia.   The author explains at the
level of first-order analysis such themes as morphology, ritual,
myth, doctrine and prophetic leadership.   Translated into
English by Lisa Sergio and published in 1963 by MacGibbon and
Kee of London as *The Religions of the Oppressed*.

0204 Lauer, Robert H. "Socialization into Inequality: Children's
Perception of Occupational Status." *Sociology and Social Research*
58 (1974): 176-183.

Occupational status provides the measure of socialization into
social inequalities and this process is monitored developmentally
according to grade level at school.   In this study children
attending Catholic and public schools are separately reported,
thereby giving an indication of the religious factor in
socialization.   Catholic children are found to give a progressive
emphasis to income and the functions of labor whereas public
school children gave progressively greater recognition to the
place of achievement.

0205 Lourdusamy, Stan. "India's Needs and the Indian Church: Can
the Church Play the Needed Role? A Sociological Reflection."
Impact 14 (1977): 196-200.

Using case study material from an Indian village, it is suggested
that the Catholic Church's dependence upon the landowning class
for material support precludes its adoption of the perspective of
the poor.   This argument is elaborated in terms of the
institutional church's lack of understanding and credibility.

0206 MacLaren, A.Allen. *Religion and Social Class: The Disruption Years in Aberdeen.* London: Routledge & Kegan Paul, 1974.

Social class in mid-nineteenth century Aberdeen was reflected in religious practice and observance, particularly within the Presbyterian denominations, which in turn affected social change. MacLaren relates the Disruption in the Church of Scotland and the emergence of the Free Church in the 1840s to the development of the industrial economy and changes in the old social structure.

0207 McLeod, Hugh. "Class, Community and Region: The Religious Geography of Nineteenth-Century England." *A Sociological Yearbook of Religion in Britain* 6 (1973): 29-72.

McLeod makes an extensive analysis of census data to characterize English religiosity for comparison with that of other European states.   It is found, for example, that in England there is a relatively low correlation of religious allegiance with political allegiance whereas in France the parties of the Right had drawn support from mass-attenders and those of the Left from mass-abstainers.   In the mid-nineteenth century there were marked variations in church attendance between county and county (attendance being much lower in the north of the country) and between class and class; in these respects.   What was true within the Church of England was also true of high-status nonconformists such as the Wesleyans, but there were marked differences of denominational distribution based upon class.   Regional peculiarities identifiable in the nineteenth century have largely dissolved: the social class bases of denomination have been confused by amalgamations, such as that of the Methodists; and massive population movement, not least as a consequence of post-war immigration, has affected the geographical pattern of religious activity.

0208 McLeod, Hugh. "The Dechristianisation of the Working Class in Western Europe (1850-1900)." *Social Compass* 27 (1980): 191-214.

This is a densely informed historical account of the progressive exclusion from religious participation of the proletariat of England, Germany and other countries in Europe.   The period covered is one of intensive missionary effort but McLeod shows the Christian churches to have been losing the battle.

0209 Michelat, Guy and Simon, Michel. *Classe, Religion et Comportement Politique.* Paris: Presses de la Fondation National des Sciences Politiques et Éditions Sociales, 1977.

The authors make a detailed study of the political orientations of Catholic and non-religious respondents, on the basis of which they develop a typology of religious orientation and political views.   The social class of respondents, both subjective and objective, is similarly related to religious integration and political orientation.   See also 0512.

0210 Mueller, Charles W. and Johnson, Weldon T. "Socioeconomic Status and Religious Participation." *American Sociological Review* 40 (1975): 785-800.

The usefulness of this contribution is not in verifying the positive relationship of social class and religious participation but in qualifying it. The association of these two variables is found to be stronger for males than for females, and is negative for Jews. The authors suggest that the predictive potential of socioeconomic status has been overestimated.

0211 Nesti, Arnaldo. "Religion et Classe Ouvrière dans les Sociétés Industrielles: une Hypothèse de Recherche." *Social Compass* 27 (1980): 169-190.

The essence of this article is an identification of the type of popular religion characteristic of the proletariat in an industrial society. It is also an attempt to relate social class allegiance to religious forms and a general overview of cognate research.

0212 Opazo Bernales, Andrés. "Les Conditions Sociales du Surgissement d'une Église Populaire." *Social Compass* 30 (1983): 175-209.

The empirical base of this article is the popular Church of societies in central America. It is concerned with the tension between life and death and the interplay of these in symbolic systems and in religious discourse.

0213 Roof, Wade Clark. "Socioeconomic Differentials among White Socioreligious Groups in the United States." *Social Forces* 58 (1979): 280-289.

In social, occupational and economic status Catholics have in recent years enjoyed continuous improvement and it has been suggested that they now rank above Protestants. This possibility is tested from survey data of the National Opinion Research Center but it is found that Protestants retain their superior ranking.

0214 Terrenoire, Jean-Paul. "Groupes Socio-professionels Pratiques des Culturelles Catholiques." *Archives de Sciences Sociales des Religions* 37 (1974): 117-155.

This article is a piece of religious demography. The data base is provided by the Catholic Church in France which has through its dioceses conducted religious censuses in the 1950s and 1960s. These are analyzed by region and by occupational grouping of respondents for variations in church attendance patterns, and comparisons are made diachritically. It transpires that the matter of causality is more complicated than available explanatory models can accommodate.

0215 Terrenoire, Jean-Paul. "Population Active, Pratiques
Religieuses et Espaces de Référence." *Archives de Sciences
Sociales des Religions* 44 (1976): 137-161.

This study reports research using sophisticated statistical methods
to discover a relationship between the internal variations of the
occupational structure of the labor force and fluctuations in
Catholic participation in such obligations as Easter duty, mass
attendance and regular communion. The research field was in
rural France and the theory explored is that of a significant
relationship of the economy and religious practice.

0216 Van Roy, Ralph F.; Bean, Frank D.; and Wood, James R. "Social
Mobility and Doctrinal Orthodoxy." *Journal for the Scientific Study
of Religion* 12 (1973): 427-439.

This essay examines the effects of (generationally differentiated)
occupational status upon orthodoxy of individual beliefs. Of
three hypotheses proposed, it is that of "acculturation" which is
most confirmed. That is, the effects of social mobility are to
generate a proportionate increase of secularization since
individuals in passage from one social stratum to another do not
conform to the orthodoxy of intermediate groups.

0217 Willems, Emilio. "Religiöser Pluralismus und Klassenstruktur
in Brasilien und Chile." *Internationales Jahrbuch für
Religionssoziologie* 1 (1965): 190-209.

This article is particularly concerned with the pentecostal sects
which have developed in Brazil and Chile since 1920.   The structure
of these is diometrically opposed to that of traditional agrarian
society.   In Brazil, the situation is further complicated by two
further religious organizations competing for the allegiance of
the lower classes, Spiritualism and Umbanda.   Appears in English
in Robertson (0049).

0218 Williams, Bill. "The Beginnings of Jewish Trade Unionism in
Manchester, 1889-1891." In *Hosts, Immigrants and Minorities*,
edited by Kenneth Lunn, pp.263-307. Folkestone, Kent: Dawson, 1980.

The case of Manchester is used to illuminate the circumstances
in which Jewish trade unions emerged in the late nineteenth century
and the attitudes toward them expressed by non-Jews. It is
suggested that previous explanations have centered too much on
the dimension of ethnicity and Williams endeavors to broaden his
analysis to take account of wider economic, social, political
and cultural factors.

0219 Yishai, Yael. "Israel's Right-wing Jewish Proletariat."
Jewish Journal of Sociology 24 (1982): 87-98.

The 1977 election in Israel saw a shift of working-class alignment
from the Labour to the Likud party: this was confirmed in the 1981
election.   The author accounts for this by suggesting that
Oriental Jews blamed Labour for years of hardship and felt that

Likud offered them better prospects for the future.   But of
greater sociological interest is the suggestion that they found
in a right-wing alignment an assertive expression of religious
observance.

G.   MARXIST CRITIQUE

0220 Bosse, Hans. *Marx-Weber-Troeltsch.* Munich: Chr.Kaiser Verlag,
1970.

This is a German study of marxist ideology and the sociology of
religion in the light of the work of three great thinkers.
Politics and ethics are examined with reference to Weber and
Troeltsch and Bosse goes on to explore the critique of religion to
which all contribute.

0221 Houtart, François and Lemercinier, Geneviève. "Religion et
Mode de Production Tributaire." *Social Compass* 24 (1977): 157-170.

Houtart and Lemercinier assess the role of religion in tributary
societies and its relationship to production.   It is argued that
the place of religion in precapitalistic societies is more complex
than has hitherto been assumed.

0222 Mayrl, William W. "The Christian-Marxist Encounter: From
Dialogue to Detente." *Sociological Analysis* 39 (1978): 84-89.

Mayrl here reviews recent literature on the dialogue between
Christianity and marxism and concludes that neither belief system
is represented in a typical form.   The thrust of debate is
explanation: that is to say, Christians and marxists endeavor
to reject each others' positions by controlling them in the course
of explanatory analysis.

0223 Nesti, Arnaldo. "Gramsci et la Religion Populaire." *Social
Compass* 22 (1975): 343-354.

The work of the Italian father of Eurocommunism, Antonio Gramsci,
passes through three phases as far as his thought on the position
of religion is concerned.   Initially, Gramsci argued for
socialism as a new religion which would succeed Christianity.
Under the influence of Benedetto Croce he refined this view and
talked of a faith in civilization which would attract adherents
from the traditional religions.   In the latter phase he
analyzed religion as a social fact, thereby recognizing its
persistence.   Nesti draws from Gramsci a cluster of problems which
command the attention of sociologists of religion, such as the
significance of religions of the lower classes.

0224 Opazo Bernales, Andrés. "La Fonction de l'Église dans la
Lutte Pour l'Hégémonie." *Social Compass* 26 (1979): 237-260.

The author interprets the Church as an instrument devoted to the development of a class hegemony and analyzes the variable function of the Church in a context of class struggle.

0225   Orsolic, Marco.   "La Sociologie de la Religion d'Inspiration Marxiste en Yougoslavie." *Social Compass* 20 (1973): 73-82.

The development of the sociology of religion in Yugoslavia is a post-war phenomenon.   In the ten or fifteen years of its infancy it was crude, dogmatic and marxist.   Exponents followed Marx, Lenin, Kautsky and others in supposing that with the advent of science and the enjoyment of socialism religion would wither away.   The author condemns this period and approach as barren, and applauds the more empirical manner of subsequent developments in Yugoslav sociology of religion.

0226   Robbe, Martin.   "Marxismus und Religionsforschung." *Internationales Jahrbuch für Religionssoziologie* 2 (1966): 157-182.

This article considers the critical and revolutionary analyses of religion as expressed by Marx and Engels.   It is argued that not only religion but also irreligion and its rational articulation in atheism are objectively conditioned and the author points to a neglect among marxists of the scientific study of religion.

0227   Turner, Bryan S.   *Religion and Social Theory: A Materialist Perspective*.   Aldershot, England: Gower, 1983.

This textbook considers a variety of theories about the social functions of religion which are central to both marxist and sociological theory.   By offering a "materialist perspective" the book pays particular attention to the role of religion as an institutional link between economic and human reproduction.

0228   Vidal, Daniel.   "Pour une Lecture Marxiste du Prophétisme: Champ Autre et Champ Outre." *Social Compass* 22 (1975): 355-380.

A marxist analysis of the social function of prophetic utterance which is shown to be an instrument of domination over the popular classes and of the neutralization of conflicts and tensions in social relationships.   The use of prophecy under Calvinism in Languedoc-Cévennes from 1685 to 1715 provides the empirical base for Vidal's work.

H.   EVERYDAY LIFE; RELIGION AND VALUES; PROTESTANT ETHIC

0229   Ahlstrom, Sydney.   "National Trends and Changing Religious Values." *Daedalus* 107 (1978): 13-29.

Ahlstrom studies the evolution of morality in the United States culminating in a period of satisfaction in the 1950s only to be succeeded by a decade of moral and spiritual turmoil.   During the

1960s new moral issues became prominent including peace and war, race, sexuality and environmental problems. Simultaneously there emerged new religious movements, many of them syncretist in character. The nationalism which had marked American morality gave way to a more global perspective.

0230 Alston, Jon P.; McIntosh, William A.; and Wright, Louise M. "Extent of Interfaith Marriages among White Americans." *Sociological Analysis* 37 (1976): 261-264.

Survey data are used to show that only seventeen per cent of the white population of America marry outside their denominational allegiance; this practice correlates with lower levels of organizational commitment and participation. The authors use the General Social Survey Program which takes in a national example.

0231 Anderson, Charles H. "Religious Communality among White Protestants, Catholics and Mormons." *Social Forces* 46 (1968): 501-508.

Anderson's coverage of white Protestant and Catholic communality extends the literature of this subject while his data on the involvement of Mormons constitute a new departure. The survey is conducted in three American cities and all three religious faiths give evidence of substantial involvement.

0232 Aries, Philippe. "Les Grandes Étapes et le Sens de l'Evolution des nos Attitudes devant la Mort." *Archives de Sciences Sociales des Religions* 39 (1975): 7-15.

Aries introduces, elaborates and applies to history an evolutionary scheme of the image of death. He relates each stage to an historical period but indicates also that they survive within certain social classes in the modern world. For example, the notion of death as tamed belongs to the remote past but lives on in certain sections of the lower classes. See also Freund (0245) and Vovelle (0287).

0233 Beemsterboer, Kees. "La 'Semaine pour la Paix' aux Pays-Bas: Action et Evaluation." *Social Compass* 21 (1974): 473-488.

An analysis of a "Week for Peace" held in the Netherlands. The action is evaluated in respect of its impact upon public opinion. Although the event is an annual one it is shown in a survey of the population of Arnheim to pass by about a third of the people; only fourteen per cent declared themselves relatively acquainted with the Peace Week activities and only six per cent declared an involvement.

0234 Bellah, Robert N. "Reflections on the Protestant Ethic Analogy in Asia." *Journal of Social Issues* 19 (1963): 52-60.

Bellah investigates the possibility that Weber's idea of the Protestant ethic is applicable to the Asian situation and the cases considered are in Japan the Jōdo and Zen Buddhists and the Hōtoku and Shingaku movements, in Java the Santri Moslems, in India the

Jains and Parsis.   Reprinted in Bellah's collection of Essays,
Beyond Belief (0003): 53-62.

0235 Bouvier, Leon F. "The Fertility of Rhode Island Catholics
1968-1969." *Social Analysis* 34 (1973): 124-139.

Interviews were conducted among the Catholics and non-Catholics
of Rhode Island in 1968 and 1969 and findings compared with the
results of earlier surveys.   Catholic expectations of fertility
were greater than those of non-Catholics but the difference
between the actual fertility of the two groups was less pronounced.
The practice of birth control is found upon investigation to have
increased among Catholics and this is speculatively related to
the loss of minority-group status.   See also Brackbill and
Howell (0236).

0236 Brackbill, Yvonne and Howell, Embry. "Religious Differences
in Family Size Preferences among American Teenagers." *Sociological
Analysis* 35 (1974): 35-44.

The emphasis of this study is upon differences between Catholics
and non-Catholics and the survey was conducted in 1971 in
Washington, D.C.   Results point to the importance of the religious
factor in issues concerning girls' careers and the size of the
preferred family; it was more powerful than other controlled
variables such as gender, age, race and socioeconomic status.
See also Bouvier (0235).

0237 Buckley, Anthony D. "Walls Within Walls: Religion and Rough
Behaviour in an Ulster Community." *Sociology* 18 (1984): 19-32.

In an Ulster community images of the siege of Derry, the household,
the Church and certain secret societies are articulations of one
paradigm.   What is thought good in relation to one ideal image
is thought bad in relation to another.   Paradigms vary according
to social groups and the choice of frames reflects social status.

0238 Crespi, Franco. "Impegno Religioso e Pregiudizio." *Rivista di
Sociologia* 10 (1972): 109-140.

The sample used in this survey was almost entirely engaged in
Catholic activities and the distinctions afforded were not between
denominations but between progressives and conservatives.
Religious conservatism was shown to be positively related with
authoritarianism and racial prejudice but progressivism in the
religious sphere correlates with an absence of prejudice and
authoritarianism.   Even within the one Church, therefore, religion
is shown to be ambivalent in these respects.

0239 Curtis, James E. and Lambert, Ronald D. "Status Dissatisfaction
and Out-group Rejection: Cross-cultural Comparisons within Canada."
Canadian Review of Sociology and Anthropology 12 (1975): 178-192.

This is yet another essay in search of significant relationships
between selected variables.   This time the samples are anglophone
and francophone Canadians, the former Catholic and Protestant and

the latter only Catholic.   Within the French sub-sample there is
found to be a direct and significant relationship between status
dissatisfaction and prejudicial attitudes toward Blacks and
Jews.

0240 Davidson, James D.   "Religious Belief as an Independent
Variable." *Journal for the Scientific Study of Religion* 11 (1972):
65-75.

The author is concerned with the religious functions of comfort and
challenge, the extent to which these are performed by religion and
their relationship with forms of belief.   The empirical work was
conducted with Baptists and Methodists in Indiana.   Comfort was
found to be related to beliefs involving a superior and
transcendant being, called "vertical" beliefs in this paper.
Challenge was posed by religion in its prophetic function and
related to "horizontal" beliefs governing relationships with fellow
human beings.   Only in a minority of cases, however, was religion
the basis for social involvement, whereas the majority of
respondents looked to their religion for comfort.

0241 Dearman, Marion.   "Christ and Conformity: A Study of Pentecostal
Values." *Journal for the Scientific Study of Religion* 13 (1974):
437-453.

The study is conducted within the United Pentecostal Church, a
unitarian sect recognizing the speaking in tongues as the proof of
conversion.   Such a conversion, the author finds, is accompanied
by a dramatic change from deviant to rational and conformist
behavioral orientations.   It is suggested that the counter-
revolutionary tendency of such a religious form has implications
in the political affairs not only of the United States but also in
the underdeveloped world.

0242 De Neuter, Patrick.   "Amour, Sexualité et Religion." *Social
Compass* 19 (1972): 365-387.

The work is based on a questionnaire survey among college students
complemented by the use of Image Apperception Tests. De Neuter
is concerned to assess the love relationship as a model or
reference for a relationship with God and he explores this problem
by investigating the religious valuation of human love. Subjects
are classified according to the strength of their religious belief
into two groups, and thus afford comparisons of attitudes and
behavior associated with the love relationship.

0243 Enroth, Ronald M.   "The Homosexual Church: An Ecclesiastical
Extension of a Subculture." *Social Compass* 21 (1974): 355-360.

Enroth analyzes the Metropolitan Community Church and other
religious organizations of or for homosexuals as the religious
extension of the gay subculture in the United States. The gay
churches offer a refuge for a disaffected social group but also
serve a deeper social function in legitimizing a marginal lifestyle and offsetting the effect of social disapproval.

0244 Fox, William S. and Jackson, Elton F. "Protestant-Catholic Differences in Educational Achievement and Persistence in School." *Journal for the Scientific Study of Religion* 12 (1973): 65-84.

The authors report an analysis of a 1957 survey data. No overall differences in educational backgrounds are found but within groups controlled for age, ethnicity, region of birth and father's occupation Protestants enjoy consistent advantages. Men with high status origins constitute the most conspicuous group and are the most likely to persist in college and gain degrees.

0245 Freund, Julien. "La Signification de la Mort et le Projet Collectif." *Archives de Sciences Sociales des Religions* 39 (1975) 31-44.

This paper juxtaposes the theme of death as it surfaces in religion and in politics. It is observed that there is a tendency to ignore death and thereby to assert human emancipation. Politics and religion are in contention for the management of this phenomenon. See also Aries (0232) and Vovelle (0287).

0246 Goodridge, R. Martin. "The Secular Practice and the Spirit of Religion." *Social Compass* 20 (1973): 19-30.

Indulgence in worldly pleasures is an expensive pursuit whereas abstinence allows the accumulation of material wealth. The sanctification of an ascetic lifestyle is the principle of what Weber identifies as the protestant ethic. In this article, however, Goodridge traces the roots of ascetic religion to a period of centuries before the Reformation and to secular practice in Europe. The economic principle elaborated by Weber is acknowledged but its association with protestantism is challenged.

0247 Greeley, Andrew M. "Influence of the 'Religious Factor' on Career Plans and Occupational Values of College Graduates." *American Journal of Sociology* 68 (1963): 658-671.

Findings of a 1961 survey do not substantiate Lenski's submission (0068) that Catholics score low on measures of economic rationality. In each of Greeley's tests Catholics' and Protestants' performances are comparable and he suggests that the discrepancy between his and Lenski's findings is attributable to ethnic factors.

0248 Haddad, Juliette. "Sacré et Vie Quotidienne: Perspectives sur une Société Arabo-musulmane Moderne." *Social Compass* 29 (1982): 311-333.

The Aqaba and Karak regions of Jordan provide the field for a study of the impact of modernity upon the traditional religious system of a primitive society with nomadic tendencies. This study of the impact since circa 1950 of modernity upon traditional structures illuminates subsequent resistance, often manifested in violent expressions. The complexity of nomadic religion is explored and there is seen to be an ossification of social and religious structures with the urbanization of former nomads.

0249 Hastings, Philip K. and Hoge, Dean R. "Religious Trends among Students, 1948-79." *Social Forces* 60 (1981): 517-531.

The trend in the religious participation and involvement among American college students passed through three phases in the period studied.   Surveys evidenced a decline until 1967 and then **stability until the survey of 1974**; since then there has been a slight but certain increase.   The trough in student affections for religious institutions ran from 1972 to 1975.   The authors cannot confirm the hypothesis that this disaffection was a dimension of a more generalized disenchantment with institutions.

0250 Higgins, Paul C. and Albrecht, Gary L. "Hellfire and Delinquency Revisited." *Social Forces* 55 (1977): 952-958.

Studies in particular parts of the United States by Hirschi and Stark and later by Burkett and White suggest that there is no relationship, either positive or negative, between delinquency and religiosity.   Higgins and Albrecht took this further in 1970, operationalizing religiosity as church attendance and delinquency as behavior, both variables as reported by 1383 students in tenth grade.   This investigation revealed a moderately negative relationship and they suggest an explanation of regional variations.

0251 Homan, Roger. "The Problem with Asa's Feet: Religious Responses to Worldly Medicine." *Actes de C.I.S.R.*   17 (1983): 176-188.

When in the Old Testament King Asa was "diseased in his feet", he made what the Chronicler judged to be a mistake in seeking advice from medical men rather than from the priests: in consequence, we read, "he slept with his fathers".   The recourse to worldly medicine has likewise in the modern period contradicted the official doctrine of certain fundamentalist sects such as Jehovah's Witnesses, Christian Science, pentecostal groups and the lesser known Plumstead Peculiars.   This paper examines these organizations and the public indignation and litigation which have been used to control them.   Much of the observation is based in the nineteenth century and anticipates the reaction in the twentieth to new religious movements as documented by James Beckford (0357) and others.   See also Montague (0412).

0252 Houtart, François and Lemercinier, Geneviève. "Conscience Religieuse et Conscience Politique en Amérique Centrale." *Social Compass* 30 (1983): 153-174.

A study of the role of religions in the colonization and transformation of societies in central America.   As the class struggle in rural areas moves into a new phase, so Vatican II inaugurates changes in pastoral structures within the Church.   In the most recent period religious commitment is popularly mediated within existing organizations by political consciousness.

0253 Hunt, Larry L. and Hunt, Janet G. "Black Religion as Both Opiate and Inspiration of Civil Rights Militance: Putting Marx's Data to the Test." *Social Forces* 56 (1977): 1-14.

The Marx in the title is not the Marx usually associated with talk of religion as an opiate but Gary Marx who in 1964 investigated the relationship of black religiosity and civil rights militancy. The secondary analysis of Hunt and Hunt reveals that black militancy is dissipated within sectlike orientations, whereas within religious organizations of the church type and those such as Catholic and Presbyterian which are largely white, greater militancy is sustained. These findings run contrary to expectations and to Marx's earlier interpretation. See also 0535.

0254 Hutjes, J.M. "Dutch Catholics on Birth Control and Sexuality." *Sociologia Neerlandica* 11 (1975): 144-158.

This article is the report and analysis of a 1969 survey conducted among nearly seven hundred married couples who were baptized Catholics. The prevailing attitude toward the Church's teaching was a critical one: many respondents ignored it in their own practice and relatively few allowed their consciences to be troubled by it. Results are presented as statistical data and in one of the tables attitudes to coitus are cross-tabulated with strength of commitment to the Church; as Nietzsche would have us expect, those putting emphasis upon "desire" declare a relatively weak religious commitment. See also Van Kemenade (0285), Bax (0469) and Thurlings (0536).

0255 Ikeda, Daisaku and Wilson, Bryan R. *Human Values in a Changing World*. London: Macdonald, 1984.

This book consists of a dialogue on the social rule of religion between a leading sociologist of religion and the Japanese leader of the world's largest lay Buddhist organization. The book is presented in the form of a symposium, representing edited conversations ranging across the social role of religion, ethics in the modern age, the threat to world peace, the function of personal morality, the limits of rationality, principles of non-violence, the ethics of suicide and capital punishment, and the character of nationalism. If of its nature such a volume is fragmentary, it is rendered more accessible by an extensive index.

0256 Isambert, François A. "Vie Quotidienne, Éthique et Religion." *Social Compass* 28 (1981): 441-445.

Isambert offers an overview of religion and everyday life as examined in an issue of *Social Compass* specially devoted to that subject. He endeavors to account for the interest which everyday life currently commands among sociologists of religion and to account for the place of ethics in that study.

0257 Itturra, Raul. "Marriage, Ritual and Profit: The Production
of Producers in a Portuguese Village." *Social Compass* 32 (1985):
73-92.

Itturra brings to his study of the Portuguese peasantry insights
developed by him earlier in Chile. He is interested in peasant
rationality in economics and then in marriage as a ritualized
system of redistributing and reproducing labor for the land.
His thesis flies in the face of more romantic perceptions as
sanctified in religious ceremonies.

0258 Lefever, Harry G. "The Value-Orientations of the Religious
Poor." *Sociological Analysis* 43 (1982): 219-230.

Talcott Parsons' framework of pattern variables is used to
analyze data collected in a low income white neighborhood in
Atlanta, Georgia. The value-orientations found to exist were
affectivity, self-orientation, particularism and quality.

0259 Loux, Françoise. "Pratiques Médicales Préventives et
Recours Religieux: Les Soins aux Enfants en Haute-Normandie."
Archives de Sciences Sociales des Religions 44 (1977): 45-58.

A study based in the cantons of Normandy which deals with the
recourse to religious therapies and preventions such as early
baptism and pilgrimage. Such a phenomenon of alternative
medicine is treated with some reservation by the Catholic
Church, which thereby reinforces the traditionalism of the
religion of those who have recourse to it.

0260 Lucas, Philippe. *La Religion de la Vie Quotidienne.* Paris:
Presse Universitaire de France, 1981.

This is an essay on the religion of everyday life which
identifies certain religious processes and institutions in the
structure of the private domain. If fragmentary in its
presentation, it is a worthwhile contribution to an area of
sociological concern that has been developed by predominantly
quantitative studies.

0261 McConahay, John B. and Hough, Joseph C. "Love and Guilt-
oriented Dimensions of Christian Belief." *Journal for the
Scientific Study of Religion* 12 (1973): 53-64.

This paper is interesting less for what it tells us about the
sample of students in Californian seminaries than for its
demonstration of a number of scales and its exploration of love-
oriented, guilt-oriented and culture-oriented dimensions of
religious belief. The author sets out the various relationships of responses in these dimensions to scaled attitudes
towards church involvement.

0262 McRae, James A. "Changes in Religious Communalism Desired by Protestants and Catholics." *Social Forces* 61 (1983): 709-730.

This reports and compares results of area studies conducted in Detroit in 1958 and 1971. The focus is the changing desire of religious believers to live with those of like faith. The strength of such a preference has diminished overall; communal arrangements have passed from fashion and the faithful who sustain this preference are seen in the second study to be more tolerant of the proximity of the faiths of co-residents to their own. The author relates this shift to the exposure of the young to the ecumenical movement and notes that the least flexible subjects are those with northern farm backgrounds.

0263 Maranell, Gary M. "An Explanation of Some Religious and Political Attitude Correlates of Bigotry." *Social Forces* 45 (1967): 356-362.

A survey was conducted among groups of undergraduates in four American universities in order to assess the correlation of anti-semitism and prejudice against Negroes. In all constituencies there was a strong correlation of bigotry with political conservatism.

0264 Mayeux, Marie Rose. "Catholicisme et Coopération - L'Image de la Coopération, son Ambiguité et sa Polyvalence dans la Doctrine Sociale de l'Église Catholique." *Archives Internationales de Sociologie de la Coopération et du Développment* 33 (1973): 57-83.

This is a detailed study of the official Catholic line on cooperatives as evidenced by the pontifical statements from those of Leo XIII to those of Paul VI. Aspects treated include the strategy of cooperation, the social justice achievable in shared economic relations of employment and labor, the personalization of work and psychological and motivational factors such as satisfaction. The pontifical statements show an awareness of such a range of considerations and there are several passages of support for the practice of cooperatives.

0265 Mews, Stuart P. "Urban Problems and Rural Solutions: Drink and Disestablishment in the First World War." In *The Church in Town and Countryside*, edited by Derek Baker, pp.449-476. Oxford: Blackwell, 1979.

Drink and disestablishment are among the principal themes that occupy students of the nineteenth century during which they were the subject of renewed agitations in Britain. They feature less in the twentieth but are still important. In the analysis given here the conventional model of social class derived from Marx is overlain with other dichotomies, notably rural-urban and Anglican versus Nonconformist. The drink issue was so bound up with religious allegiance that generally speaking "Churchmen... distrusted the man who did not like his glass of ale."

0266 Michel, Barbara. "Le Bon Voisin, le Mauve Voisin: Ebanche d'une Sociologie de l'Ethos de Voisinage." *Social Compass* 28 (1981): 357-379.

In order to minimize conflict and stress among themselves, occupants of any neighborhood devote time and energy to the maintenance of "neighborly" relations: the character of this endeavor constitutes the interest of Barbara Michel in this paper.   She identifies and explores the mechanisms by which values are negotiated in neighborhood contexts.

0267 Middleton, Russell. "Do Christian Beliefs Cause Anti-semitism?" *American Sociological Review* 38 (1973): 33-52.

The causal relationship of Christian orthodoxy and negative attitudes toward Jews was postulated by Glock and Stark. Middleton scrutinizes this hypothesis and isolates attendant variables such as socioeconomic status and a number of social and personality factors. With these removed the direct relation-ship of Christian belief and anti-semitism is statistically much diminished.   Glock and Stark offer a rejoinder in the pages that follow (53-59) to which Middleton responds (59-61). For a comparable study see Roof (0275).

0268 Moberg, David O. "The Salience of Religion in Everyday Life: Selected Evidence from Survey Research in Sweden and America." *Sociological Analysis* 43 (1982): 205-217.

The research reported is a survey of 1081 respondents in Sweden and America.   Data indicate the importance of religious faith for decision-making, the impact of religious belief on lifestyle and so on.   The major differences found were not between the two national groups of respondent but between denominational categories - Catholics, evangelicals, atheists and agnostics; in all counts of the influence of religious beliefs, evangelicals ranked highest.

0269 Morgan, S.Philip. "A Research Note on Religion and Morality: Are Religious People Nice People?" *Social Forces* 61 (1983): 683-692.

The research reported and interpreted here involves the operationalization of "religious" in terms of the frequency of prayer behavior - an indicator which some would not judge to be reliable - and that of "nice" as friendly and co-operative behavior in everyday life.   The faithful will be pleased to learn that the author confirms a positive relationship.

0270 Nelsen, Hart M. "Intellectualism and Religious Attendance of Metropolitan Residents." *Journal for the Scientific Study of Religion* 12 (1973): 285-296.

The basis for the study is the general assumption that intellectualism and church attendance are inversely related: that is to say, religious participation is a behavior perceived as unbecoming in individuals with intellectual pretensions.

This notion was tested in 1963-1964 with a sample of over two thousand residents of New York City.   Differences were found between generations and denominations and when these were controlled there was no relationship between intellectualism and attendance.

0271   Nuttall, Geoffrey, F. *The Puritan Spirit*. London: Epworth Press, 1967.

This is a substantial volume of essays and addresses, some more pertinent to the book's title than others.   The dominant perspective is historical and there are essays on the spread of Arminianism in England, on Erasmus, on Walter Cradock, Richard Baxter, John Bunyan, Philip Doddridge, Quakers and Primitive Methodists.   Of more explicitly sociological interest are later essays on the ecumenical movement, the devotional life of the professional minister and changes in the social teachings of the churches, most particularly respecting the justification of war.

0272   Pawelczynska, Anna. *Values and Violence in Auschwitz*. Berkeley: University of California Press, 1979.

Pawelczynska provides a sociological contribution to the literature of the holocaust.   The concentration camp is studied as a social system based on criminal intent and practice.

0273   Pickering, William S.F. "Quelques Résultats d'Interviews Religieuses."   In *Vocation de la Sociologie Religieuse: Sociologie des Vocations*, by E.Collard; J.Dellepoort; J.Labbens; G.Le Bras; and J.Leclercq, pp.54-76.   Paris: Conférence Internationale de Sociologie Religieuse, 1958 (0694).

Pickering reports and analyzes interview data acquired in two industrial towns in England and covering the content of beliefs represented in several churches and religious groups.   The analysis includes a discussion of the social conditions affecting religious affiliation and the effect of compulsory religious education in state schools.

0274   Remy, Jean. "Vie Quotidienne, Production de Valeurs et Religion." *Social Compass* 29 (1982): 267-281.

The sociology of everyday life is assessed as a study informing the generation and stabilization of values.   Remy explores and employs the concept of everyday life as a religious category.

0275   Roof, Wade Clark.   "Religious Orthodoxy and Minority Prejudice: Causal Relationship or Reflection of Localistic World View?" *American Journal of Sociology* 80 (1974): 643-664.

This paper is concerned with the nature of the relationship between negative or prejudicial attitudes to minority groups and religious orthodoxy.   A causal analysis is offered on the basis of survey data from North Carolina; it is suggested that

religious orthodoxy and prejudicial attitudes are together
functions of a parochialism in world-view that admits only
near horizons and entertains the prospects of neither mobility
nor adjustment. For a comparable Study see Middleton (0267)
and Thompson (0282).

0276 Sabagh, Georges and Lopez, David. "Religiosity and Fertility:
The Case of Chicanas." *Social Forces* 59 (1980): 431-439.

This study compares the effectiveness of two agencies of socialization, the family and the Roman Catholic Church. In 1973
some 1100 Mexican American women (Chicanas) were interviewed
in Los Angeles and responses were computed to show the effects
of upbringing and conformity to religious norms in respect of
fertility. The importance of upbringing, the authors suggest,
must not be underestimated and there are important differences
between those who were brought up in the United States and those
reared in Mexico.

0277 Schoenfeld, Eugene. "A Preliminary Note on Love and Justice:
The Effect of Religious Values on Liberalism and Conservatism."
Review of Religious Research 16 (1974): 41-46.

The author asserts love and justice as the dominant values of
the Judaeo-Christian tradition and relates these to political
conservatism and political liberalism respectively. Love, he
argues, directs the individual to alleviate the problems of his
fellows and the author's contention is that this will be
directed more at treatment than at prevention.   Justice,
however, issues in a concern with the uses and abuses of power
which for the author corresponds to a liberal ideology. Although
some passages of this argument are highly contentious, it at
least offers a new basis for the analysis of the relation of
religious values to political orientations. See also Stellaway
(0279).

0278 Starr, Jerold M. "Religious Preference, Religiosity and
Opposition to War." *Sociological Analysis* 36 (1975): 323-334.

This reports and analyzes a 1974 survey among college students in
Pennsylvania. Religiosity was measured by frequency of
attendance and the sample was broken down by denominational
affiliation. Subjects declining to express a religious preference were those most opposed to war and Jews ranked second.

0279 Stellaway, Richard J. "The Correspondence between Religious
Orientation and Socio-political Liberalism and Conservatism."
Sociological Quarterly 14 (1973): 430-439.

Data were collected in the rural Midwest and demonstrated strong
correlations of religious liberalism and sociopolitical liberalism and likewise of religious conservatism with status quo
orientations and political conservatism. This relationship was
found to be still more pronounced among those whose career
aspirations had not been realized. See also Schoenfeld (0277).

0280 Swanson, Guy E. "Life with God: Some Variations of Religious Experience in a Modern City." *Journal for the Scientific Study of Religion* 10 (1971): 169-199.

The survey was conducted with a sample of over seven hundred Detroit adult white Catholics, white Protestants and black Protestants. Various dimensions of religious belief and participation are measured and interpreted in relation to selected demographic variables.

0281 Swiecicki, Andrzej. "La Religiosité, Les Valeurs et Les Motivations." In *Religiousness in the Polish Society Life*. edited by Witold Zdaniewicz, pp. 73-82. Warsaw: Pallottinum, 1981 (0181).

Swiecicki here reports a 1978 investigation in the Polish region of Jaroslaw which was concerned with religious beliefs and practice, moral principles and behavior and values: results are reported by occupational group, age and standard of education.

0282 Thompson, Robert C.; Michel, Jerry B.; and Alexander, T. John. "Christian Orthodoxy, Authoritarianism and Prejudice." *Rocky Mountain Social Science Journal* 7 (1970): 117-123.

In tests on samples of undergraduate students there was found to be a strong relationship between authoritarianism and prejudice toward ethnic groups but the relationship between religious orthodoxy and prejudice was not strong. See also Middleton (0267) and Roof (0275) for comparable studies.

0283 Tittle, Charles R. and Welch, Michael R. "Religiosity and Deviance: Toward a Contingency Theory of Constraining Effects." *Social Forces* 61 (1982): 653-682.

The authors operate nine types of deviance and relate these to religiosity by examining contextual variables of a socio-demographic kind which appear to condition such deviance. The authors predict, as many might have done without their close analysis, that the impact of religious constraints is increased when controls in the secular domain are less forceful.

0284 Tygart, Clarence E. "Social Movement Participation: Clergy and the Anti-Vietnam War Movement." *Sociological Analysis* 34 (1973): 202-211.

The article indicates what social and ideological character- istics accompanied opposition to the Vietnam war in a sample of 486 Protestant ministers. It is found that those who expressed opposition to American involvement in Vietnam tended to define themselves as "liberal", both politically and theologically; they were also active in civil rights campaigning and were characterized as non-authoritarian.

0285   Van Kemenade, J.A.   "Roman Catholics and Their Schools."
Sociologia Neerlandica   7 (1971): 15-27.

The need for separate identity and institutional isolation is
a declining feeling among Dutch Catholics.   In a spirit of
prescription not common among modern sociologists of religion,
the author suggests that the time has come for a more integrated
system of religious education in the cause of greater social
pluralism.   See also Hutjes (0254), Bax (0469) and Thurlings
(0536).

0286   Vaughan, Ted R.; Smith, Douglas H.; and Sjoberg, Gideon.
"The Religious Orientation of American Natural Scientists."
Social Forces   44 (1966): 519-526.

The authors provide a study of the religious beliefs and
practices of a putatively representative sample of natural
scientists working in American universities.   The authors
characterize their subjects' religious orientations as
"neo-orthodox", in contrast to their fellow professionals
outside universities whose orientations are more traditionally
orthodox.   For discussions of the relationship of religiosity
and academic discipline, see also 0293 and 0300.

0287   Vovelle, Michel.   "Les Attitudes devant la Mort, Front
Actuel de l'Histoire des Mentalités." *Archives de Sciences
Sociales des Religions*   39 (1975): 17-29.

Vovelle's paper is a research review concerned with work on
attitudes to death.   The author selects certain themes such
as the importance of mental habits and treats research to
date for methods deployed, approaches - whether descriptive,
impressionistic or whatever - and interpretations.   Vovelle
compares his own model with that developed by Aries (0232).
See also Freund (0245).

0288   Wallis, Roy.   *Salvation and Protest: Studies of Social and
Religious Movements*.   New York: St.Martin's Press, 1979.

This useful essay takes stock of universal features of
social and religious movements and investigates certain cases
of moral crusade such as the National Viewers' and Listeners'
Association, which is established in Britain by Mary Whitehouse
to monitor television and radio broadcasts, and the Nationwide
Festival of Light, a campaign against the perceived decline of
Christian values.

0289   Weddell, Sallie Cone.   "Religious Orientation, Racial
Prejudice and Dogmatism: A Study of Baptists and Unitarians."
Journal for the Scientific Study of Religion   11   (1972):
395-399.

Small matched samples of Unitarians and Southern Baptists are
used in the assessment of religious orientations and racial
prejudice projected towards blacks.   The Baptists are found

to be the more prejudiced and the more dogmatic of the two
groups monitored.

0290 Wilson, Glenn. "Why Are Christians Prejudiced?" *New Society*
558 (1973): 617-619.

The question that Wilson addresses is not as simple as his title.
He measures attitudes in a number of groups of subjects and
finds prejudices varying from strong to insignificant.   It is
the explanation of these variations that warrants attention.
Fundamentalist belief, he suggests, is a basis for prejudice
only if unaccompanied by a deeper involvement in the life of
the church: his Dutch Reformed Church (South Africa) group
showed strong prejudices whereas the Salvation Army group, who
were much involved in their organization and in the world, were
innocent of prejudicial attitudes.

0291 Zahn, Gordon C. "War and Religion in Sociological
Perspective." *Social Compass* 21 (1974): 321-431.

The Christian position in respect of war is examined in
chronological historical perspective.   Modern pacifism, while
having antecedents in Christian history, is a phenomenon
arising in the inter-war period of the twentieth century and
is seen here as a reaction to the prospect of war inhibited
at the time by the threat of Nazism.   The ethical dimension,
however, is only one of a number of components commanding the
attention of the sociologist.   War is a theme of the
relationship of Church and State and is also to be studied as
a principle of social control.

I. RELIGIOSITY; RELIGIOUS BEHAVIOR; ATTITUDES; DIMENSIONS

0292 Barrish, Gerald and Welch, Michael R.   "Student Religiosity
and Discriminatory Attitudes Toward Women." *Sociological Analysis*
41 (1980): 66-73.

It is suggested that at least among the highly educated as
represented by a sample of college students drawn from three
schools there is not the strong link often alleged between
high levels of religiosity and the adoption of stereotypical
attitudes to gender roles.

0293 De Blauwe-Plomteux, Magda. "L'Attitude des Adolescents
et des Jeunes Adultes envers le Christ." *Social Compass* 19 (1972):
415-430.

This is the progress report of a research project on young
people's attitudes towards Christ.   Findings point to the
significance of age as a factor in coping with the character
of Christ as both human and divine, an ambivalence with which
younger respondents had difficulty.   Among university students,
however, the age factor signifies less than the sphere of study,

and the uniqueness of Christ appeals more to students of social than of natural sciences.   Some 88.7 per cent declared a belief in the divinity of Christ but only one third of students monitored reckoned that Christ played an important role in their lives.   See also Lehman (0300).

0294 De Jong, Gordon F.; Faulkner, Joseph E.; and Warland, Rex H. "Dimensions of Religiosity Reconsidered: Evidence from a Cross-cultural Study." *Social Forces* 56 (1976): 866-889.

The authors apply a cluster of dimensions of religiosity to groups of German and American students.   Their findings confirm the desirability of utilizing multivariate measures and they notice a general independence of certain dimensions (notably religious knowledge and social consequences) from the others (individual moral consequences, religious belief, religious experience and religious observation).   For an appreciation of Glock's dimensions see Faulkner and De Jong (0295).

0295 Faulkner, Joseph F. and De Jong, Gordon F. "Religiosity in 5-D: An Empirical Analysis." *Social Forces* 45 (1966): 246-254.

On a sample of over three hundred college students the authors apply, assess and favor the theory of Glock that religious involvement may be measured within five dimensions - the ideological, the ritualistic, the experiential, the intellectual and the consequential.   For a discussion of the interdependence of these dimensions see 0296.

0296 Johnson, Arthur L.; Brekke, Milo L.; Strommen, Merton P.; and Underwager, Ralph C. "Age Differences and Dimensions of Religious Behavior." *Journal of Social Issues* 30 (1974): 43-67.

This reports and interprets part of an extensive survey in which a large battery of questions was put to a national sample of over four thousand Lutheran Church members in the United States. Items investigated ranged across religious beliefs and practices and the responding sample was divided into age groups for analysis.   In the younger groups there was a marked heterogeneity of behavior which appeared to be reduced with age, while the older groups were characterized by relative homogeneity.   The effects of cohort and congregational solidarity are explored in the analysis of this tendency.

0297 King, Morton. "Measuring the Religious Variable: Nine Proposed Dimensions." *Journal for the Scientific Study of Religion* 6 (1967): 173-190.

This article is a contribution to the analysis of the multidimensionality of religion, a problem area explored by Glock and Stark (0122).   There is much verbatim quotation of responses to exemplify the dimensions King proposes which are:

1. Creedal assent and personal commitment.
2. Participation in congregational activities.
3. Personal religious experience.
4. Personal ties in the congregation.
5. Commitment to intellectual search despite doubt.
6. Openness to religious growth.
7a. Dogmatism.
7b. Extrinsic orientation.
8a. Financial behavior.
8b. Financial attitude.
9. Talking and reading about religion.

0298 Klemmack, David L. and Cardwell, Jerry D. "Interfaith
Comparison of Multidimensional Measures of Religiosity."
Pacific Sociological Review 16 (1973): 495-507.

Tests were conducted with a student constituency to explore the
variation across denominations of manifestations of the
dimensions of commitment; these are then related in the analysis
to the formal beliefs and emphases of the respective
denominations.   The authors find that structural religiosity
for Catholics is akin to that for Baptists but patterns of
commitment vary.   Contrasting perceptions of youth and
adults led to a discovery of the Protestant emphasis upon
youth-orientations while Catholics stressed adult-orientations.

0299 Kostovski, Stefan. "Tipovi Religionznosti u Seoskim
Nascijima Donjeg Pologa." *Sociologija Sela* 10 (1972): 35-36.

Donjeg Pologa is a small village in Macedonia.   Kostovski's
starting point is the marxist interpretation of religion as an
expression of alienation and he applies this in his typification
of forms of rural religiosity.   Of every six members of his
rural population, one is characterized as inconsistently
religious and four are consistent believers in the traditional
sense; the other is atheist, whether by virtue of disinterest
or as a consequence of deliberate and rational contemplation.
Evidence is adduced to confirm the marxist view that atheists
are to be found principally among the more educated groups
whereas traditional religiosity flourishes among the less
educated.   The strong influence of the family over the religious
orientation of the young is attested in all groups but is more
pronounced among Moslems than in Orthodox families.

0300 Lehman, Edward C. "Academic Discipline and Faculty
Religiosity in Secular and Church-related Colleges." *Journal for
the Scientific Study of Religion* 13 (1974): 205-220.

It is often supposed that the academic discipline pursued by
a student or teacher has an effect upon religious orientations.
Questionnaire data suggest that in schools not related to
churches those pursuing the sciences are more religious than
those in non-scientific subjects.   In church-related colleges,
however, the reverse is true and the religiosity of those in

the humanities is greater than those in the sciences.   This
does not necessarily demonstrate the causal effect of academic
discipline.   It is likely that those with a prior inclination
toward religion gravitate toward the church colleges; and
humanities courses and social sciences will attract all those
intending to find a profession in the religious sphere.
See also De-Blauwe-Plomteux (0293).

0301 Moberg, David and McEnery, Jean N.   "Changes in Church-
related Behavior and Attitudes of Catholic Students." *Sociological
Analysis* 37 (1976): 53-62.

Over the period studied there appeared to be a decline among
Catholic students of mass attendance, the habit of prayer and
resort to the confessional.   This decline was accompanied by
a relaxation of attitudes concerning personal morality and
responsibility, while there was an increased tendency to take
into account the rights and sensitivities of others.   The
authors interpret these trends as a gradual emancipation from
the formal and traditional values of the Roman Catholic Church
and the greater influence upon prevailing value systems of
peer group and contemporary American culture.

0302 Thurstone, L.L. and Chave, E.J. *The Measurement of Attitude:
A Psychophysical Method and Some Experiments with a Scale for
Measuring Attitude Toward the Church*.   Chicago: University of
Chicago Press, 1929.

The work of Thurstone and Chave survives as a classic in this
field.   They develop, operate and evaluate a scale of attitudes
toward the Church which has considerable utility in the
measurement of attitudes of different groups and opinions about
different organizations.   Their work ranges over the measurement of belief and attendance and they include the
questionnaire design for attitudes.

0303 Wuthnow, Robert, ed. *The Religious Dimension: New Directions
in Quantitative Research*. New York: Academic Press, 1979.

This is a summary work which employs Andrew M.Greeley and
others to bring up to date the discussions on indicators of
religiosity and the correlates of religious commitment.   There
are position papers too on religious affiliation against
socioeconomic status and religion and social change.

0304 Wuthnow, Robert, and Glock, Charles Y. "Religious Loyalty,
Defection and Experimentation Among College Youth." *Journal for
the Scientific Study of Religion* 12 (1973): 157-180.

A survey of Berkeley students is interpreted to suggest that
religious experimentation is rooted in broader cultural
disaffections.   The most significant factors in religious
defection among college students appear to be intellectual
sophistication and psychological stress.   This work emanates
from a period characterized by religious pluralism, with

intellectual, cultural and spiritual alternatives being available
in their fullest variety at school level.   For fuller treatment
see Wuthnow (0465).

J.   TYPOLOGIES OF RELIGIOUS ORGANIZATION

0305   Beckford, James A.   "Sociological Stereotypes of the Religious
Sect." *Sociological Review*   26 (1978): 109-123.

Beckford argues that "the supposedly objective and neutral
conceptualisation of sect-type and church-type among sociologists
is...based on assumptions deeply rooted in prejudiced folk
knowledge" and that Weber is largely to blame.   Drawing upon his
work on Jehovah's Witnesses (Beckford, 0356), he challenges in
particular the notions of sects as religious movements of the
disprivileged classes and as organizations of protest and
rejection in a world perceived to be oppressive.   See also
the work of Alston and Aguirre (0348).

0306 Bokhorova, S.S.   "Problema Tipologii Religioznykh Ob'edinenii
v Burzhnaznoi Sotsiologii Religii." *Vestnik Moskovskogo Universiteta,
Filosofiya*   27 (1972): 78-87.

Bokhorova presents an analysis of the problem of the typology
of religious organizations in "bourgeois" sociology of religion
as exemplified by Niebuhr, Thomas O'Dea, Bryan Wilson and others.
Soviet sociologists view with approval the process of secularization which western sociologists view more often with concern than
with indifference.   The church-type and sect-type are familiar
categories in the Soviet sociology of religion but the concept
of denomination is seldom rehearsed and Bokhorova commends its
application to religious organizations that would be thought
heterogeneous in a western context - Baptists, Methodists,
Seventh Day Adventists, Jehovah's Witnesses, Mennonites,
Pentecostals.

0307 Brothers, Joan. *Religious Institutions*.   London: Longman,
1971.

Joan Brothers introduces the sociological perspective on religion
and, with particular reference to Great Britain, the development
and type of religious institutions.   Seminal contributions to
the sociology of religion are noted in summary form and there is
a lucid survey of a range of empirical studies, in particular
concerning social class and the "religious factor".   The book
treats extensively of religion in minority communities, but
makes no pretence to be other than an elementary account.

0308 Dynes, Russell R.   "Church-Sect Typology and Socio-Economic
Status." *American Sociolical Review*   20 (1955): 555-560.

This is a classic typological study rendered the more distinguished
by being addressed in part to the question of the influence of

social stratification.   Furthermore, Dynes introduces a scheme
of scaling, using the typologies of Weber and Troeltsch as a
basis for measuring attitudes across the protestant population
of Columbus, Ohio.   Reprinted in Yinger's *Religion, Society
and the Individual*   (0070).

0309 Fernandez, J.W.   "African Religious Movements - Types and
Dynamics." *Journal of Modern African Studies* 2 (1964): 531-549.

This is an attempt to establish an elementary typology of
religious movements in Africa, with a special study of the
particular configuration and dynamics of the "syncretist"
movements of equatorial Africa.   Fernandez endeavors to assess
the place of these religious movements in the political processes
leading to nationalism, Africanism and Pan-Africanism.   It is
suggested that they embody many cultural imperatives, primarily
expressive techniques facilitating the adjustment to modernization, just as they provided adjustment to the colonial
situation.   Reproduced in Robertson (0049).

0310 Garelli, Franco.   "Gruppi Giovanili Ecclesiali: The Personale
e Politico, tra Franzione Educativa e Azione Sociale." *Quaderni
di Sociologia* 26 (1977): 275-320.

Garelli studies church groupings of young people and in the light
of recent literature develops a typology.   The groups he
characterizes as types include countercultural groups with
internally consistent value-systems, and those which are
distinguished by prepolitical or political activity such as
involvement with labor unions.   Cases studied include Communion
and Liberation, the Scout movement and the Italian Catholic
Action.

0311 Hill, Michael.   "Typologie Sociologique de l'Ordre Religieux."
Social Compass 18 (1971): 45-64.

This offers a review of ideal-types of religious organization
and proceeds to the particular study of religious orders.   Close
parallels are found between the religious order as observed and
the sect as typified by Bryan Wilson.   It is suggested that the
religious order corresponds to Wilson's notion of a "sect within
a church" and this compelling point of comparison is explored and
illustrated.   A critical difference is that the order exists
to serve the church as a whole whereas the sect is exclusive to
its own members.   See also Bryan Wilson's *Religious Sects* (0462).

0312 Johnson, Benton.   "A Critical Appraisal of the Church-Sect
Typology." *American Sociological Review* 22 (1957): 88-92.

This is an early endeavor to reappraise the assumptions underlying
the compelling distinction between church and sect which
sociologists had tended to operate on the basis of differences
in organization, and on the dynamic opposition of the two types.
Johnson emphasizes the importance of the theological variable
in determining the character of the two forms and in legitimizing
their distinctive postures to the world and to each other.

Reprinted with an editorial comment in the volume of papers collected by Newman (0040) pp.240-249.

0313 Johnson, Benton. "Church and Sect Revisited." *Journal for the Scientific Study of Religion* 10 (1971): 124-137.

Johnson surveys the lack of consensus on the nature of the church-sect distinction and raises problems concerning the conventional view that sects lose their purity and compromise their ideology in the course of growth. He checks the conceptual baggage that one generation of sociologists passes on to another and suggests that some of it can be declared excess. For an extension of this argument see Beckford (0305).

0314 Martin, David. "The Denomination." *British Journal of Sociology* 13 (1962): 1-14.

The sociological concept of denomination likens it to a political party that is permanently in opposition. It is a religious form that is peculiar to the United States and the British commonwealth. It flourishes as a progressive factor in conditions in which social progress proceeds at a steady rate and wherein the Church represents a source of continuity and stability. For the use of the concept in a Soviet context see Bokhorova (0306).

0315 Séguy, Jean. "Les Problèmes de la Typologie dans l'Étude des Sectes." *Social Compass* 12 (1965): 165-170.

Séguy draws attention to the problems deriving from the formulation of typologies in particular temporal and spatial contexts which do not obtain in other constituencies where they are applied. Wach's typology is commended for its inherent historical and comparative properties and for the scope it allows for sub-classification. For the work of Joachim Wach see 0058.

0316 Snook, John B. "An Alternative to Church-Sect." *Journal for the Scientific Study of Religion* 13 (1974): 191-204.

Finding the conventional church-sect typology inadequate, Snook proposes an alternative from the starting point that religious institutions are structures for the organization of religious experience. He then suggests four dimensions for the analysis of such institutions: these are intensity, pervasiveness, structure and symbolism. The potential of these dimensions is then explored and commended by application to diverse cases.

0317 Sommerville, C.John. "Religious Typologies and Popular Religion in Restoration England." *Church History* 45 (1976): 32-41.

Sommerville here covers the historical period 1660 to 1711 and works by content analysis of major religious materials then being published. He distinguishes between Anglican and dissenting works and correlates these two groups with some conventional typologies such as church-sect, authoritarian-liberal, conversionist-moralist and Old Testament oriented-New Testament

oriented.   Statistical significance is found for differences
between the two groups.

0318 Swatos, William H.   "Church-Sect and Cult: Bringing Mysticism
Back In." *Sociological Analysis* 42 (1981): 17-26.

It is suggested that the asceticism-mysticism continuum can throw
more light on the origins and development of the new religious
movements than does the church-sect typology.   For a theory of
formative organizational processes Swatos urges a cult-order
typology in place of church-denomination-sect.

0319 Wilson, Bryan R.   "Typologie des Sectes dans une Perspective
Dynamique et Comparative." *Archives de Sociologie de Religion* 16
(1963): 49-63.

Wilson suggests here a seven-fold classification of sects which
extends the typologies offered in his earlier work: he distinguishes
conversionist, revolutionary, introversionist, manipulationist,
thaumaturgical, reformist and utopian types.   These he
exemplifies both in the Christian world and in "the mission
territories".   This typology has been widely noted and deployed.
This article appears in English in Robertson (0049).   For further
exemplification of these types see Wilson's *Religious Sects*
(0462).

K. SECT DEVELOPMENT

0320 Bainbridge, William Sims and Stark, Rodney.   "Cult Formation:
Three Compatible Models." *Sociological Analysis* 40 (1979):
283-295.

The three models typified in this paper are:

- the psychopathology model: this emphasizes the pathology of
  the individuals for whom the cult provides articulate
  expression and plausible resolutions to common problems;

- the entrepreneur model by which the cult is seen to provide
  the means to spiritual and even material ends;

- the subculture-evolution model: herein members find scope
  within the religious community to develop and practise
  notions of an alternative and radical society.

0321 Beckford, James A.   "The Embryonic Stage of a Religious Sect's
Development: The Jehovah's Witnesses." *A Sociological Yearbook of
Religion in Britain* 5 (1972): 11-32.

The early organizational development of Zion's Watch Tower Tract
Society, from which Jehovah's Witnesses descended, does not conform
in Beckford's interpretation with any of the available
sociological models of religious group formation.   Beckford insists

upon the close study not only of the role of the charismatic
founder, of schism and of organized revival but also of the
founder Russell's position as editor of the magazine, president
of the publishing enterprise and nominal "Pastor" of the majority
of Bible student classes in the U.S.A.   Both at the embryonic stage
and in recent times, the pattern of organization of Jehovah's
Witnesses has differed markedly from that of other evangelistic
groups.   Beckford's monograph on Jehovah's Witnesses is *The
Trumpet of Prophecy* (0356); and for further implications for
conventional conceptions see Beckford (0305).

0322   Bloch-Hoell, Nils.   *The Pentecostal Movement: Its Origins,
Development and Distinctive Character.*   Oslo: Universitetsforlaget,
1964.

This work is particularly useful for its developmental treatment
of modern pentecost.   It picks up the story with Holiness
meetings in America at the turn of the century; when pentecost
was established in the States it attracted visitors from Europe,
where it was in due course imported.   In the subsequent phase
of development, the pentecostal churches missionize the world.
In recent years some of the most flourishing pentecostal churches
have become established in the underdeveloped world.   See also
Hollenweger (0384).

0323   Desroche, Henri and Reymarkers, Paul.   "Départ d'un Prophète:
Arrivée d'une   Eglise."   *Archives de Sciences Sociales des Religions*
42 (1976): 117-162.

The authors select and present key documents illuminating the
circumstances of the death in prison in 1951 of the Congolese
prophet Simon Kimbangu, his death-bed conversion to the Roman
Catholic Church and the survival of his spirit in a church
bearing his name and led by one of his sons.

0324   Flanagan, Thomas.   "Social Credit in Alberta: A Canadian
'Cargo Cult'?"   *Archives de Sciences Sociales des Religions*   34
(1972): 39-48.

The Social Credit League emanates from the period of economic
crisis following World War I and its ideas are owed to a British
engineer, Clifford Hugh Douglas (1878-1952).   In the misery of
the moment Social Credit is optimistic and issues the hope of
a glorious future.   Flanagan studies Social Credit as a case
of millenarianism and relates its development to social and
economic disorientation.

0325   Hill, Christopher; Reay, Barry; and Lamont, William.   *The
World of the Muggletonians.* London: Temple Smith, 1983.

The Muggletonians constitute a religious movement generated in
the social and religious ferment of the mid-seventeenth century
in England.   Their founder and principal ideologist was John
Reeve but they take their name from the organizer of the movement
Ludowick Muggleton.   The articles in this group analyze the

genesis of Muggletonianism and give breakdowns of adherents by economic and occupational status.

0326 Isichei, Elizabeth Allo. "From Sect to Denomination in English Quakerism, with Special Reference to the Nineteenth Century." *British Journal of Sociology* 15 (1964): 207-222.

A detailed study of English Quaker history raises questions about the straightforward linear sect-to-denomination progression which typifies received sociological wisdom.   Isichei suggests that sectarian and denominational tendencies co-exist within a religious group and that a sect is likely to move through successive phases of outward and inward orientation.   Reproduced in Wilson (0344) pp.161-181. See also Isichei (0393).

0327 Jacobson, Cardell K. and Pilarzyk, Thomas J.   "Croissance, Développement et Fin d'une Secte Conversioniste: Les Jesus People de Milwaukee." *Social Compass* 21 (1974): 255-268.

This article documents the rise and fall of a conversionist sect, the Jesus movement in Milwaukee.   The unit of organization is the commune and the typification of the movement as a "conversionist sect" derives from the work of Bryan Wilson (0319, 0462).   The problems of community maintenance included that of routinizing the ideals of a charismatic nucleus.   The tendency to disintegrate and reaffiliate to mainstream churches is one which the student of the Milwaukee case predicts as a general trend.

0328 Larsen, Egon. *Strange Sects and Cults: A Study of Their Origins and Influence.* London: Arthur Barker, 1971.

This is not a deeply scientific or analytical work and it draws little upon the sociological literature for its interpretations. Indeed, the range of religious organizations treated itself precludes anything but a superficial and documentary introduction. But it brings together some instructive vignettes of sect develop- ment and presents a number of cases that have not commanded the scholarly interest they might warrant.   The Assassins and the Thugs are here, as exemplars of the notion of murder as a sacred duty. The Castrators and the Doukhobors provide illustrations of Russian sects.   And attention is given to new religious movements engaging in political affairs: these include the Soka Gakkai of Japan and the African Cherubim and Seraphim, viewed according to its manifestations in England.

0329 Mauss, Armand L. and Petersen, Donald W. "Les 'Jesus Freaks' et le Retour à la Responsibilité." *Social Compass* 21 (1974): 283-301.

This is a study of the social functions of the Jesus movement of the late 60s and early 70s as a manifestation of the Prodigal Son syndrome.   The authors detect the routinization of a deviant religious movement and anticipate the rehabilitation of its members within mainstream Christianity.   These speculations are confirmed in the course of an interview survey.

0330 Muelder, Walter. "From Sect to Church." *Christendom*
(1945): 450-462.

Religious organization being associated with social class,
Muelder looks at the effects of changes in one dimension upon
the other and makes an early study of the evolution of
sociological structure in a group as it develops from sect
to church. Abridged and reprinted in Yinger (0070).

0331 Niebuhr, H.Richard. *The Social Sources of Denominationalism*.
New York: Holt, 1929.

Niebuhr's essay is a classic in the sociology of religion by
a Protestant theologian who recognizes the limitations of
doctrine as a criterion by which to differentiate the
(American) denominations.   He groups these not by theological
characteristics but as "the churches of the disinherited",
those of the middle class and those of immigrants: his account
is centered upon nationalism and "the color line". Niebuhr
was among the first to perceive sectarianism in terms of
political and cultural disintegration and this book is for
that reason a landmark.

0332 O'Toole, Roger. "'Underground' Traditions in the Study of
Sectarianism: Non-Religious Uses of the Concept 'Sect'." *Journal
for the Scientific Study of Religion* 15 (1976): 145-156.

The author draws delineations of the sect-type from the marxist
tradition and from the "collective behavior" tradition
associated with Simmel, Blumer, Kurt Lang, Lewis A.Coser and
others.   These non-religious applications of the concept of
sect are then related to formulations developed with reference
to religious movements.

0333 Redekop, Calvin. "A New Look at Sect Development." *Journal
for the Scientific Study of Religion* 13 (1974): 345-352.

The author notices among sociologists a neglect of radical
sects developing within intolerant societies.   In consequence,
in his view, little is understood of the mutually rejecting
relationship of sect and "world".   He provides case studies
of the development of Old Colony Mennonites and Mormons.

0334 Rogerson, Alan. "Témoins de Jéhovah et Étudiants de la
Bible. Qui Est Schismatique?" *Social Compass* 24 (1977): 33-43.

Rogerson makes a study in sect development and schism which is
based on the activities of the Watch Tower Society between
1919 and 1932.   During this time, under the leadership of
Rutherford, there were changes in all aspects of the sect and
it was during this time that Jehovah's Witnesses emerged from
the Bible Student community.   See also Beckford (0321, 0356).

0335   Stark, Werner. *The Sociology of Religion: A Study of Christendom 2. Sectarian Religion.* London: Routledge and Kegan Paul, 1967.

The second volume of Stark's encyclopaedia is given to the origins and development of sectarianism, and to the nature and variety of religious sects.   For a typology Stark juxtaposed the retrogressive with the progressive sect, the rigoristic with the antinomian and the violent with the non-violent.   He surveys conditions affecting the decline of sectarianism, including denominationalization, schism and social conflicts of various kinds.

0336   Theobald, Robin.   "Seventh-day Adventism and the Millennium." *A Sociological Yearbook of Religion in Britain* 7 (1974): 111-131.

Theobald conducts a study of the development of the Seventh-day Adventist movement and an analysis of its eschatology.   The author discovers ways in which the movement departs from the ideal-typical adventist sect.   See also Theobald (0337).

0337   Theobald, Robin.   "The Role of Charisma in the Development of Social Movements: Ellen G.White and the Emergence of Seventh-day Adventism." *Archives de Sciences Sociales des Religions* 49 (1980): 83-100.

This paper applies Weber's typology of authority to the rise and fall of Mrs Ellen G.White among the antecedents of the Seventh-day Adventists.   Mrs White's initial leadership was confirmed through her exercise of charismatic gifts, notably the gift of prophecy.   But in the late 1880s this gave way to authority of the rational-legal type and Mrs White's influence waned. See also Theobald (0336).

0338   Treece, James William.   "Theories on Religious Communal Development." *Social Compass* 18 (1971): 85-100.

With special reference to the Bethany Fellowship of Minneapolis of which the author is a student, this article surveys various theories of religious communal development and particularly commends the theory of Ethnic and Status proposed by Don Martindale.   It is argued that other theories are partial but Martindale's is universal.

0339   Turner, Bryan S. and Hill, Michael.   "Methodism and the Pietist Definition of Politics: Historical Development and Contemporary Evidence." *A Sociological Yearbook of Religion in Britain* 8 (1975): 159-180.

The essay surveys conflicting interpretations of the early history of Methodism and its role in or against capitalist development.   There is then an examination of evidence of recent trends in English Methodism.   When the pietist rejection of secular politics as inherently sinful ceases to be possible, there are two courses to be taken.   Either Methodism confirms and supports existing governments as in Wesleyan Toryism, or

else it declares a moral coup d'état as it does by expulsions
of the Nonconformist conscience. The authors find that the
Methodist stance on the Vietnam war, for example, has a
distinctively ethical basis.

0340 Wallis, Roy. "The Cult and its Transformation." In
Sectarianism: Analyses of Religious and Non-religious Sects, edited
by Roy Wallis, pp.35-49. London: Peter Owen, 1975.

It is argued that a definition of cult and sect on the basis
of content of doctrine is irrelevant to the sociological
problems posed by these types of ideological collectivity.
A distinction is proposed in terms of the conception of access
to the truth or salvation incorporated in the belief-system -
that is, whether it is seen as uniquely or pluralistically
legitimate.

0341 Wallis, Roy. "Scientology: Cult to Religious Sect."
Sociology 9 (1975): 89-100.

Wallis offers a study of the sectarianization of a religious
collectivity confronted with problems of management and
community maintenance. Sectarianization is expressed as a
strategy of internal dynamics and external relationships and
the author explores the process with reference to authority
and access to truth. For the major study on Scientology by
Wallis, see *The Road to Total Freedom* (0448).

0342 Wilson, Bryan R. "An Analysis of Sect Development."
American Sociological Review 24 (1959): 3-15.

This article is an examination of the tensions besetting the
maintenance of original value orientations which offers
characterizations of distinctive types of sect. Of these it is
suggested that "adventist" and "introversionist" types are
relatively resistant to denominationalization whereas
"conversionist" types transform with ease. Reproduced in an
amended form in Wilson (0344): pp.22-45.

0343 Wilson, Bryan R. "The Exclusive Brethren: A Case Study in
the Evolution of a Sectarian Ideology." In *Patterns of Sectarianism: Organisation and Ideology in Social and Religious Movements*,
edited by Bryan R.Wilson, pp.287-342. London: Heinemann, 1967
(0344).

Wilson's paper is a rare study of an inaccessible group
conducted by interviews with lapsed members. Far from
denominationalizing, the Exclusive Brethren's sectarianism
has intensified with successive generations and new doctrinal
emphases have the effect - perhaps intended - of reinforcing
this exclusiveness.

0344 Wilson, Bryan R., ed. *Patterns of Sectarianism:*
Organisation and Ideology in Social and Religious Movements.
London: Heinemann, 1967.

This volume is a collection of case studies of the development
of sect organization and of the inter-relationship of ideology
and structure in sect-type movements. Essays range across
the English Quakers, Holiness, the Salvation Army, the Churches
of God and the Exclusive Brethren. They are all
conscientiously empirical. Certain recurrent tendencies
are identified such as the early developmental stage of
"ecumenical counter-sect" in which the group asserts itself in
opposition to sectarianism.

0345 Wilson, John. "The Sociology of Schism." *A Sociological*
Yearbook of Religion in Britain 4 (1971): 1-20.

John Wilson applies Neil Smelser's theory of collective
behavior to the withdrawals from parent bodies of the Primitive
Methodist Church and the Hicksite Quakers and the fission of
the Plymouth Brethren in 1848. The model is a linear one
and it is possible to describe religious schism as a natural
sequence of interdependent stages with the linkage that
Smelser calls "value added".

0346 Wright, Beryl. "The Sect that Became an Order: The Order of
Ethiopia." *A Sociological Yearbook of Religion in Britain* 5
(1972): 60-71.

This paper is concerned with schism from the mission churches
in South Africa in the late nineteenth century, and in particular
with the revolt against European guidance which came to be
called "the Ethiopian Movement". The event of schism is studied
in the light of conditions and factors identified by Smelser and
Wilson (0345).

L. SECTS; CULTS; NEW RELIGIOUS MOVEMENTS

0347 Allan, Graham. "A Theory of Millennialism: The Irvingite
Movement as an Illustration." *British Journal of Sociology* 25
(1974): 296-311.

The author is concerned with the early years of a Scottish
sect which later became the Catholic Apostolic Church. He
regards millennial movements as organized endeavors to recognize
and reinforce the aspirations of members who feel otherwise
undervalued. Allan emphasizes that millennial movements can
only be understood in relation to the social contexts in which
they arise and he points to the constraints of the real world
and the reinterpretation of these afforded by millennialist
doctrines.

0348 Alston, Jon P. and Aguirre, N.F. "Congregational Size and the Decline of Sectarian Commitment: The Case of the Jehovah's Witnesses in South and North America." *Sociological Analysis* 40 (1979): 63-70.

An examination of the process of denominationalization among Jehovah's Witnesses conducted in a wide constituency over a quarter of a century.   On the whole the conventional sociological hypotheses about sect development are confirmed and there is broad evidence of pretensions to church-like behavior as congregations flourish.   But there are exceptions such as Jehovah's Witnesses in Paraguay and Brazil.   The authors suggest implications for the revision of conventional typologies.   Beckford (0305) similarly bases upon the case of Jehovah's Witnesses a challenge to existing sociological stereotypes.

0349 Andrews, Edward Deming. *The People Called Shakers: A Search for the Perfect Society*. New York: Dover, 1953.

This is a comprehensive sociological and historical account of a millennial sect founded by Ann Lee, whose leadership is a subject of study in this volume.   Internal order, the regulation of worship, tensions with "the world", the management of labor and Shaker communism are all treated.   The author studied the decline of the order in recent years and the appendices include a fascinating statement of Shaker rule. For example, "Slamming doors and gates, loud talking and heavy walking in the dwelling house, should not be practised by Believers."   See also Andrews (0350).

0350 Andrews, Edward Deming. *The Community Industries of the Shakers*. Philadelphia: Porcupine, 1972.

The economy of the American Shakers was centered around a cluster of agricultural industries such as dried sweet corn, dried apples, garden seeds, herbs, leatherwork, buckles, buttons, copper work and blacksmithing.   All trades are related to the basically agricultural economy and their conduct is regulated by a system of values emanating from a simple religious faith. See also Andrews (0349).

0351 Baechler, Jean. "Mourir à Jonestown." *European Journal of Sociology* 20 (1979): 173-210.

The Jones sect committed mass suicide in Guyana on 18 November 1978.   This is an endeavor to analyze the charisma of its leader the Revd Jim Jones and his capacity to engage the commitment of his followers even to the point of self-sacrifice for the sake of the cult.   The paper is psychological as well as sociological in its interpretation.   See also Gutwirth (0380).

0352 Baer, Hans A. "Black Spiritual Churches: A Neglected Socio-
religious Institution." *Phylon* 42 (1981): 207-223.

In the author's account the spiritual churches within the black
community are observed to synthesize disparate religious
traditions in a new religious formation.   He estimates that there
are thousands of spiritual groups within the black community
and commends them as a subject for serious study.

0353 Balswick, Jack. "The Jesus People Movement: A Generational
Interpretation." *Journal of Social Issues* 30 (1974): 23-42.

The Jesus People were prominent in the scene of new religious
movements in the post-Hippie period of the early 1970s and
they receded therefrom soon afterwards.   This paper analyzes
the phenomenon as the religious expression of a generational
counterculture and points to its studied informality, spontaneity
and contemporary style of communication as the symbolization of
such an identity.   To the extent that this work was researched
by participant observation, it is a timepiece.   The author
anticipates either that the movement will become institutionalized as a formal religious organization or that existing churches
will respond by incorporating some of its appealing qualities.
In the event the latter prediction has been the more true and
the charismatic movement draws from the Jesus People and
contemporary religious countercultures the emphasis upon freedom
within a law of faith, the centrality of the Holy Spirit,
informality in expression and yet biblical fundamentalism.

0354 Barker, Eileen. "New Religious Movements in Britain: The
Context and the Membership." *Social Compass* 30 (1983): 33-48.

The subject is introduced in its historical context and in the
context of religion in contemporary Britain.   There is a general
explanation of youth movements in Britain, a characterization
of persons who join movements and an examination of full-time
membership as demanded by some of the new religious movements.
Recruitment is reported by the usual demographic variables
such as age, sex and social class.

0355 Barker, Eileen, ed. *New Religious Movements: A Perspective
for Understanding Society*. New York: Edwin Mellen, 1982.

This work appears as volume 3 in the series "Studies in Religion
and Society". Far from offering one brief case study after
another, it engages broad comparative themes such as the
individual and society, disengagement, assimilation and social
resources.   David Martin writes on the peace sentiment in
historical perspective, Roy Wallis on the new religious movements as social indicators, Colin Campbell on the new
spirituality, and Bert Hardin and Gunter Kehrer on rejection.

0356 Beckford, James A. *The Trumpet of Prophecy: A Sociological
Study of Jehovah's Witnesses*. Oxford: Blackwell, 1975.

This is the major sociological study of the Watch Tower movement.
This treats in a scholarly way of origins, crises in development, organization, doctrine, ideology, moral and religious
teachings.   Far from deferring to conventional models of the
sect-type, Beckford uses his research as the basis for
challenging existing stereotypes (Beckford, O305).   Particular
attention is paid to the movement's track-record in recruitment
which is analyzed in the context of contemporary secularization.

0357 Beckford, James A. *Cult Controversies: The Societal Response
to New Religious Movements*. London: Tavistock, 1985.

Here is a meticulously researched account of anti-cult expressions
with particular but not exclusive reference to the situations in
Britain, France and West Germany.   Controversies have centered
on recruitment strategies and procedures for induction; and
opposition has been expressed in violence towards cult members,
in initiatives to investigate and control new religious movements,
in the excited interest of the press and in increased litigation.
Beckford interprets the sensational interest in new religious
movements in terms of a general tendency toward privatization in
the religious domain; at the more formal level, the interest of
politicians and legislators is explained as a manifestation of
the growth of the "therapeutic state".   See also Beckford (O362)
and Shupe and Bromley (O434); and for a comparative study see
Bromley (O367).

0358 Beckford, James A. "Organization, Ideology and Recruitment:
The Structure of the Watch Tower Movement." *Sociological Review* 23
(1975): 893-909.

Far from conforming to the general trend of secularization,
Jehovah's Witnesses have held their own.   Beckford seeks an
explanation of this relative success and finds it in a highly
distinctive organizational structure.   Dimensions of the
relationship between organizational style and capacity for
recruitment include the mobilization of recruiting agents, the
sanctification of their activities, the centralization of power
and absence of an intermediate sector in decision making and
finance.

0359 Beckford, James A. "Two Contrasting Types of Sectarian
Organization." In *Sectarianism: Analyses of Religious and Non-
religious Sects*, edited by Roy Wallis, pp. 70-85. London: Peter
Owen, 1975 (O454).

The cases studied are religious organizations with contrasting
beliefs but like objectives, the Watch Tower movement and the
Unified Family of Sun Yan Moon, Beckford identifies mass-
movement features of the Watch Tower organization and the
"community intensity" of the Moonies. Both groups were
expanding at a time when many were suffering losses and Beckford
moots the possibility that the cultural appropriateness of a
religious movement may have as much to do with the form of its
organization as with the set of its teachings.

0360 Beckford, James A. "Explaining Religious Movements."
International Social Science Journal 29 (1977): 235-249.

Beckford examines new perspectives and new sensitivities in
sociological accounts of the development of religious movements.
These are related much more than previously to elements in
sociological theory as well as to the organizational contexts of
the religious movements themselves. Beckford's appreciation of
the new perspective arises out of what he calls the "conventional
problematic".

0361 Beckford, James A. "The Watchtower Movement World-wide."
Social Compass 24 (1977): 5-31.

The purpose of this article is in part introductory and the
account includes historical insights as well as details of current
organization and practice. The Jehovah's Witness movement is
remarkable as a missionary organization not least for the energies
of its devoted adherents. In other respects, however, the
movement eludes the conventions of sociological analysis and
Beckford is interested to point out aspects in which it deviates
from familiar models; for further treatment see Beckford (0356).

0362 Beckford, James A. "The Public Response to New Religious
Movements in Britain." *Social Compass* 30 (1983): 49-62.

The new religious movements in Britain have attracted excited
attention in the media and the religious establishment. Anti-
cult campaigns have been followed by government initiatives and
again by defensive lobbies. Beckford gives a comprehensive account
of this continuing conflict and interprets the strategies deployed.
See also Beckford's *Cult Controversies* (0357).

0363 Bennett, John W. *Hutterian Brethren: The Agricultural Economy
and Social Organization of a Communal People*. Stanford: Stanford
University Press, 1967.

Bennett's research is rigorous, systematic and reported with
several statistical tables and diagrams. His sensibility is
keenly sociological and he provides insights on the stratification
of the Hutterite community, the operation of social control,
internal organization, sect-world relations, and the management
of labor and enterprise. The work is relatively uninformative
on religious faith, for which the reader should instead see
Hostetler (0392).

0364 Berger, Peter L. "The Sociological Study of Sectarianism."
Social Research 21 (1954): 467-485.

This is a timepiece and the response to it now constitutes a
major component of empirical research on religious sectarianism.
Berger takes stock of scientific research to date and opens up
the possibility of further work at practical and theoretical
levels. He calls for careful monographs on sectarian movements
in America previously neglected by sociologists and initiates an
interest in organizational processes within the sects. And he

wants a clearer picture of the American religious scene and of the place of sectarianism within it.

0365   Bibby, Reginald W., and Brinkerhoff, Merlin B.   "The Circulation of the Saints: A Study of People Who Join Conservative Churches." *Journal for the Scientific Study of Religion* 12 (1973): 273-283.

The study reveals a high level of mobility between the memberships of the American churches. Among twenty evangelical congregations the authors found that over seventy per cent of new members were recruited from other churches and twenty per cent were the children of members.   It is suggested that the relatively high growth rate of the conservative churches relates to their superior ability to retain their children and mobile members.

0366   Bocock, Robert J.   "Anglo-Catholic Socialism: A Study of a Protest Movement within a Church." *Social Compass* 20 (1973): 31-48.

The constituency studied is the Church of England in the late nineteenth and twentieth centuries, and the perspective of analysis is provided by the typology of Joachim Wach.   The beliefs, values and rituals of the movement are related to its historical and social situation.   And the author recognizes the contribution of the Anglo-Catholic movement to the formation of the English Labour Party and the Trades Union Movement.

0367   Bromley, David G. and Shupe, Anson D.   "The Tnevnoc Cult." *Sociological Analysis* 40 (1979): 361-366.

The authors demonstrate the self-repetition of history by examining the Tnevnoc cult of the nineteenth century which, like the new religious movement burgeoning in the last decade, deployed methods of induction and socialization that incurred public antipathy and controversy.   In techniques and in public relations the parallels are close.   For comparison see Beckford's *Cult Controversies* (0357) and Beckford (0362).

0368   Campbell, Colin.   "Clarifying the Cult." *British Journal of Sociology* 28 (1977): 375-388.

This is an essay in conceptual clarification with the particular purpose of conforming the concept of "cult" as practised in the sociology of religion to something of an ideal-type.   Campbell reverts to the contribution of Ernst Troeltsch and points out distinguishing characteristics of the cult-type such as the peculiar belief system, internal organization and "the mystic collectivity".

0369 Clark, Elmer T. *The Small Sects in America*. New York: Whitmore & Smith, 1937.

This is an early documentary study and classification of sects in the United States which takes account of a wide range of analytical problems and attempts a first-order explanation.   Clark studies the religious constituency of America with particular reference to the sectarian spirit that has beset it.   He explores

the economic conditions of sectarianism and proposes a typology
of American sects, case studies of which occupy the remainder of
his study.   In his submission sects may be:

1.   pessimistic or adventist, including Jehovah's Witnesses
     the Millerite movements and Seventh-day Adventism;

2.   perfectionist or subjectivist: here he treats of Negro
     Methodism, Holiness groups and others;

3.   charismatic and pentecostal: such as the Assemblies of
     God, the Churches of God, the Kentucky revival and
     Father Divine's Peace Mission;

4.   communistic: the Oneida Perfectionists, Shakers, the
     House of David;

5.   legalistic or objectivist: small sects here include the
     Dunkers, the River Brethren, Christadelphians and the
     Separate Baptists.

Clark identifies universal features such as puritan ethic,
emotional deprivation, and the poverty of sectarians.   A revised
edition was published in 1949 by Pierce & Smith.   See also Bryan
R.Wilson's *Patterns of Sectarianism*   (0344).

0370   Davis, Rex and Richardson, James T.   "The Organization and
Functioning of the Children of God." *Sociological Analysis*   37 (1976):
321-339.

This is a highly informative documentary account of the international organization of the Children of God, a zealously Christian
communitarian movement which flourished in the late 1960s and early
70s.   The domestic unit, the commune, represents the lowest of a
number of levels of organization which rise as a pyramid to the
King's Counselorship.   Financial support, sought partly through
the selling of magazines, is a further theme of the authors'
investigation and they offer details of types of Children of God
communes.

0371   Desroche, Henri.   *Les Shakers Américains: D'un Néo-Christianism
à un Pre-socialisme*.   Paris: Éditions de Minuit, 1955.

Desroche relates economic, organizational and religious principles
in the development of the American Shakers.   Shaker millenarianism
is related to European forms.   From a sociological perspective,
Desroche proposes a phased chronology and topology of the Shaker
community.   The work is highly analytical and densely informed.
An extended edition was published in English in 1971 by the
Massachusetts University Press.

0372   Desroche, Henri.   "Oneida, Puritaine et Libertaire: De
l'Acculturation d'une Utopie Écrite aux Contreacculturations d'une
Utopie Pratiquee." *Archives de Sciences Sociales des Religions* 36
(1973): 3-34.

An analytical study of the Oneida community which has become well-known among sociologists as a contemporary and observable case of a utopian religious movement.   Desroche develops an interest in the foundation of the community and investigates it as a case of counter-acculturation.   See also Clark (0369).

0373 Downton, James W. *Sacred Journeys: The Conversion of Young Americans to Divine Light Mission.* New York: Columbia University Press, 1979.

The Divine Light Mission was very visible in the early 1970s as one of a group of new religious cults affected by eastern philosophy.   Downton uses the testimonies of four converts to illuminate the psychological dimensions of religious experience offered by the cult, in particular in the extension of sensory perception.   Of greater sociological interest is his account of organizational metamorphosis, defection from membership and the loss of momentum in the later 1970s.   See also Foss and Larkin (0375).

0374 Ellwood, Robert S. *Religious and Spiritual Groups in Modern America.* Englewood Cliffs: Prentice-Hall, 1973.

The number of groups treated in this survey is considerable and they are conveniently classified as Theosophical and Rosicrucian traditions, Spiritualism and UFO cults, neo-paganism, Hindu and other oriental movements.   These are interpreted within an historical context of religious alternatives and the quest of new religions.

0375 Foss, Daniel A. and Larkin, Ralph W. "Worshiping the Absurd: The Negation of Social Causality among the Followers of Guru Maharaj Ji." *Sociological Analysis* 39 (1978): 157-164.

The Divine Light Mission was a religious movement which burgeoned among the young of the 1960s and had a vogue eastern connection in the charismatic leadership of the youthful Guru Maharaj Ji. Foss and Larkin portray the crisis for doctrine and beliefs engendered by the subsequent decline of the cult and look closely at problems of causality and meaning in the ideology of Divine Light.   See also Downton's *Sacred Journeys* (0373).

0376 Frideres, James S. "The Death of Hutterite Culture." *Phylon* 33 (1972): 260-265.

The author's central thesis is that Hutterite culture has been attenuated in Canada by a systematic program of the provincial governments of Alberta, Saskatchewan and Manitoba.   Anti-Hutterite state initiatives include legislation on communal property rights and economic controls related, at least at the level of propaganda, to adverse effects of the Hutterites upon local communities.   Karl A.Peter has published a rejoinder to this article in the same journal (0417). See also Bennett (0363) and the major work of Hostetler (0392).

0377   Goodman, Felicitas D.   *Speaking in Tongues: A Cross-cultural Study of Glossolalia.*   Chicago: University of Chicago Press, 1972.

The author uses taped material of tongues - utterances by congregations and gatherings whose mother-tongues are in some cases English and in others Portuguese.   She joined Maya Indians in the Yucatan and an Apostolic congregation in Mexico City.   Her analysis of behavior and language reveals compelling continuities between groups of distinctive cultural backgrounds.   See also Hine (O383), Holm (O385) and Holm (O386).

0378   Gordon, David F.   "The Jesus People: An Identity Synthesis." *Urban Life and Culture*   3 (1974): 159-178.

The author is concerned with the implications and character of changes in personal identity associated with conversion to a religious movement.   The case of the Jesus People instances a peculiar type of change which the author calls "consolidation": this involves the reconciliation of two dissonant prior identities experienced by the convert.   The effect of consolidation is to confirm the beliefs of those who had considered themselves Christians before admission to the Jesus commune and to reconcile child-oriented and youth-oriented morality.

0379   Guizzardi, Gustavo.   "New Religious Phenomena in Italy: Towards a Post-catholic Era?" *Archives de Sciences Sociales des Religions*   42 (1976): 97-116.

Guizzardi makes a study of the post-war burgeoning of extra-ecclesial religious movements in Italy which has parallels else-where.   The author characterizes the Italian experience and attempts an explanatory scheme to account for new movements being predominantly youthful, ideological and middle and upper class. Guizzardi's explanatory model relates to six factors: changes in the class system, secularization, marxism, youth protest, the institutional church and social and cultural pluralism in Italian society.

0380   Gutwirth, Jacques.   "Le Suicide-massacre de Guyana et Son Contexte." *Archives de Sciences Sociales des Religions*   47 (1979): 167-187.

The cult of Reverend Jim Jones took root in California before moving to its apocalyptic phase in Guyana.   Sociologists tended to take it more seriously after its self-extermination than during its development and first-hand interpretive accounts are rare. This is a review article drawing on the work of Krause and Stern and of Kilduff and Javers.   See also Baechler (O351).

0381   Hardin, Bert.   "Quelques Aspects du Phénomène des Nouveaux Mouvements Religieux en République Fédérale d'Allemagne." *Social Compass*   30 (1983): 13-32.

The new religious movements present a dilemma for the West German government which has constitutional and moral commitments both to the principle of religious freedom and to the protection of

the young and the institution of the family.   Hardin underlines
the need for scientific research on the new religions in the
German context by pointing to the predominance of unsystematic
research and emotive charges and the privileged access to the
media of certain interest groups.

0382 Harrison, Michael I.   "The Maintenance of Enthusiasm: Involvement in a New Religious Movement." *Social Analysis* 36 (1975):
150-160.

Harrison makes a study of the structures for induction and socialization through which a new religious movement - in this case the
pentecostal movement within the American Catholic Church - sustains
commitment and involvement.   The organization is one which affords
maximal participation through attendance and performance at
regular meetings and the practice of skills defined as emanating
from the Holy Spirit.

0383 Hine, Virginia H.   "Pentecostal Glossolalia: Toward a Functional
Interpretation." *Journal for the Scientific Study of Religion* 8
(1969): 211-226.

Psychologically based explanations of the speaking in tongues are
examined and found wanting: so too are accounts which present
glossolalia as the function of social disorganization and deprivation.   In their place, Hine argues that glossolalia is a form of
learned behavior, performance in which celebrates commitment
to the pentecostal movement and its stances on personal and social
change.   See also Goodman (0377), Holm (0385) and Holm (0386).

0384 Hollenweger, Walter J. *Enthusiastisches Christentum: Die
Pfingstbewegung in Geschichte und Gegenwart.* Zurich: Zwingli Verlag,
1969.

This formidable volume is an encyclopaedic survey of the pre-
history, twentieth century development and current practice of
pentecostal churches throughout the world.   Although the book is
incidentally informed by sociological insight throughout, its
disciplined sociological assessment is confined to one chapter
in which Hollenweger examines the social function of pentecostal
eschatology, charts a growing social and educational commitment
among pentecostals and reports a survey of the social origins
of four hundred pentecostal pastors.   See also Nils Bloch-
Hoell (0322).   Published in English as *The Pentecostals.*
London: S.C.M. Press, 1972.

0385 Holm,Nils G.   "Ritualistic Pattern and Sound Structure of
Glossolalia in Material Collected in the Swedish-speaking Parts of
Finland." *Temenos* 11 (1975): 43-60.

Holm gives an observational study of the ritual context and
functions of speaking in tongues together with a detailed
linguistic analysis of glossolalia and vernacular. See also
Holm (0386), Goodman (0377) and Hine (0383).

0386   Holm, Nils G.   "Functions of Glossolalia in the Pentecostal Movement."   *Psychological Studies on Religious Man*, edited by Thorvald Källstad, pp.141-158. Uppsala: Almqvist & Wiksell, 1978.

Holm treats of the speaking in tongues as a "pseudolanguage" performable by any person competent in a first language. Here he analyzes the functions of glossolalia in ritual contexts; it has an integrating function for those already initiated by baptism in the Spirit and provides a model for those who aspire to full membership.   See also Felicitas Goodman (0377), Holm (0385) and Hine (0383).

0387   Holmes, Barbara.   "Status Hierarchy and Religious Sanctions: A Report on the Krishna Cult."   *Human Mosaic*   7 (1974): 31-45.

The cult of Krishna Consciousness was one of the most conspicuous and colorful of the new religious movements generated in the late 1960s and representing the attraction of younger generations in the western world to the lifestyles and philosophy of the east.   Holmes' study was conducted by participant observation and interview and it highlights the degree of social stratification within a small Krishna community emanating from the routinization of community life (practical domestic tasks and daily schedules) and the system of socializing new members. Status within the stratified community is used to motivate the convert to conformist behavior within it.

0388   Holt, John B.   "Holiness Religion: Cultural Shock and Social Reorganization."   *American Sociological Review*   5   (1940): 740-747.

This is a discussion of the effects of migration from rural to urban communities with particular reference to the south-eastern states of America.   Holiness religion is seen as a social movement in the sense of being an attempt on the part of groups suffering acute social maladjustment to recover security through religious revival and reform.   Reprinted in abridged form in Yinger (0070): 463-470.

0389   Homan, Roger.   "Interpersonal Communications in Pentecostal Meetings."   *Sociological Review*   26 (1978): 499-518.

This is a survey of the schemes within which interpersonal relations are developed in pentecostal meetings.   Expressions of sympathy and appreciation and the recognition of individual merit are made not directly between persons but indirectly in the form of public prayer and testimony.   The indirectness of interpersonal transactions accords with the theocentricity of the pentecostal world-view and the conscientious denial of personal competence.

0390   Homan, Roger.   "Crises in the Definition of Reality."   *Sociology*   15 (1981): 210-214.

This paper is an analysis in the tradition of W.I.Thomas in which are considered the functionary skills and prerogatives deployed in the process of framing, negotiating and establishing

conditions for action in pentecostal assemblies.   It is
based upon overt non-participant observation and interviewing in
sixty-six pentecostal institutions in England and Wales, Canada
and the United States.   Its focus is upon the crises that
arise either when the prerogative of definition is contested
by two or more "special definers" or when there is a compelling
resemblance of phenomena in the sacred domain to realities
familiar in the profane.   The skills which enable the professional functionary to sustain sacred definitions during such
conflicts include competence in the sacred language, the
management of laughter and the sacred gift of "discernment".

0391   Hostetler, John A.   *Amish Society*.   Baltimore: Johns Hopkins
University Press, 1963.

   The Amish society is a Mennonite group concentrated in
   Pennsylvania with large communities in other states such as
   Illinois.   Its resistance to cultural change celebrated by
   conspicuously traditional styles of dress and a taboo upon
   motor transport and the use of electricity has attracted
   curious sociologists, for whom Hostetler provides a comprehensive account.   He is interested in structural problems,
   culture maintenance, social isolation, inter-generational
   tensions and evolving conceptions of the outside world.   A
   revised edition appeared in 1968.   See also Stoltzfus (0442).

0392   Hostetler, John A.   *Hutterite Society*.   Baltimore: Johns
Hopkins University Press, 1974.

   The earlier work on the Hutterian brethren by Bennett (0363)
   is here complemented by an examination which takes more account
   of the religious factor in community organization and ideology.
   There is an extensive study of the Bruderhof in Europe before
   its migration to the United States and the process of adaptation is well documented.   This throws into highlight a
   number of sociological problems such as insulation from "the
   world", language maintenance and ritual integration.   See also
   Frideres (0376) and Peter (0417).

0393   Isichei, Elizabeth Allo   "Organization and Power in the
Society of Friends, 1852-59."   *Archives de Sociologie des Religions*
19 (1965): 31-49.

   In contrast to nineteenth century Quakerism in America, that in
   England was barely schismatic.   Isichei explores the tension
   between Quaker democracy and individualism on the one hand
   and the notion of divine influence on the other.   Fox's theory
   of the Light Within made all forms of ecclesiastical constraint
   seem intolerable; yet there prevailed such a vigilance against
   abuses of democracy that there was in adopted procedures an
   implicit conservative bias which acted as a check upon reform-
   ists whose initiatives might produce schism.   Reprinted in
   Wilson (0344): 182-212.

0394 Janosik, Robert J. "Religion and Political Involvement: A
Study of Black African Sects." *Journal for the Scientific Study
of Religion* 13 (1974): 161-175.

In modernization and political development there has been
greater activity by religious sects of the Kikuyu than among
the relatively acquiescent Zulu sects. The author brings to
his study of this comparison some of the insights and techniques
conventionally applied to the study of more explicitly
political organizations such as labor unions. In his analysis
the factors affecting the political orientation of African
sects include the variable of bureaucratization,the degree of
emphasis upon local customs and the openness of recruitment.

0395 Jones, Dean C. "The Management of Cleavage Potential in
a Religious Sect." *Journal for the Scientific Study of Religion*
1o (1971): 384.

This study provides a focus and analysis of the management skills
of the minister of a Holiness congregation. The strategy
adopted to obviate schism within the congregation involved the
studious avoidance of ideological issues which had the potential
of division and the majoring instead on consensual issues.
Such a strategy is familiar to students of ecumenism who observe
the avoidance and subordination of the issues that divide and
an elevation of the importance of issues that unite.

0396 Jones, Robert Kenneth, ed. *Sickness and Sectarianism:
Exploratory Studies in Medical and Religious Sectarianism.*
Aldershot: Gower, 1985.

This collection signifies an interesting departure in the sociology
of religion. In his own contribution the editor treats of the
development of medical sects and operates the concept of sect
that has previously been applied to political organizations, as
by O'Toole (0416) and Wallis (0454). There are studies of the
therapeutic functions of new religious movements and of the
mental health of religious extremists.

0397 Jones, Robert Kenneth. "The Catholic Apostolic Church: A
Study in Diffused Commitment." *A Sociological Yearbook of Religion
in Britain* 5 (1972): 137-16o.

The Catholic Apostolic Church arose as a charismatic movement
in the 182os and is perhaps best known for the manifestations
of glossolalia which were first heard in Scotland in 183o.
Jones traces the emergence of the movement as a sect with a
peculiarly well-developed liturgy and architectural hierarchy
and a primitive belief in the imminence of the millennium, the
elusiveness of which has been a major factor in the movement's
twentieth century decline. Jones is inclined to attribute
the emergence of the Catholic Apostolic Church to the impotence
of the middle classes to disapprove - let alone restructure -
the social situation of the 182os and subsequent decades.

0398   Jones, Robert Kenneth.   "The Swedenborgians: An Interaction-
ist Analysis."   *A Sociological Yearbook of Religion in Britain* 7
(1974): 132-153.

This is a rare sociological treatment of Swedenborgianism.
The author traces the development of the sect from its genesis
in the late eighteenth century and documents a familiar pattern
of schism.   He treats of order, liturgy, organization, doctrine,
exegesis, social and historical background of the sect and
aspects of social interaction within the "New Church".

0399   Kiernan, Jim P.   "Authority and Enthusiasm: The Organization
of Religious Experience in Zulu Zionist Churches."   In *Religious
Organization and Religious Experience,* edited by J.Davis, pp.169-179.
London: Academic Press, 1982 (0013).

The chain of authority which the author analyzes is a simple
one running from preacher to minister to bishop.   At "band"
level enthusiasm is checked by a tightening of the reins, but
it also erupts as a way of slipping the reins and is then a
check upon or even threat to the authority system within the
church.   See also Kiernan (0588).

0400   Klibanov, A.I.   "Piatdesiat' Let Nauchnogo Issledovaniia
Religioznogo Sektantstva."   *Soviet Sociology* 8 (1969): 239-278.

This is a Russian account of "fifty years of scientific study
of religious sectarianism".   The keynote is said to have been
struck by Lenin and religious sectarianism is considered as a
product of the contradictions of capitalism and landlords.
Klibanov treats not only of the scientific study of religious
sectarianism in Russia but of its political control and so
the migration of the Doukhobors is one of the problems that
occupies him.

0401   Koss, Joan D.   "El Porque de los Cultos Religiosus: El
Caso del Expiritismo en Puerto Rico."   *Revista de Ciencias
Sociales* 16 (1972): 61-72.

The purpose of this paper is to explain in historical perspective the development of cults with particular reference to the
case of Puerto Rican Spiritualism.   The pattern of recruitment
to Spiritualism in the nineteenth century suggests that its
attractions were greater for professionals than for lower
classes and greater for Creoles than for Spaniards; a factor
in the latter tendency was the association of Spiritualism
with social welfare and with the resistance of Spanish colonialism.   From a middle-class power base Puerto Rican
Spiritualism broadened its appeal.   This article provides a
useful complement to the literature of cults and a basis for
comparative study; the disorientation of the educated classes
which this case illustrates has compelling parallels in the
study of new religious movements in recent times.

0402   Lalive d'Epinay, Christian.   "L'Héritage et la Dynamique
Externe du Changement."   *Archives de Sciences Sociales des
Religions*   36 (1973): 35-70.

This is a study conducted by participant observation and
interviewing among the Iris Community, a Waldensian group in
the *pampas* of Chile and Argentina.   The author analyzes the
role of the community in the   socioeconomic history of the
region.   The missionary community is examined in a dynamic
relationship with the world in which it is established.

0403   Lans, Jan M. van der and Derks, Frans.   "Les Nouvelles
Religions aux Pays-bas: Contexte, Appartenance, Réactions."
Social Compass   30 (1983): 63-83.

This is an overview of the new religions current in the
Netherlands such as Ananda Marga and Divine Light.   These
are interpreted to signify a cultural syncretism of East and
West.   The new religions had at the time of writing the
article been the subject of wider attention than was
warranted by their size: but while they had become prominent
in the media there was a reluctance to comment being shown
by the churches, the government and the helping professions.

0404   Leger, Danièle.   "Charisma, Utopia and Communal Life."
Social Compass   29 (1982): 41-58.

Leger makes a study of neorural apocalyptic communes in
France with particular reference to the process of initiation
and to everyday life within the communes.   As its title
suggests, this article draws upon Max Weber's theory of
forms of domination.

0405   Levi, Ken, ed.   *Violence and Religious Commitment:
Implications of Jim Jones's People's Temple Movement.* University
Park, Penn.: Pennsylvania University Press, 1982.

In November 1978 the Revd Jim Jones of Jonestown died of a
gunshot wound amid the bodies of 911 members of the People's
Temple.   This mass suicide sent shock waves through the
American public from whom the Jones cult had migrated.   This
volume offers a sociological post mortem and endeavors to
understand reactions to Jonestown.   See also Richardson
(0422).

0406   Lofland, John.   *Doomsday Cult: A Study of Conversion,
Proselytization and Maintenance of Faith.*   Englewood Cliffs:
Prentice-Hall, 1966.

Lofland conducts an observational study of cult activity and
maintains a special interest in career passages and structures.
This includes the characterization of converts, strategies of
recruitment and socialization and promotion opportunities
within the cult organization.   The problem of sustaining hope,
often in spite of major events in the life of the cult,

occupies Lofland as it did Festinger. The conduct of field work
is described in some detail.

0407 Long, Theodore E. and Hadden, Jeffrey K. "Sects, Cults and
Religious Movements." *Sociological Analysis* 40 (1979): 280-282.

Long and Hadden write the editorial introduction to a special
issue of *Sociological Analysis* concerned with the predominantly
counter-cultural religious movements of the 1960s. Among the
more prominent of these were the Jesus People, the Divine
Light Mission and various syncretist movements which celebrated
the western interest in eastern philosophy that had burgeoned
in the secular antecedent of these religious movements, Hippie
culture.

0408 Martin, Bernice. "The Spiritualist Meeting." *A Sociological
Yearbook of Religion in Britain* 3 (1970): 146-161.

This article offers a descriptive account and close commentary
on the structure and conduct of the spiritualist meeting and
then draws from anthropological analyses of shamanism and
such phenomena to suggest models for integrating the religious
significance of the meeting and the medium.   The distance of
Spiritualism from the Judaeo-Christian tradition accounts for
the inadequacy of conventional categories such as sect and cult,
prophet and priest; on the other hand, shamanism is operative
as an adjunct to priestly religion while Spiritualism is claimed
to be self-sufficient.   Parallels with shamanism are assessed
in terms of the calendar of rites, concern for the cultural
system, individualism and community, and the authorization
of functionaries.

0409 Marty, Martin E. "Sects and Cults." *Annals of the American
Academy of Political and Social Science* 332 (1960): 125-134.

In contemporary America sects and cults are perceived as a
religious category complementing Protestantism and Catholicism.
While sects are groupings with peculiarly negative orientations,
cults have the tendency of a positive orientation and charismatic
leadership.   Marty emphasizes the importance in analysis of
religious context as well as religious content.   Sects and cults
provide a haven and a counter-current and their members do not
wish to be drawn into the mainstream.

0410 Marty, Martin E. "The Occult Establishment." *Social
Research* 37 (1970): 212-230.

Marty's interest in this paper is what he calls the "no-gods
land" between the conventional or "high" religions of the world
and the recognized secular ideologies such as marxism.   It is
a land of magic, superstition and bewildering opinions, clair-
voyance, astral bodies, spiritualism and so on.   In Marty's
analysis the development of spiritualist and kindred movements
represents a response to secularized denominational religion:
they provide a haven for the disenchanted as the sects are
normally reckoned to offer a refuge for the dispossessed.

Such an interpretation accords with a number of sociological comments on the new religious movements of the late 1960s and early 70s.

0411   Masefield, Peter. "The Muni and the Moonies." *Religion* 15 (1985): 143-160.

Muni is a Pali term for "sage" frequently used in conjunction with the Buddha. Masefield recognizes certain continuities and discontinuities between ancient traditions and new religious movements and highlights some universal characteristics of religious leadership.

0412 Montague, Havor. "The Pessimistic Sect's Influence on the Mental Health of its Members: The Case of Jehovah's Witnesses." *Social Compass* 24 (1977): 135-147.

The author cites published research to show that mental disorders are more frequent among Jehovah's Witnesses than in the population as a whole. This is partly attributable to the high incidence of mental disturbance among recruits prior to their conversion. Other factors include the great pressure to conform to sect norms and the emotional strain of belief-structures. Further, the faithful who suffer are urged to avoid worldly counsel and to consult instead their own Elders whose guidance consists in primitive threats of divine vengeance. Montague suggests that here is the root of a high incidence among Witnesses of aggressive crime. See also Homan (0251).

0413 Nelsen, Hart M. "Sectarianism, World View and Anomie." *Social Forces* 51 (1972): 226-233.

Nelsen works with a sample of southern Appalachian Presbyterians to identify the operational character of the relationship between sectarian orientation and social and economic deprivation. In the analysis of this paper the mode of world rejection which characterizes members of religious sects has a direct appeal for individuals of low social class, reading age and unprivileged place of residence. This interpretation differs from the conventional view that social and economic deprivation beget anomie from which sectarianism provides a refuge.

0414 Nelson, Geoffrey K. "The Membership of a Cult: The Spiritualist National Union." *Review of Religious Research* 13 (1972): 170-177.

The inquiry involved members of the National Spiritualists Union in the west midlands of England, who were tested on a group of social and psychological variables in an endeavor to characterize cult membership. Major factors affecting affiliation include curiosity concerning "psychic gifts" and disenchantment with the belief systems of mainstream religious organizations.

0415   Oh, John Kie-chang.   "The Nichiren Shoshu of America."
Review of Religious Research   14 (1973): 169-177.

The Nichiren Shoshu is a cult of Japanese origin observed by
the author to be enjoying considerable success in attracting
American converts.   Its faith, ethical and doctrinal
principles are unsophisticated and the missionary zeal it
induces in its adherents compare with those observed among
Mormons and Jehovah's Witnesses.   Oh reports studies in
three urban areas (New York, Los Angeles and Chicago) and
finds that the appeal of Nichiren Shoshu is particularly to
the young and better educated.   Such a tendency has also
been observed in new Christian movements and in studies of youth
cultures in the late 1960s (Rigby and Turner, 0676).

0416   O'Toole, Roger.   *The Precipitous Path: Studies in Political
Sects*.   Toronto: Peter Martin, 1977.

The stereotype of sect is well rehearsed and exemplified in
the literature of the sociology of religion.   Roger O'Toole
explores the concept by empirical study of a number of
political organizations including the Social Labour Party,
the League of Social Action and the Internationalists, all
of them marxist organizations in Toronto, Canada.   O'Toole's
documentation and interpretation are compelling sources for
the student of religious sects and the parallels both in
doctrine and in strategy and organization are close.   It is
a study in political sociology undertaken in the intellectual
tradition of the sociology of religion.

0417   Peter, Karl A.   "The Death of Hutterite Culture: A Rejoinder."
Phylon   40 (1979): 189-194.

Peter replies to an article by James S.Frideres published in
1972 (0376).   He recognizes the fact of restrictive
legislation based on patriotic and economic sentiments and
directed at the Hutterite community but suggests that Frideres
overestimates its magnitude in writing of cultural genocide.
Peter reads the high prices at which Hutterites acquire land
not as a discriminatory control but as an effect of market
forces.   See also Hostetler (0392).

0418   Pin, Emile Jean.   "En Guise d'Introduction, ou Comment se
Sauver de l'Anomie et de l'Alienation: Jesus People at
Catholiques Pentecostaux."   *Social Compass*   21 (1974): 227-239.

A study of Catholic pentecostals and Jesus People as examples
of "how to save oneself from anomie and alienation".   Although
the two groups are related in this paper as like products of
an insecure society - that of the United States in the 50s and
60s - they are treated comparatively.   Both groups perpetuate
sets of counter-cultural characteristics and yet provide
alternatives to the secular movements and are performing, it
is anticipated, an important function of social reintegration.

0419 Plowman, Edward E. *The Underground Church*. Elgin,
Illinois: Cook, 1971.

In the absence of substantial scientific accounts of the Jesus
movement of the late 1960s and early 1970s, chronicles of this
kind serve to document the development of an enthusiastic
religious counterculture. Its adherents were fundamentalist
in theology but radical in political and social programs.
The work was subsequently published in England as *The Jesus
Movement: Accounts of Christian Revolutionaries in Action*.

0420 Queiroz, Maria Isavra Pereira de. *O Messianismo no Brasil
e no Mundo*. São Paulo: Editora da Universidade de São Paulo,
1965.

This extensive work provides a systematic study of primitive
messianic movements in Melanesia and Brazil and of the
nineteenth century developments. The cases studied are
classified in terms of organization and political orientation.
See also Queiroz (0421).

0421 Queiroz, Maria Isavra Pereira de. *Réforme et Révolution
dans les Sociétés Traditionelles*. Paris: Éditions Anthropos,
1968.

This offers a history and ethnology of messianic movements
in traditional societies and includes examinations of cases
among the Aborigines, Amer-Indians, African and Pacific
societies. The work is densely documentary within a
consistent style of interpretation and there is a preface by
Roger Bastide. See also Queiroz (0420).

0422 Richardson, James T. "People's Temple and Jonestown:
A Corrective Comparison and Critique." *Journal for the Scientific
Study of Religion* 19 (1980): 239-255.

The cult of the Reverend Jim Jones has been widely discussed
as a phenomenon of the new religious movements syndrome.
Richardson offers observations of a sociological character
to suggest that it is functionally distinguishable and does
not belong to the company of new religious movements. See
also Levi (0405), the note on which gives principal historical
details.

0423 Richardson, James T. "New Religious Movements in the
United States: A Review." *Social Compass* 30 (1983): 85-110.

Poll results and other data are used to demonstrate trends in
interest and participation and the political orientations of
members are perceived by themselves before and after affiliation.
The cults are then studied in their political context and the
author details media attention and official interventions.

0424 Rigby, Andrew and Turner, Bryan S. "Findhorn Community,
Centre of Light: A Sociological Study of New Forms of Religion."
A Sociological Study of Religion in Britain 5 (1972): 72-86.

Findhorn is a non-Christian de-institutionalized commune in
Scotland which developed from a pioneering venture on a
caravan park in the early 1960s.   This study of its various
processes and beliefs was a response to the complaint of
Berger and Luckman (0008) that the sociology of religion
had been too preoccupied with institutionalized forms.

0425   Roback, Judith.   "The White-robed Army: An Afro-Guyanese
Religious Movement." *Anthropologica* 16 (1974): 233-268.

The paper is an examination of a syncretic renewal movement
also known as the Jordanite Movement: far from being a
reaction against an imperial past, the belief system incorporates recognizable features of Protestant fundamentalism.
Sectarian characteristics include worldly isolationism, the
pursuit of purity and the provision of a social milieu and
high morale for the underprivileged.

0426   Robbins, Thomas; Anthony, Dick and Curtis, Thomas E.
"The Limits of Symbolic Realism: Problems of Empathic Field
Observation in a Sectarian Context." *Journal for the Scientific
Study of Religion* 12 (1973): 259-271.

After Bellah the authors distinguish between two responses
to social behavior: empathy is defined as an intuitive response
and sympathy as the intellectualization of that response.
They then warn against the exclusiveness of the empathic
response in the observation of such religious sects as the
Jesus People, who were being much noticed at the time of
publication as a new religious movement in the hippie tradition
but with strictly fundamentalist religious views.   Among such
subjects the signification of empathy is interpreted as a
readiness for conversion which involves the researcher in
undue strain and misleads his subjects into an unfounded
optimism.

0427   Robbins, Thomas; Anthony, Dick; Doucas, Madeline and
Curtis, Thomas E.   "The Last Civil Religion: Reverend Moon and
the Unification Church." *Sociological Analysis* 37 (1976):
111-125.

This offers a mass society theory of contemporary culture and
exemplifies the erosion of the intermediate level of society
leaving macro-public and the micro-private institutions isolated
from each other.   The development of a youth culture within
the vacated zone is instanced by the Unification Church which
here, after Bellah (0883), is studied as an authoritarian
civil religion sect.

0428   Robertson, Roland.   "The Salvation Army: The Persistence
of Sectarianism." In *Patterns of Sectarianism*, edited by Bryan R.
Wilson, pp.49-105. London: Heinemann, 1967 (0344).

It is argued that the Salvation Army has not undergone the
tendency of denominationalization which is normal in the
evolution of sects.   With the exception of one short period,

the Army has not expanded and it has not had to accommodate
"the world" to which it has ministered.   In explanation,
Robertson recognizes the conservative function of a dominant
"old-guard" committed to original value orientations; on the
other hand, there are "acceptors" who adopt a characteristically denominational posture and "modernists" who counsel
organizational reforms for greater effectiveness.

0429 Rogers, Philip G. *The Sixth Trumpeter: The Story of Jezreel
and his Tower*. London: Oxford University Press, 1963.

Rogers gives an illuminating and entertaining account of a case
of charismatic leadership of an eccentric millennial movement
based in the Medway towns of Kent, England.   The New House of
Israel flourished here in the 1870s and 1880s and developed
an economic base producing and trading in household provisions
and requisites such as soap, patent furniture, bakery and
confections and "Jezreel's Magic Polish".   A tower or
sanctuary was built to give access to heaven but the project
was abandoned before it reached its destination. Jershom
Jezreel, as the leader James White called himself, was found
bankrupt and without his leadership the sect dwindled.   Queen
Esther and others who succeeded the Sixth Trumpeter lacked his
charisma.

0430 Rolim, Francisco Cartaxo. "Pentecôtisme et Société au
Brésil." *Social Compass* 26 (1979): 345-372.

Modern pentecost arrived in Brazil in 1910 but did not gain
momentum until the 1930s.   In this article its popular appeal
is seen to be located within the capitalist class structure of
contemporary Brazil.   It is within this line of interpretation
that the author discusses the ideology of the pentecostal
movement.   See also Ribeiro (0522).

0431 Rolph, C.H. *Believe What You Like*. London: Deutsch, 1973.

Rolph reflects on a conflict between the Church of Scientology
and the (British) National Association for Mental Health. The
former wants religious immunity while the latter is cast in
the role of the legalistic Pharisees.   The book includes a
report of the libel action in 1970 against Mr Geoffrey Johnson-
Smith, the Member of Parliament for East Grinstead where the
Scientologists have their British headquarters.   The main
event is the High Court action involving the NAMH and the
ensuing judgement of Mr Justice Megarry.

0432 Ruff, Ivan Julian. "Baha'i - The Invisible Community."
New Society 623 (1974): 665-668.

Baha'i is a curiosity to the sociologist of religion for it
eludes so many of the conceptual frames deployed in sociological analysis.   It was founded in Iran where it is now
persecuted and there are some affinities to Islam; but the
intention was to transcend existing religions and offer a new
religion in their stead.   The credal system is loose, even

inchoate. Worship and prayer have their place but the standard meeting is the "fireside", an intimate gathering in the home of one or more of the faithful. Baha'i is organized as a world-wide and thinly dispersed system of small groups of a minimum of nine members each. The cohesion and persistence of this international movement are remarkable and the recent persecution of Baha'is since this article was written will have done much to consolidate identity.

0433   Shupe, Anson D.   "Toward a Structural Perspective of Modern Religious Movements." *Sociological Focus* 6 (1973): 83-99.

The focus of this paper is upon the Shinko Shakyo or new religious movements in Japan and contemporary forms in the United States.   The analysis of these relates their development to societal factors.   The author draws from media coverage of the new religious movements the view - which in Shupe's work becomes an hypothesis or perspective - that such organizations have as their raison d'être a kind of sublimated avarice.   He relates the new religious movements also to the cargo cults which, though serving rather more traditional societies, provide a comparable line of communication between the individual and the supernatural with material wealth having a similar symbolic significance.

0434   Shupe, Anson D. and Bromley, David G.   "The Moonies and the Anti-cultists: Movements and Counter-movements in Conflict." *Sociological Analysis* 40 (1979): 325-334.

The Unification Church provides the major focus of a paper which treats of other examples and endeavors to identify the structures within which religious counter-movements flourish. It includes a sociological interpretation of the methods of socialization for which the Moonies have been widely noticed. See also Beckford's *Cult Controversies* (0357), Beckford (0362) and Bromley (0367).

0435   Shupe, Anson D. and Bromley, David G.   "Shaping the Public Response to Jonestown: People's Temple and the Anticult Movement." In *Violence and Religious Commitment: Implications of Jim Jones's People's Temple Movement*, edited by Ken Levi, pp.105-132. University Park, Penn: Pennsylvania University Press, 1982 (0405).

The mass suicide of the Jones cult in 1978 acted as a catalyst to anti-cult   feeling in the United States, from which the cult had migrated.   The authors trace the development of the anti-cult movement and its direction of public opinion in the aftermath of the Jonestown tragedy.   See also on Jonestown Levi (0405) and Richardson (0422); and on anti-cult movements see Beckford's *Cult Controversies* (0357).

0436   Simard, Jean.   "Cultes Liturgiques et Devotions Populaires dans les Comités de Portneuf et du Lac Saint-Jean." *Sessions d'Etudes: Société Canadienne d'Histoire de l'Eglise Catholique* 43 (1976): 5-14.

This is a presentation of survey results on liturgical cults and popular devotions in two counties of Quebec with comparative analysis of some cults in France in the 1970s.

0437 Simmonds, Robert B.; Richardson, James T. and Harder, Mary W. "Organizational Aspects of a Jesus Movement Community." *Social Compass* 21 (1974): 269-281.

This is a documentary account of the organization of a Christian commune occupying and administering a small farm and providing a case for comparison with the kibbutz model.   There are two authority systems, the legal and the spiritual, which have their own hierarchies and are organized relatively independently. The commune encourages specialization in economic and domestic functions and there is much role differentiation by gender. The Jesus movement was particularly visible in the early 1970s and the commune model is a cultural inheritance of the late 1960s.

0438 Simpson, George Eaton.   "Black Pentecostalism in the United States." *Phylon*   35 (1974): 203-211.

Modern pentecost was born out of Holiness at the turn of the century and regards as the initial event of the twentieth century outpouring the experience of a black Holiness group in Los Angeles.   Pentecost spread quickly across the world and most of those who enjoyed it in the early years were white. Simpson's historical account engages themes of sociological interest such as the tendency of denominationalization; he notices that the pentecostals are no longer to be numbered entirely among the dispossessed and that social affairs feature with increasing prominence among their concerns.

0439 Sorrell, Mark. *The Peculiar People*. Exeter: Paternoster, 1979.

The Peculiar People organized as an austere Protestant sect on the north and south banks of the river Thames and have in recent years lost independent identity by union with the Fellowship of Independent Evangelical Churches.   In the late nineteenth century one faction, the Plumstead Peculiars, achieved notoriety and suffered imprisonment for refusing medical attention on behalf of their children who languished and in some cases died.   Sorrell gives a detailed documentary account and resourcefully portrays the Peculiars in their early years.

0440 Stark, Rodney; Bainbridge, William Sims and Kent, Lord. "Cult Membership in the Roaring Twenties: Assessing Local Receptivity." *Sociological Analysis* 42 (1981): 137-162.

The authors use 1926 data from the U.S.Census Bureau to examine the nature of membership of cults such as Christian Science, Mormons and the National Spiritualist Association.   Their purpose is largely to draw attention to census data as a useful source and they find remarkable stability in the activites of American cults between the 1920s and 1970s.

0441 Stephan, Karen H. and Stephan, G.Edward. "Religion and the
Survival of Utopian Communities." *Journal for the Scientific
Study of Religion* 12 (1973): 89-100.

> Forty utopian communities, largely established in the nineteenth
> century, were investigated for the conditions that might account
> for their persistence or extinction.   Of the factors considered,
> the strongest appeared to be the unity of faith among members;
> those communities whose members showed a plurality of religious
> beliefs stood less chance of survival.

0442 Stoltzfus,Victor. "Amish Agriculture: Adaptive Strategies
for Economic Survival of Community Life." *Rural Sociology* 38
(1973): 196-206.

> This study is based in three counties of the state of Illinois
> in which the Amish are settled.   It is concerned with changing
> social and economic conditions in the outside community and with
> the adaptation of the Amish to these changes.   The Amish have
> been widely noticed for their ideological insularity but in
> spheres of agriculture and economics there is an expedient
> response to the vicissitudes of the outside world.   See also
> the work of John A.Hostetler (0391).

0443 Theobald, Robin. "The Politicization of a Religious Movement:
British Adventism under the Impact of West Indian Immigration."
British Journal of Sociology 32 (1981): 202-223.

> Seventh-day Adventism has been more widely recognized by American
> than by British sociologists as an important form of black
> religiosity.   Whereas black and white pentecostals have operated
> as separate organizations, in some cases having assemblies next
> door to each other, black Adventists have joined the indigenously
> populated Adventist church in Britain.   There have been tensions
> within the organization and at one point there was the prospect
> of a schism on racial lines; these are the problems that occupy
> Theobald in this paper.

0444 Thóden van Velzen, H.U.E. "The Gaan Gadu Cult: Material
Forces and the Social Production of Fantasy." *Social Compass* 32
(1985): 93-109.

> The Gaan Gadu cult made its appearance deep in Surinam in 1890
> and rapidly developed, exorcizing Surinam of its traditional
> witch crafts, attracting numerous converts and establishing its
> own shrines and pilgrimages.   The author studies alongside the
> cult's social consolidation the elaboration of a collective
> fantasy expressing both its psyche and its economic aspirations.

0445 Vatro, Murvo. "Messianism in Russia: Religious and
Revolutionary." *Journal for the Scientific Study of Religion* 10
(1971): 277-338.

> This work complements that of Roger O'Toole (0416) in drawing
> attention to parallel features of religious and secular movements
> in organization and doctrine.   Those which Vatro discusses

operated in conditions of extreme social upheaval following the
Russian Revolution of 1917.   Both types trade upon an
optimistic eschatology and both utilize a notion of the collectivity in social organization.

0446   Vosper, Cyril. *The Mind Benders.* London: Spearman, 1971.

Though lacking the disciplined analytical power of Roy Wallis's
The Road to Total Freedom (0448), this is an informative account
at the documentary level of controls in Scientology such as
auditing, training, ethics and promotion.   There is also a
chapter on the organization of Scientology.   The book is
written to be highly readable.

0447   Walker, Andrew.   "The Theology of the 'Restoration' House
Churches."   In *Strange Gifts?* edited by David Martin and Peter
Mullen, pp.208-216.   Oxford: Blackwell, 1984 (0510).

The charismatic movement in Britain passed its zenith in the
late 1970s; one of its most interesting sociological characteristics was its penetration of the sacramental churches as
well as the protestant denominations.   It has been widely
succeeded by the inadequately so-called "Restoration" movement, a seminal doctrine of which concerns the restoring of a
proper relationship with God.   The movement commands very
large followings in certain English centers such as Hove,
Bradford and Ewell.   Though insistently anti-denominational
it is rooted in protestant sectarianism.   Walker provides
here an informative documentary account and interpretation,
and he points to its typical sectarianism in organization and
doctrine.

0448   Wallis, Roy.   *The Road to Total Freedom: A Sociological
Analysis of Scientology.*   London: Heinemann, 1976.

The enquiries of Roy Wallis into Scientology have been the
subject of complaints by his subjects and this volume is at
the center of a controversy well documented by Beckford
(0357).   The author's methods and interests are faithfully
sociological.   He uses Scientology to reassess conventional
stereotypes of cult and sect.   He examines internal processes
of induction, control and the transmission of belief.   He
investigates relations between the Church of Scientology and
the State, discovering there a pattern quite different from the
rejection of the world by the traditional sect.   Appendices
include statements relating to the conduct of Roy Wallis and
sociological enquiries in general, as perceived by
Scientologists. See also Wallis (0449).

0449   Wallis, Roy.   "Religious Sects and the Fear of Publicity."
New Society   557 (1973): 545-547.

Both Christian Scientists and Scientologists have in their day
been quickly litigious in an endeavor to confine the scrutiny
of their doctrines and religious practices to within their
own organizations.   Wallis introduces this historically and

goes on to document his own case in which Scientologists
proceeded against him following his research work on this cult
(0448).   In his analysis the reasons for sectarian defensive-
ness are twofold.   Both sects studied in this article are
authoritarian in structure and fear that external scrutiny by
outsiders, especially scientific inquiry, might undermine
their authority.   Further both sects claim a privileged
access and responsible custodianship of truth and regard
commentary by outsiders as likely to corrupt that truth.
Perhaps the second reason is merely a legitimation of the
first.   See also Beckford's *Cult Controversies* (0357).

0450 Wallis, Roy. "The Sectarianism of Scientology."
A Sociological Yearbook of Religion in Britain 6 (1973):
136-155.

A case study is made of Scientology in the light of a series
of characteristics conventionally associated with sects -
exclusiveness, self-conception as elect, asceticism, total-
itarianism, the priesthood of all believers, voluntary and
achieved membership.   This is used to illuminate sociological
understanding of the sect as a minority group organized around
a belief-system regarded by its adherents as a unique and
privileged mode of access to the truth or salvation.   The
major work on Scientology by Wallis is *The Road to Total
Freedom* (0448).

0451 Wallis, Roy. "The Aetherius Society: A Case Study of the
Formation of a Mystagogic Congregation." *Sociological Review*
22 (1974): 27-44.

The concept of mystagogue is derived from Weber and is applied
by Wallis to George King, born 1919, the founder and leader of
the Aetherius Society.   It is argued that the institutionalization of his mystagogic congregation was related to his
success in monopolizing access to charismatic legitimation,
elaborating a theodicy, and subordinating spiritual healing
to evangelistic and ritual goals.   Reprinted in Wallis (0454):
17-34.

0452 Wallis, Roy. "Observations on the Children of God."
Sociological Review 24 (1976): 807-829.

Wallis conducts a wide ranging observation comprehending the
history, organization, beliefs and economics of a post-war
millennial movement.   Particular attention is paid to the
tension between evangelism and the proclamation to the world
that its end is imminent and, on the other hand, withdrawal
from the world for the preservation of purity: accordingly,
history of the movement is marked by changes in organization
and strategy.   See also Wallis (0453).

0453 Wallis, Roy. "The Social Construction of Charisma."
Social Compass 29 (1982): 25-39.

The Children of God constitute the empirical field of this study, which is an attempt to show that the problematic notion of charisma is not so much an inherent property of the individual as a social relationship situationally generated. See also Wallis (0452).

0454 Wallis, Roy, ed. *Sectarianism: Analyses of Religious and Non-religious Sects*. London: Peter Owen, 1975.

This is a collection of essays on a range of organizations of the disenchanted, both religious and secular. Cases studied include the Aetherius Society (a flying saucer cult), Krishna Consciousness, Scientologists, Maoists, De Leonists, and therapeutic groups like Recovery, Inc. and Neurotics Nomine.

0455 Weiser, Neil. "The Effects of Prophetic Disconfirmation Committed." *Review of Religious Research* 16 (1974): 19-30.

Prophetic disconfirmation is a traumatic event for the faith and personality of the believer and for the legitimacy of cult leaders. Festinger's *When Prophecy Fails* stands on its own as an analysis of disconfirmation and its effects upon the community of the faithful. Weiser points to the limitations of Festinger's application of the principle of cognitive dissonance but at the same time suggests that its application might be extended to primitive eschatologically-oriented sects.

0456 Wermlund, Sven. "Religious Speech Community and Reinforce- ment of Belief." *Acta Sociologica* 3 (1958): 132-146.

Wermlund studies language learning as a dimension of social- ization within the religious community and speech performance as the means by which commitment and belief are confirmed. Examples of such performance include singing and unisonous credal statements.

0457 Westley, Frances. *The Complex Forms of the Religious Life: A Durkheimian View of New Religious Movements*. Chico, Ca.: Scholars Press, 1983.

There is a routine review of Durkheim's sociology of religion followed by a penetrating classification of "cult of man groups" and "harmonial cults" and an application to new religious movements of the familiar church-sect dichotomy. The author's treatment of "cult of man" rituals and her account of activities inside "the control room" add important elements to the sociological literature of modern cults.

0458 Whalen, William J. *Armageddon around the Corner: A Report on Jehovah's Witnesses*. New York: John Day, 1962.

This is an illustrated work on the activities of Jehovah's Witnesses in a worldwide context. It is written in a purposely light and readable style and has about it the air of an exposé. Its treatment of the theology of Jehovah's Witnesses points to

inherent heresies and the question "who are Jehovah's Witnesses?"
is not answered in a scientific way with dutiful correlation with
demographic variables.   Nevertheless, the book offers some
useful vignettes of sect leaders in the formative years and an insight into its missionary activity.   For a more rigorous
scientific study see *The Trumpet of Prophecy* by James A.Beckford
(0356).

0459   Whitworth, John McKelvie.   "Communitarian Groups in the World."
In *Sectarianism*, edited by Roy Wallis, pp.117-137.   London: Peter
Owen, 1975 (0454).

The groups Whitworth here studies are those of the Shakers who
broke away from the Society of Friends in England in 1747 and
migrated to North America.   The Shakers were long-lived, but
the life-expectancy for communitarian groups in western
industrial societies is suggested by Whitworth to be short,
while totalitarian societies offer them virtually no prospects
at all.   Introversionist and utopian groups are most likely to
arise and flourish, he suggests, in those countries of the Third
World in which tribal affiliations are breaking down, religious
conceptions or styles of thought persist and the State is weak,
tolerant or indifferent enough to allow sufficient freedom.
See also Whitworth (0460).

0460   Whitworth, John M.   "The Shakers - Ideological Change and
Organizational Persistence."   *A Sociological Yearbook of Religion
in Britain*   8 (1975): 78-102.

Whitworth traces the development and structure of Shaker
communitarianism from its English origins through migration to
America and relates organizational forms to early utopian
definitions of mission.   He studies revisions of these
definitions and other changes in ideology in the context of the
vicissitudes of the community.   At the time of his writing
there survived only two societies of Shakers which had a
combined membership of fifteen women.   See also Whitworth
(0459) and the major work of Desroche (0371).

0461   Wilson, Bryan R.   *Sects and Society: A Sociological Study
of Three Religious Groups in Britain.*   London: Heinemann, 1961.

Wilson's is a pioneering study in the sociology of sect life,
which remains an authoritative account and masterly analysis
of the histories and dynamics of three religious groups, the
Elim Foursquare Gospel Church (now the Elim Pentecostal
Church), Christian Science and the Christadelphians.
Much had been written (by Troeltsch, Niebuhr, Yinger and others)
on the general characteristics of sects and of normal patterns
of sect development.   Wilson's distinctive contribution was
his meticulous attention to details of structure and
institution, of control and leadership, of social class
composition, of recruitment, allegiance and service and of the
management of conflicts within the groups studied.   The work
is researched by extensive observation and interviewing and by
a thorough reading of sect literature and is written in the

succinct and perceptive style that has since come to distinguish
Bryan Wilson as one of the world's foremost scholars in the
sociology of religion.   In conclusion Wilson tests the
organizations he chooses against existing paradigms and
recognizes in world-rejection, voluntarism in membership,
individuality in faith, charismatic leadership, and total-
itarianism in organization, a general conformity to ideal-types,
though Christian Science does not confirm the notion of sect
as the church of the disinherited   (for further treatment see
Beckford,(0305). Particular attention is drawn to sect eschatology
as   the most emphatic expression of their basic orientation".
See also Wilson (0462).

0462   Wilson, Bryan R. *Religious Sects: A Sociological Study*.
London: Weidenfeld & Nicolson, 1970.

The format, typeface and liberal use of photographs serve to
excite interest in the study of sects but this is also a scholarly
survey by a leading scholar on this subject.   In international
terms the scope is broad and the author ventures to classify the
many examples he describes as introversionist, manipulationist,
revolutionist, thaumaturgical.   And there is a special study of
two societies which "appear to be the most prolific spawning
grounds of sectarianism", South Africa and Japan.   See also
Wilson (0461).

0463   Wilson, Bryan R. *Magic and the Millennium*.   London:
Heinemann, 1973.

This is a sociological study of religious movements of protest
among tribal and Third World peoples.   While it is the religion
of the western world that provides the ideal-types of "sect" and
"church", it is possible to operate and adapt these in respect
of deviant religious movements in the under-developed world.
The author investigates thaumaturgical movements in Papua,
Umbanda (see Willems, 0217), possession cults in Brazil, responses
to the missions of Protestant and Catholic Churches, Cargo
cults as cases of "commodity millennialism" and the arguably
introversionist Peyote cult.   Magic is represented as an early
form of religion and millennialism as an evolved form.

0464   Wilson, Bryan R.   "Aspects of Kinship and the Rise of
Jehovah's Witnesses in Japan." *Social Compass* 24 (1977): 97-120.

This article presents and interprets interview data on various
aspects of recruitment, on family relationships of Jehovah's
Witnesses and on occupational groups.   Among the themes
recurring in responses is a sense of liberation from materialist endeavors which membership of the movement allows; this
may immediately be related to the prevalence of materialist
concerns in contemporary Japanese society.

0465 Wuthnow, Robert. *Experimentation in American Religion: The New Mysticisms and their Implications for the Churches.* Berkeley: University of California Press, 1978.

Wuthnow documents and analyzes a variety of religious orientations, whether toward eastern philosophies or in connection with psychological and scientific phenomena, such as extra-sensory perception.   Religious countercultures are seen to be burgeoning in American campus life and to relate there to a defection from conventional religion.   Among less recently developed alternatives, Wuthnow examines the appeal of astrology and he studies the relationship of the new mysticisms to politics. See also Wuthnow (0304).

0466 Zygmunt, Joseph P. "Jehovah's Witnesses in the U.S.A. 1942-1976." *Social Compass* 24 (1977): 45-57.

The year 1976 was a significant one because Jehovah's Witnesses did not expect to reach it.   The anticipation of the millennium had been a dominant theme in the preceding years and features in this account along with organizational problems of the Watch Tower movement.

M. DENOMINATIONS AND CHURCHES; MOVEMENTS WITHIN CHURCHES

0467 Ball, Peter. "Dimensions of Neopentecostal Identity in the Church of England." *European Journal of Social Psychology* 11 (1981):   349-363.

It is found that charismatics within the Church of England identify themselves mainly in terms of conventional religious markers such as conversion, belief and prayer habits. Glossolalia played a more limited role than was expected and denominational affiliation had no significance at all.   It is suggested that neopentecostals perceive their own status in the mainstream churches as marginal, aim to distinguish themselves from "nominal" Christians and identify with all devout believers in preference to asserting neopentecostal distinctiveness which does not afford favorable enough social comparisons.

0468 Bastenier, Albert. "Paul VI et la Paix: Analyse de Sept Discours Pontificaux." *Social Compass* 21 (1974): 489-501.

Bastenier conducts a discourse analysis of seven pontifical statements informing the aspect on the problem of peace taken by Pope Paul VI.   The evidence suggests that the pontiff eschewed engagements of the subject at the social and political levels except where there was already a consensus established among the authorities.   Instead his statements were expressed in the abstract or else as a charge to the individual.

0469 Bax, Mart. "Religious Infighting and the Formation of
Dominant Catholic Regime in Southern Dutch Society." *Social
Compass* 32 (1985): 57-72.

This is a study which asserts the autonomy of the religious
variable in the process of social change in a rural society. It
offers an examination of the tensions inherent in the hierarchical
structure of Dutch Catholicism and the struggle for power.   See
also Hutjes (0254), Van Kemenade (0285) and Thurlings (0536).

0470 Beeson, Trevor. *The Church of England in Crisis*. London:
Davis-Poynter, 1973.

The author is a prominent clergyman in the Church of England and
this analysis is largely concerned with spiritual and other
dimensions of the Church's current problem.   However, the
third chapter usefully documents "the statistics of decline" and
deals with trends in membership and the supply of suitable
candidates for the ordained ministry.   Other themes treated
which are of interest from a sociological point of view include
the liturgical movement, the dissemination of ideas, clergy in
the parishes and the comprehensiveness of the Church of England.

0471 Benson, J.Kenneth and Hassinger, Edward W. "Organization
Set and Resources as Determinants of Formalization in Religious
Organization." *Review of Religious Research* 14 (1972): 30-36.

Over five hundred rural Missouri churches contributed to this
research project which attempts to explain why churches in a
simple and traditional community context adopt styles of
organization appropriate to more complex social conditions.
It is suggested that the urban context generates the models
of organization adopted throughout a given church by all its
congregations and that available resources support this model.

0472 Berzano, Luigi. "Ideologia e Utopia nella Diocesi di Roma:
Analisi di Communita e Gruppi Ecclesiali non Instituzionalizzati."
Critica Sociologica 32 (1974): 71-84.

The inquiry was conducted between 1968 and 1973 and covered
nine dissident Catholic groups in Rome.   It is hypothesized
that the ascendancy of a group conscience is a concomitant of
a new biblical exegesis and that there is a place within the
context of Church reform for the maintenance of dissident group
identity.   The study informs on the genesis of religious
groups and their institutionalization and differentiation.

0473 Boling, T.Edwin. "Sectarian Protestants, Churchly Protestants
and Roman Catholics: A Comparison in a Mid-American City."
Review of Religious Research 14 (1973): 159-168.

This is the report and interpretation of a 1969 interview survey
conducted in Springfield, Ohio.   It points to churchlike and
sectlike characteristics of Roman Catholics.. In their
perspective toward the world Roman Catholics share that of

churchlike Protestants; Catholicism, it is found, is not associated with the mode of rejection.   See also Collins (0557).

0474 Brewer, Earl D.C. "Sect and Church in Methodism."
Social Forces 30 (1952): 400-408.

Brewer applies conventional church-sect typologies to the pattern
of American religion and endeavors to locate within such
typologies certain religious organizations in transition.   With
some adaptations he confirms the appropriateness of available
ideal-types and he characterizes Methodism as a denominational
form that has reached the mature stage of church-type.

0475 Church Information Office. *Facts and Figures About the Church
of England.* London: Church Information Office, 1962.

The Church of England collects and periodically publishes
information about itself, its membership and finances.   This
volume presents in maps, histograms and statistical tables
details of the geographical distribution of infant baptisms,
the ages of the clergy, candidates for holy orders, children
of parochial clergy, choirmasters and choristers.   For those
interested in population movements among church mice, this
is the place to come for precise information .

0476 Cross, Robert D. ed. *The Church and the City 1865-1910.*
Indianapolis: Bobbs-Merrill, 1967.

The period covered was one which demanded major adaptations by
the churches to changing social conditions.   The relations
between them were strained and one of the contributors to this
collection speaks of "the fratricide of the churches".   While
old faiths were reasserted, new ones like Christian Science
came into being and there were changing organizational styles
such as the emergence of the "neighborhood church".   Cross
collects nearly twenty extracts from contemporary works.

0477 Dann, Graham Michael Stuart. "Religious Belonging in a
Changing Catholic Church." *Sociological Analysis* 37 (1976):
283-297.

The notion of organizational bureaucracy, it is suggested, has
ceased helpfully to illuminate the character of affiliation in
the Roman Catholic Church.   Since Vatican II the element of
bureaucracy is increasingly rejected by avowed members and
Catholic religiosity has dimensions that are not organized.
Dann perceives in the Catholic Church a pluriform rather than
a uniform entity, with tensions between center and individuals,
with allegiances compromised by ecumenical associations, and
with the emergence of church parties.

0478 Davidson, James D. "Patterns of Belief at the Denominational and Congregational Levels." *Review of Religious Research* 13
(1972): 197-205.

An inquiry involving members of four Baptist and Methodist
congregations is reported and analyzed. What emerges is the
high degree of belief heterogeneity shown in both denominations
and the author discusses the problematic character of this in
organizational crises.

0479 Dyson, Anthony O. "The Church's Educational Institutions."
Theology 80 (1977): 273-279.

The Church of England sustains an historic involvement in the
provision of schools, both for the children of its members and
for others. The resources, human and material, are
considerable and it is arguable that a better strategy would
be to convince government and others of the necessity of such
provision. Having surrendered other spheres of influence,
the Church is reluctant to give up its educational role.

0480 Ferris, Paul. *The Church of England.* London: Gollancz,
1962.

Paul Ferris's account attracted much notice in its day and
remains a challenging statement. It is a mixture of
sociological distance and personal impression and its overall
effect is critical. Ferris treats of the clerical role and
organization within the parishes, notes the advent of
bureaucracy, points to parties and partisans and finds theology
to be insulated in a world of its own. Such provocations have
their place in establishing an agenda for more scientific
research of the kind subsequently conducted by Coxon (0696) and
Towler (0759).

0481 Fichter, Joseph H. "Liberal and Conservative Catholic
Pentecostals." *Social Compass* 21 (1974): 303-310.

Whereas traditional Protestant pentecostals tend to be of lower
socioeconomic status and of more conservative social and
political orientation, the pentecostals within the Catholic
Church are characteristically and by contrast middle-class,
better educated and of liberal outlook. Fichter investigates
variations within the Catholic constituency and finds that
those who are liberally minded have the better education, more
often in Catholic schools, whereas conservatives have had a
secular education and less of it. However, sociopolitical
orientations are not allowed to divide the fellowship of
Catholic pentecostals.

0482 Field, Clive D. "The Social Structure of English Methodism:
Eighteenth-Twentieth Centuries." *British Journal of Sociology*
28 (1977): 199-225.

The author is concerned to test four propositions which are
widely accepted in the historiography of Methodism. First,
it is believed that the Wesleyans made their most significant
gains among the manual workers and the destitute: Field finds
this to be a gross exaggeration. Second, he adduces evidence
to suggest that Victorian Wesleyanism was rather less

respectable and bourgeois than is commonly believed.   Third,
he finds that the Primitive Methodists were not wholly or
exclusively proletarian and did not therefore usurp the early
mission of the Wesleyans.   But fourth, he confirms the
view that in the twentieth century Methodism has lost contact
with its working-class base.

0483   Gallup Organization.   *A General Survey of Episcopalian
Laity, Clergy, Bishops, Convention Deputies and Alternates.*
Princeton: Gallup, 1985.

The report presented here follows a national poll conducted in
April and May 1985 and commissioned by the Prayer Book Society
of the United States.   The questionnaire, which is given as an
appendix, covers a broad spectrum of topical ecclesiastical and
moral problems including, for example, preferences in the matter
of liturgy, the ordination of women and homosexuals, standard
doctrines such as the Resurrection, proposals for mergers with
other churches and the church's potential role as an agent for
political change.   The laity are invariably more supportive
of the current political status quo and more critical of the
church's engagement in politics.   However, the theological
views of the clergy are the more orthodox.   There is a full
account of technical problems in the research, including
sampling, methodology and the tolerance of error.

0484   Greeley, Andrew M.   "The 'Religious Factor' and Academic
Careers."   *American Journal of Sociology*   78 (1973): 1247-1255.

This paper points to a little noticed phenomenon and calls for
serious investigation of it; the author adduces evidence to
show that in spite of powerful socioeconomic and other factors
the number of Roman Catholics seeking careers in academic life
is increasing.

0485   Greeley, Andrew M.;   McCready, William C. and McCourt,
Kathleen.   *Catholic Schools in a Declining Church.*   Kansas City:
Sheed and Ward, 1976.

Between 1963 and 1972 the demographic, economic and political
changes suffered by the Catholic Church in the United States
were dimensions of a general scenario of decline.   Religious
change is observed to be greater than political change.   In
this context Catholic education exercises an important
stabilizing function.   It disposes Catholics to follow the
religious leadership, accept changes within the Church and to
give financial support.   Catholic schools are sought after
by parents although the number of schools and therefore the
extent of enrollment declined during the period studied.

0486   Halévy, Elie.   *The Birth of Methodism in England.*   Chicago:
University of Chicago Press, 1971.

The volume contains two essays by Halévy translated from the
French by Bernard Semmel.   As well as that which gives its
title to the book, there is included "Methodism and

Revolution".   In Halevy's analysis the germ of Methodism was
for some time dormant in the Church of England before Wesley
began his public sermonizing.   Halevy distinguishes different
types of early Methodism, each with peculiar perspectives on
the establishment.

0487 Harper, Charles L.   "Spirit-filled Catholics: Some
Biographical Comparisons." *Social Compass* 21 (1974): 311-324.

Autobiographical accounts of Catholics involved in the
charismatic movement are used to develop a characterization
of Catholic pentecostals signifying social and motivational
characteristics.   Participants tend to be reacting against
a secularizing trend in modern society and attempting to
recover a religious foundation to the prevailing system of values.

0488 Hassinger, Edward W.; Benson, J.Kenneth; and Holik, John
S. "Changes in Program and Suborganization of Rural Churches in
Missouri in a Fifteen-year Period." *Rural Sociology* 37 (1972):
423-435.

It is not a genuine longitudinal study that is presented here
but the comparison of results from 1952 and 1967 surveys of
rural churches in Missouri classified on a church-sect
typology and by size of congregation.   The authors are
interested in the provision by these churches of various
Sunday and weekday opportunities for worship.   They note a
general tendency toward weekly patterns of worship and in
the sphere of suborganization find some evidence of a
convergence of church and sect types.

0489 Heimer, David D.   "Abortion Attitudes among Catholic
University Students." *Sociological Analysis* 37 (1976): 255-260.

University education and Roman Catholic allegiance act as
opposing factors in the formation of attitudes to such issues
as abortion and it is reckoned that acceptance of abortion is
a function of higher education.   In Catholic schools, however,
the influence upon students is conservative and the religious
factor prevails.

0490 Hill, Michael, and Wakeford, Peter.   "Disembodied
Ecumenicalism: A Survey of the Members of Four Methodist Churches
in or near London." *A Sociological Yearbook of Religion in Britain*
2 (1969): 19-46.

The authors report a questionnaire survey with a focus upon
the prospect of Methodist union with the Church of England.
Age was the most significant variable, the younger groups
favoring unity with the greater enthusiasm; infrequent
attenders, married respondents and Conservative and Liberal
voters all thought unity more desirable than did their
counterparts.

0491 Hinings, C.Robin and Foster, Bruce D. "The Organization Structure of Churches: A Preliminary Model." *Sociology* 7 (1973): 93-106.

The authors draw from work at the University of Aston a causal model for the analysis of organizations, previously deployed in examination of industries. The model is then applied to churches. The authors postulate the primacy of belief systems in determining operational goals and such character- istics as size, on the basis of which organization structures are established. The contribution of the sociology of organizations is to lay less stress on belief and more upon resources.

0492 Hoge, Dean R. and Faue, Jeffrey L. "Sources of Conflict over Priorities of the Protestant Church." *Social Forces* 52 (1973): 178-194.

This essay is based upon surveys of Presbyterian ministers, laypersons and students in theological colleges and is concerned with finding causes and cases of conflict within the Presbyterian Church. While religious education and congregational life provide spheres for consensus, conflicts of view arise in respect of the role of the Church in the world, its capacity for mission and the sectarian (or otherwise) character of its posture toward the world. The authors examine views on these subjects in respect of background and theological orientation and conclude that conflicts observed are theological in origin.

0493 Hood, Ralph W. "Normative and Motivational Determinants of Reported Religious Experience in Two Baptist Samples." *Review of Religious Research* 13 (1972): 192-196.

Subjects were classified as extrinsic and intrinsic on Allport's scale of Religious Orientation. The likelihood that religious experiences would be reported was greater among Southern Baptists than American Baptists and greater among intrinsically oriented subjects than among extrinsically oriented. Hood commends his "Religious Experience Episodes Measure" as an instrument sensitive to the characteristics monitored in this research.

0494 Hornsby-Smith, Michael P.; Lee, Raymond M.; and Reilly, Peter A. "Social and Religious Change in Four English Roman Catholic Parishes." *Sociology* 18 (1984): 353-365.

The research was conducted in the mid-1970s and included non-Catholic as well as Catholic members of the electoral registers in the four English parishes chosen. The authors expected to find Catholics enjoying rather more upward social mobility than non-Catholics but this expectation was not realized. More significant findings were obtained elsewhere in the survey, however, and this paper reports the relative independence of religious authority asserted by the middle

class and the salience of the parish in matters of sexual
morality.

0495 Kelley, D. *Why the Conservative Churches Are Growing*. New
York: Harper and Row, 1972.

The rejection of the State as secular and ungodly is as
significant a phenomenon among the American churches as
among Orthodox Jews in Israel.   Hitherto, such a posture
has been confined to relatively marginal sects.   Kelly
observes the recent expansion of the conservative churches
at a time when the mainline churches are losing impetus.
This trend is interpreted as a sectarian tendency in American
religion.

0496 Kersten, Lawrence K. *The Lutheran Ethic: The Impact of
Religion on Laymen and Clergy*. Detroit: Wayne State University
Press, 1970.

Religious beliefs, practices and involvements affect attitudes
and alignments in the outside world respecting the local
community, blacks, Jews, Catholics and nonbelievers, social
and moral issues such as smoking, dancing, divorce, the role
of women and deviance.   Data are presented in tables of
statistics and some findings, such as the images of man
prevailing among Lutherans, are compared with other denominations.   From this survey there stem issues not directly
related to it but of certain interest to sociologists of
religion.   These include the schism, as it is found to be,
between laity and clergy.   The author notes a trend away from
religious commitment and toward humanism and suggests, in
reflection, a new approach for the sociology of religion.

0497 Lane, Ralph. "The Catholic Charismatic Renewal Movement
in the United States: A Reconsideration." *Social Compass* 25
(1978): 23-35.

The movement is traced from its 1967 origins in the University
of Duquesne, Pittsburgh, Pennsylvania.   Its political impact
is appreciated and the author preducts that the CCR will in
due course become "routinized" after the fashion of previous
religious enthusiasms.   Nevertheless, his assessment of the
significance of CCR issues in the plea that it be maintained
on the agenda of sociological research.

0498 Lazerwitz, Bernard. "A Comparison of Major United States
Religious Groups." *Journal of the American Statistical Association*
56 (1961):   568-579.

The religious groups of the title are in fact the major denominations such as Congregationalists, Methodists, Lutherans and
Catholics and these are analyzed in terms of age composition,
sex composition and marital status, fertility, life cycles,
occupational grouping of family head, educational attainment
and family income.   The author presents findings in respect of
these variables in clear statistical tables.   The problems of

the study are analyzed in terms that would more interest
statisticians than sociologists of religion, although the data
are themselves of great sociological significance and William
M.Newman therefore includes the article in his anthology
together with an editorial comment (0040: 127-145).

0499 Lazerwitz, Bernard and Harrison, Michael. "American Jewish
Denominations: A Social and Religious Profile." *American
Sociological Review* 44 (1979): 656-666.

National survey data of 1970-1971 show marked differences in
identity and status between the various groupings within American
Judaism.   Jewish identity is strongest among the Orthodox,
socioeconomic status highest among Conservative Jews.   As in
Protestantism, behavior and attitudes to the secular domain are
differentiated according to denominational allegiance.

0500 Le Bras, Gabriel. *L'Eglise et Le Village.*.Paris: Flammarion,
1976.

The rural church has a special relationship with the community
it serves and its ritual expressions are adapted to local
sentiments.   The distinction of sacred and secular which obtains
in urban communities is less appropriate in the countryside.
This is a systematic account of the Catholic presence in rural
life.   Le Bras examines the sociological trappings of that
presence, from parish institutions to congregation to cemetery.

0501 Legrand, Michel and Meyers, Pierre. "L'Analyse Socio-
linguistique de Deux Documents Pontificaux." *Social Compass* 20
(1973): 427-457.

Two pontifical edicts provide the material of which a comparative
study is made: these are the encyclical *Rerum Novarum* (1891) and
Pope Paul VI's Letter to Cardinal Roy (1971).   Matthes'
hypothesis provides the analytical model.   Some of the differences
that come to light are purely stylistic but there is an interesting
consistency in the determination of the Church to maintain control
of its members.

0502 "Les Catholiques Français et la Religion." *Sondages* 35,4
(1973): 65-77.

This article reports, largely in tables of statistics, a survey
among French subjects fifteen years of age and over.   Some
familiar tendencies are confirmed, such as the higher proportion
of women than of men declaring religious beliefs.   The majority
regarded Catholic schools with approval and a majority of
Catholics viewed with favor the possibility of a priest abandoning
his vocation in order to marry.

0503 Lyng, Stephen G. and Kurtz, Lester R. "Bureaucratic
Insurgency: The Vatican and the Crisis of Modernism." *Social Forces*
63 (1985): 901-922.

The notion of "bureaucratic insurgency" derives from Zald and Berger and it is here tested for appropriateness upon the modernist movement in the Roman Catholic Church.   Lyng and Kurtz confirm that the model applies in the latter stages of the modernist movement.   But in respect of the early years they identify quite different dimensions of conflict and offer a "dialectical model" as an appendix to Zald and Berger.

0504   McGuire, Meredith B.   "An Interpretive Comparison of the Pentecostal and Underground Church Movements in American Catholicism." *Sociological Analysis*   35 (1974): 57-65.

Though sectarian in some aspects of their inclinations the underground church and charismatic movements of American Catholic-ism are middle-class in their appeal and do not fit standard sociological characterizations and predictions.   In all some twenty-one groups were studied in New Jersey and were followed over a four-year period.   While the two movements are similar on basic sociological variables they are differentiated on the basis of sociopsychological factors.   See also McGuire (0505) and Macioti (0506).

0505   McGuire, Meredith B.   "Toward a Sociological Interpretation of the 'Catholic Pentecostal' Movement."   *Review of Religious Research*   16 (1975): 94-104.

The pentecostal or charismatic movement within the pentecostal church commands the attention of sociologists who have been accustomed to distinguish between sect-types and church-types and now find a case of one within the other.   The appeal of the movement is predominantly to the young, the middle class and the better educated and the author attempts to explain this in terms of their need for a strong authority system in a world that is perceived by them as insecure, ambiguous and indefinite.   The system of groups according to which the Catholic pentecostal movement in the United States is organized provides the authority and the community they seek.   See also McGuire (0504) and Macioti (0506).

0506   Macioti, Maria I.   "Neo-pentecostali e Carismatici." *La Critica Sociologica*   43 (1977): 17-38.

As in other countries, the new pentecostal and charismatic move-ments in Italy have flourished principally within the urban middle class and their appeal has been to the young and the better educated.   Yet, in Macioti's analysis, the charismatic movement represents an expression of irrationalism.   At the ideological level the social and political functions of the two movements are conservative.   Gender roles are sharply defined.   The Catholic Church in Italy has been increasingly accommodating in its posture toward these groups which in turn have been keen to remain within the ranks of the Church.   See also McGuire (0504, 0505) for American comparisons.

0507 Macourt, M.P.A. *Church Attenders: Their Identification and
Their Characteristics*. University of Durham: North-east Area Study
Working Paper 27, 1976.

This work is the third in a series of methodological studies
arising out of a survey project on new towns in the north-east
of England. With particular reference to this project there
is a useful study of measures of religiosity, of the question
of church attendance and of various demographic characteristics
of attenders.

0508 Maître, Jacques; Poulat, Émile; and Terrenoire, Jean-Paul.
"L'Église Catholique et la Vie Publique en France." *Archives de
Sciences Sociales des Religions* 34 (1972): 49-99.

Here are two extensive and densely documented analyses of opinion
surveys on the relationship of the Catholic Church and French
political life. The reports are encyclopaedic, showing every-
thing from opinions on the Vietnam war to attitudes on clerical
celibacy.

0509 Martin, David. "The Political Oeconomy of the Holy Ghost."
In *Strange Gifts*, edited by David Martin and Peter Mullen, pp.54-
71. Oxford: Blackwell, 1984 (0510).

This paper is a piece of sociology which has serious implications
of a critical kind for the conduct of the Church. Professor
Martin studies the invocation of the Holy Spirit as a means of
validating new initiatives and not least those that depart from
such orthodoxies as the teaching of St Paul or the doctrines
enshrined in the English Church's Book of Common Prayer. The
Holy Spirit is cited by the hierarchs of the Church who move to
suppress its traditionalist dissidents and at the same time to
legitimize the actions of synods and benches of bishops.

0510 Martin, David and Mullen, Peter, eds. *Strange Gifts? A Guide
to Charismatic Renewal.* Oxford: Blackwell, 1984.

This is a collection of contributions by authors of diverse
backgrounds and disciplines which presents the range of
debate concerning the rise of the charismatic movement,
especially in the context of churches in England. Among
the sociological contents are David Martin's "The Political
Oeconomy of the Holy Ghost" (0509) and pieces by Andrew Walker
on the position of the Orthodox church vis-à-vis charismatic
renewal (0539) and on the Restoration House Churches (0447).
Douglas Davies writes on "The Charismatic Ethic and the Spirit
of Post-Industrialism".

0511 Maxwell-Arnot, Madeleine. "Social Change and the Church of
Scotland." *A Sociological Yearbook of Religion in Britain* 7
(1974): 91-110.

A number of changes are documented here. Candidates for the
ministry in the Church of Scotland are increasingly recruited
from the lowlands and urban areas and there is a shortage

of ministers in the highland areas.   Fewer are themselves
the sons of clergy and the age at which candidates left high
school has decreased in recent years.   This is partly
attributable to the fashion of recruiting mature entrants
in whose youth the statutory school leaving age was lower.
The author assesses the implications of these changing
patterns for the character of the church.

0512 Michelat, Guy and Simon, Michel.   "Catholiques Déclarés
et Irreligieux Communisants: Vision du Monde et Perception
du Champ Politique." *Archives de Sciences Sociales des Religions*
35 (1978): 57-111.

Interviews were conducted with two groups, the first comprising
those who declared themselves to be Catholics and the second
those who declared themselves to be irreligious, being workers
with communist tendencies.   These two constituencies clearly
represent sub-cultures rooted in French history.   For the
Catholic group ideas are organized around the Church and the
unit of reference is the individual.   The irreligious, by
contrast, manifest a consciousness that is more collective.
Religion for them is a peripheral concern, whereas for
Catholics interviewed communism is perceived as a threat.

0513 Morrow, Ralph E. *Northern Methodism and Reconstruction*.
Michigan: State University Press, 1956.

Morrow treats of Methodism in the northern United States with
particular examination of social issues such as slavery,
blacks and politics.   There are special studies within the
book of mission to the Africans and the education of freedmen.

0514 Nelsen, Hart M. and Potvin, Raymond H.   "The Rural Church
and Rural Religion: Analysis of Data from Children and Youth."
Annals of the American Academy of Political and Social Science
429 (1977): 103-114.

This analysis relies upon data from two 1975 surveys, the one
of children in Minnesota and the other involving a national
sample of adolescents.   Differences in religiosity are
assessed according to habitat.   Fundamentalism, it is found,
has a higher incidence among rural and urban than among
metropolitan Protestants.   There is some speculative discussion
of the implications of devolution in church organization and
of the future of the small rural church.

0515 Nesti, Arnaldo. "La Question Catholique et le Fascisme."
Social Compass 23 (1976): 171-196.

It is argued here that Fascism is the function of accelerated
modernization and institutionalization and that in the case of
Italy these tendencies were manifest in Catholicism; this
is demonstrated by reference to religious documents of the
period studied.   Nesti relates this to a crisis within modern
Catholicism.

0516 Pagden, Frank T. "An Analysis of the Effectiveness of
Methodist Churches of Varying Sizes and Types in the Liverpool
District." *A Sociological Yearbook of Religion in Britain* 1
(1968): 124-134.

Pagden provides an example of "religious sociology" conducted
by a Methodist Minister to discover why Methodist membership
in Liverpool was increasing while decline was the norm
elsewhere in the country. He finds that Methodism flourishes
in suburban areas and in churches with between 200 and 280
members. Smaller churches bear excessive anxieties on plant
maintenance; larger churches might overwork their ministers.
In times of church closures, amalgamations and rebuilding,
the author suggests that "the greatest service that this sort
of enquiry can do, is to assist the policy-makers of
Methodism in asking the right questions."

0517 Page, Enzo. "Charismatics and the Political Presence of
Catholics: The Italian Case." *Social Compass* 25 (1978):
85-99.

Page analyzes the significance of a group of charismatics
within the traditionally Catholic region of Veneto. He
assesses the measure and dynamics of charismatic activity
within the region. The potential for conflict and disequilibrium represented by the early charismatics in this
region has, the author suggests, been lessened by the
institutional deterrent of the Church which perpetuates its
values and, on the other hand, the redefinition by charismatics of their ideological and practical scheme.

0518 Papaderos, Alexander. "Orthodoxy and Economy: A Dialogue
with Alfred Müller-Armack." *Social Compass* 22 (1975): 33-66.

The thrust of Müller's sociological studies of the Orthodox
Church is that, in Greece at least, certain ideas and
dogmas inherent in the religion have the function of determining economic structures in the respective society. In
Müller's analysis this principle is interesting because it
connects the metaphysical with the material. But Papaderos
suggests that Müller was wrong in supposing that Orthodoxy
has maintained an attitude of indifference toward the economy
and that he wrongly based his analysis on a model of monopoly
faith appropriate in the territory of the eastern Church
but not in the west.

0519 Poulat, Emile. "L'Église Romaine: Le Savoir et le
Pouvoir." *Archives de Sciences Sociales des Religions* 37 (1974):
5-21.

The attempt of Pope Leo XIII in the nineteenth century to
impose upon the Catholic Church the philosophy of St.Thomas
Aquinas prompts a number of questions of sociological import.
Thomism featured in the papal view as a property comparable
with the Church's material endowment and so capital and
intellectual wealth are weighed together. Further,

philosophy is made subject to authority and its legitimation
in this case is extrinsic rather than intrinsic.

0520 Remy, Jean. "Opinion Publique, Groupes de Pression et Autorité
Constituée dans la Vie de l'Église Catholique: Contribution à
une Théorie de la Légitimité Religieuse." *Social Compass* 19
(1972): 155-184.

Remy's concern in this paper is with the role of public opinion
and pressure groups within the life of the Catholic Church. In
recent times these phenomena have been introduced in
ecclesiastical affairs from the political domain. Public
opinion is appealed to according to expedient and Remy
examines ways in which pressure and opinion are negotiable
in church life.

0521 Ribeiro de Oliveira, Pedro.   "Le Catholicisme Populaire en
Amérique Latine." *Social Compass* 19 (1972): 567-584.

The article provides a useful survey and assessment of typologies of Latin American catholicism by Pin, Buntig, Camargo,
Azevedo, Comblin and Rolim.   In the author's view these
various contributions stress diversity and thereby underplay
the essential unity of catholicism in Latin America.   He
pleads for a typology that is more balanced but does not
develop such a frame here.   His contribution is rather the
notion of a "constellation of acts", by which he signifies that
formula of acts by which is established a common relation of
the human to the sacred.   It is in this vein that the author
casts his definition of popular catholicism; it is a form, he
suggests, that relates the individual to the sacred and so
by-passes the institutional Church.

0522 Ribeiro de Oliveira, Pedro A.   "Le Renouveau Charismatique
au Brésil." *Social Compass* 25 (1978): 37-42.

This paper is a study of the charismatic renewal movement
within Brazilian Catholicism.   Empirical data are adduced
which show that charismatic renewal is perceived as an enlive-
ning of latent spirituality and not as conversion to a new
faith or fellowship.   The social base of the renewal movement
is shown to be in the culturally and economically privileged
sectors of the church whereas popular Catholicism has its
base among the dispossessed and less well-to-do.   Accordingly, the central principle of liberation is perceived not in
political or economic terms but in the context of the intimate
relationship with Jesus Christ.   However, the author resists
the conclusion from his data that charismatic renewal in Brazil
is a purely spiritual movement and points to its relationship
with other liberation movements which emphasize the pursuit
of the Kingdom of God.   See also Rolim (0430).

0523 Rousseau, André. "Chrétiens pour le Socialisme et Action
Catholique Ouvrière." *Social Compass* 25 (1978): 101-123.

Social, religious and political factors are considered in the
context of the fragmentation of the Catholic Church in France.
In particular the author is interested in the gravitation of
French Catholics toward socialism and he is concerned to relate
this tendency to the social background of those involved.
He studies the character and origins of the group "Chrétiens
pour le socialisme" ("Christians for Socialism") and explores
two different strategies being shown toward this group, the
strategies of "symbolic dissidence" and of "recognition".

0524 Schlangen, Joseph A. and D'Antonio, William V. "Protestant
and Catholic Perceptions of Church Structure." *Social Forces* 47
(1969): 314-322.

This article follows a questionnaire survey conducted among
Protestant and Catholic congregations in Oaklahoma. In both
constituencies the polities of the Roman Catholic Church
were perceived as hierarchical and those of the Protestant
churches as democratic.

0525 Scott, George. *The RCs: A Report on Roman Catholics in
Britain Today.* London: Hutchinson, 1967.

A documentary account, historical in places and impressionistic
in others, with research based upon extensive interviewing.
The author's particular interests range over moral and
political issues, attitudes towards Roman Catholics, recruitment and training for the priesthood, Catholic schools, women
and Protestant-Catholic conflict as manifested in rivalries
between football teams. At the time of writing there were
nearly seven million Roman Catholics in England, Wales and
Scotland and Scott distinguished and characterized Irish and
English constituencies.

0526 Segatori, Roberto. "Atteggimenti del Laicato nella Chiesa
Locali Umbra." *Revista di Sociologia* 10 (1972): 141-194.

This reports an attitudinal survey of the lay members of a
Catholic congregation in Umbria, Italy. The survey was
conducted by questionnaires and interviews in the wake of
Vatican II. The concerns of the survey cover a wide range
of contemporary Catholic issues including attitudes towards
the hierarchy, divorce, liturgical reform, clerical celibacy
and political ideologies such as Italian communism. On
essential religious values there is a consensus within the
congregation but the age factor differentiates responses on
issues concerning *aggiornamento*, the spirit of rejuvenation
within the Church breathed by the Second Vatican Council.

0527 Skinner, Michael. *House Groups.* London: Epworth, 1969.

One of the effects of radical ideas within the Christian
churches during the 1960s was the challenge of conventional
modes of organization. Congregational structures were widely
succeeded by more devolved forms which continue to flourish in
some spheres in the 1980s. This prescriptive account

delineates roles of house groups and the professional minister
and offers guidance on initiation and organization.   Skinner
directs himself to the problem of modernization which he believes
to be necessary and offers models and role delineations to that
end.

0528   Spaulding, Kent E.   "The Theology of the Pew." *Review of
Religious Research* 13 (1972): 206-211.

This article reports a cross-denominational study of nineteen
congregations, the purpose of which was to relate official
to actual beliefs.   Among Roman Catholics, United Methodists
and Presbyterians there was little agreement between lay belief
and official denominational theology; those scoring highest of
the denominations sampled were, in rank order, Free Methodists,
Baptists and Lutherans.   See also Stauffer (0530).

0529   Stark, Werner. *The Sociology of Religion: A Study of
Christendom 3.   The Universal Church*. London: Routledge and Kegan
Paul, 1967.

Stark treats separately of conservative and revolutionary
aspects, in the first case exemplifying ancient Judaism and
the mediaeval Church.   The reformist and renewal movements
featured include the Desert Fathers, the Franciscans, the
Redemptorists, the Passionists, the Benedictines and the
Protestant Reformation.   Stark speaks of the Roman Church's
"loss of unity and (its) recovery of universality".

0530   Stauffer, Robert E.   "Church Members' Ignorance of
Doctrinal Pluralism: A Probable Source of Church Cohesion."
Journal for the Scientific Study of Religion 12 (1973):
345-348.

Stauffer puts to the test the hypothesis of Glock and Stark
(0122) that since the faithful congregate in groups of like-
minded believers the problem of theological pluralism barely
surfaces.   Stauffer investigated two suburban Methodist
congregations in Chicago and found considerable diversity
of doctrine on such central issues as the presence of God
in everyday life, the Virgin Birth and biblical miracles.
Cohesion is maintained, Stauffer suggests, on the assumption
of common belief rather than on the fact of it.   See also
Spaulding (0528).

0531   Stewart, James H.   "Values, Interests and Organizational
Change: The National Federation of Priests' Councils."
Sociological Analysis 34 (1973): 281-295.

This reports a three-year study of the National Federation of
Priests' Councils, members of which are classified as
interest-oriented and value-oriented.   It is found that the
second group are more amenable to social change and the more
committed to action that might bring it about.

0532 Stoop, W. "Quatre Enquétes sur la Signification de la Vie Religieuse parmi Quatre Groupes Différents de Religieux aux Pays-Bas." *Social Compass* 18 (1971): 117-122.

Incompatible scaling and precoding of questionnaires notwithstanding, the author attempts to compare four research studies. A comparative factor analysis is possible and this centers upon the structuration of religious authority, the satisfaction or suppression of desires and aspirations among the religious, group identity and life in the religious community, the importance of prayer life and the salience of the Order.

0533 Streib, Gordon F. "Attitudes of the Irish toward Changes in the Catholic Church." *Social Compass* 20 (1973): 49-71.

Streib reports a questionnaire survey conducted in Dublin among over 700 night school and university students. Attitudes are measured for the degree of acceptance or rejection of changes in the Catholic Church since Vatican II.

0534 Takayama, K.Peter. "Administrative Structures and Political Processes in Protestant Denominations." *Publius* 4, ii (1974): 5-37.

Takayama reports a survey of the administrative structures of Protestant denominations in the United States conducted at a time when most of them were modernizing themselves by centralization, specialization and formalization. The survey suggests a convergence of formerly diverse types upon a single model independently of such variables as size and the religious basis of democratic organization.

0535 Thompson, Kenneth A. *Bureaucracy and Church Reform: The Organizational Response of the Church of England to Social Change 1800-1965.* Oxford: Clarendon, 1970.

The period studied was one of fundamental changes in the organization of the Church of England. The Church Building Act of 1818 granted one million pounds to the established church which the Lords Commissioner were appointed to administer. The period saw great changes in the character of the parish as a social unit and in the Church at large there emerged parties which survive in the present time. The Enabling Act of 1919 and the organization of the Church Assembly direct the author to some sociological conclusions on the Church of England's capacity for adaptation and preservation.

0536 Thurlings, J.M.G. "The Case of Dutch Catholicism: A Contribution to the History of the Pluralistic Society." *Sociologia Neerlandica* 7 (1971): 118-136.

The author adumbrates and explores an "hypothesis of distributed reductionism" whereby the behavior of the minority group is judged to be oriented toward its social emancipation and the elimination of its disadvantage. It is argued that the

maintenance and development of a specific cultural identity
is the characteristic of the phenomenon of Dutch Catholicism.
See also Hutjes (0254), Van Kemenade (0285) and Bax (0469).

0537   Van Billoen, Étienne. "Le Modèle d'Autorité dans l'Église."
Social Compass 20 (1973): 405-425.

One of the consequences of Vatican II has been to generate
sociocultural changes that have issued in conflicts of authority
system.   The author draws on the work of the French theorist
Pierre Bourdieu to formulate an hypothetical model of authority
within the Roman Catholic Church.   The content analysis of
speeches is a principal method used and in this respect the
author follows the work of Jean Dubois.

0538   Vrga, Djuro J. "Perception et Interprétation Subjective
des Causes de la Division Religieuse." *Social Compass* 18 (1971):
247-261.

At a superficial level religious schism is the product of
disputes over religious belief; beneath the surface, however,
it often relates to tensions on the periphery or even outside
the religious domain.   The empirical work analyzed in this
article was conducted in the Serbian Orthodox Church in
America.

0539   Walker, Andrew. "The Orthodox Church and the Charismatic
Movement." In *Strange Gifts*, edited by David Martin and Peter
Mullen, pp.163-171. Oxford: Blackwell, 1984 (0510).

This concludes as the judgement of an Orthodox on the
Christocentric theology that prevails in the charismatic
movement.   En route to that conclusion, however, there is a
useful account of the penetration - slight though it has been -
of the Orthodox Church by charismatic renewal.   In the east
the national Orthodox Churches have remained untouched and the
charismatic movement is regarded as a western phenomenon; that
ground, Walker suggests, has either been too arid or too rich
for the seed to germinate.   In the west some hierarchs have
rejected the renewal movement while others have chosen to
judge each case on its merits.

0540   West, Martin. "Thérapie et Changement Social dans les
Églises Urbaines d'Afrique du Sud." *Social Compass* 19 (1972):
49-62.

This paper offers a discussion of the therapeutic roles of
the independent churches of South Africa and analyzes the
professional-client relationships of the "prophets" who
operate in this field.   The prophet enjoys a more influential
role than the conventional doctor because of his apparently
superior competence in the definition of ills and remedial
prescription.   The therapeutic churches survive, West suggests,
by virtue of their flexibility in response to rapid urbanization.

0541 Westhues, Kenneth. "The Established Church as an Agent of
Change." *Sociological Analysis* 34 (1973): 106-123.

According to conventional sociological wisdom it is the sect-
type of religious organization that operates in critique of
the social system while the political role assigned to the
church-type is a conservative one.   This article challenges
such an assumption and through case-study of the Roman
Catholic Church in Paraguay, conducted through interviews and
document analysis, suggests that the power enjoyed by the
established church places it in a good position to effect
social change.

N. MINORITY COMMUNITIES; RELIGION AND ETHNICITY

0542 Abramson, Harold J. "Inter-ethnic Marriage among Catholic
Americans and Changes in Religious Behavior." *Sociological Analysis*
32 (1971): 31-44.

The ethnic groups constituting the Catholic Church in America
include French-Canadian, Irish, German, Polish, Hispanic and
Italian.   Religious practice as signified by mass attendance
among Irish and French-Canadians is lower among ethnically
exogamous marriages than in endogamous marriages.   This pattern
is further explored by controlling parental involvement and
educational attainment.   The decline of attendance behavior
among French-Canadians and Irish is attributed to a breaking up
of their cultural systems and dynamics of cohesion.

0543 Abramson, Harold J. "Migration and Cultural Diversity: On
Ethnicity and Religion in Society." *Social Compass* 26 (1979):
5-29.

This article offers an analysis of the relationship of the
variables ethnicity and religion and a study of the individual
migrant in respect of different forms of change.   The migrant
is successively examined as sociocultural traditionalist, exile
and isolate.

0544 Ballard, Roger and Ballard, Catherine. "The Sikhs: The
Development of South Asian Settlements in Britain." In *Between
Two Cultures: Migrants and Minorities in Britain,* edited by James
L.Watson. Oxford: Blackwell, 1977: 21-56.

The article traces the migration of Sikhs to Britain from the
immediate post-war period and analyzes social and economic
changes in the community as well as its relations with the
dominant white culture.   Initially religious practice was
minimal and even scorned, but it has since burgeoned and the
importance of this is attributed not merely to intellectual or
theological fashions but principally to the function of the
Sikh temple, the Gurdwara, in providing a meeting point at the
center of the community.

0545 Barrett, Leonard E. *The Rastafarians: The Dreadlocks of Jamaica.* Kingston: Jamaica: Sangster, 1977.

This is for the most part a general documentary introduction to Rastafarianism which locates it in Jamaican history, portrays its spiritual father Marcus Garvey, traces the development of Ethiopianism in Jamaican society and presents beliefs and practices as raw data. But it also assesses the Rastafari sect as a religious cult, observing the dispossessed status of its adherents, relating its sectarian stance to the outer society, identifying in dress, culture, music, the sacrament of "ganja" (marijuana) and other distinguishing features such as the cele- bration of withdrawal from the world. Rastafarian ideology, Prof. Barrett explains, is unsystematic, eclectic and haphazard, having an emotional basis and not being rooted in objective realities of time, space or biblical truth. See also Kitzinger (0589).

0546 Bensimon, Doris. "Aspects de l'Abandon de la Pratique Religieuse en Milieu Juif Français." *Social Compass* 18 (1971): 413-425.

France accommodates the largest Jewish community in Europe, being half a million strong. This study is based on a very small sample of sixty-five, only seven of whom were practising. Some of these wished to emigrate to Israel in order to find easier opportunities for practice. The author makes the point that the low rate of practice does not signify the loss of religious belief, still less the loss of Jewish identity.

0547 Berman, Gerald S. "Why North Americans Migrate to Israel." *Jewish Journal of Sociology* 21 (1979): 135-144.

This 1970s study compares earlier findings with a view to identify- ing shifts in the reasons for migration to Israel from the United States and Canada. Zionism continues to be an important factor, although the Zionism of the 1970s is less formally organized and more religious and idealistic than that which affected migration before the settlement of the State of Israel.

0548 Bernstein, Judith and Antonovsky, Aaron. "The Integration of Ethnic Groups in Israel." *Jewish Journal of Sociology* 23 (1981): 5-23.

The authors are specifically concerned with the African-Asian community which constitutes the largest segment of Israel's ethnic population. The indicators on the basis of which integration is assessed involve the extent to which minority group members are successful in acquiring the rewards of Israeli citizenship such as education and income. Their findings vary. On educational achievement the group is rated as successful. There is a wide gap in per capita income but this is explained in terms of differential family size.

0549 Berry, Benjamin D. "The Plymouth Congregational Church of Louisville, Kentucky." *Phylon* 42 (1981): 224-232.

Though middle-class and thereto atypical of black American
religion, the Plymouth church in many other respects represents
a model that is generalizable.   The program of which it
constitutes the center involves the development of black pride,
home ownership, educational standards, financial independence
and efficiency.   The success of the church in its mission is
related to the morale of its members.

0550 Bialor, Perry A.   "Greek Ethnic Survival under Ottoman
Domination." In *The Limits of Integration: Ethnicity and
Nationalism in Modern Europe*, edited by Oriol Pi-Sunyer, pp. 43-76.
Amherst: University of Massachusetts Research Papers, 1971.

The survival of Greek national identity through four centuries
of Turkish subjugation was effected largely by its legitimation
in the Greek Orthodox faith.   This was complicated, however, by
simultaneous commitments to Greek language, literature and the
Hellenic past and compromised by problems between the Orthodox
Church in Independent Greece and the Orthodox Patriarchate.

0551 Boling, T. Edwin. "Black and White Religions: A Comparison
in the Lower Class." *Sociological Analysis* 36 (1975): 73-80.

The research for this article was conducted in the late 1960s
in a city of the American midwest having a mixed race lower
class.   White members of religious groups within this class
manifested a tendency to display behavior patterns associated
more with church-types than with sects: religiosity pervaded
the private domain to a lesser extent than among blacks and
there was an incongruity of religious belief and institutional
allegiance.   Blacks differed in each of these respects and
were the more wholeheartedly committed to sectarian religion.

0552 Bowen, David G., ed. *Hinduism in England*. Bradford: Bradford
College, 1983.

This volume comprises a collection of seven documentary essays
which address questions of the social functions of religious
practice within minority communities, with case studies of the
Hindu communities in Bradford and Coventry, and of conflicts
between western and Hindu cultures as concerning the caste
system and the status of women.

0553 Brown, Michael. "The Beginnings of Reform Judaism in Canada."
Jewish Social Studies 34 (1972): 322-342.

The author investigates the slow early development of Canada's
three Reform synagogues and the convergence of these disparate
institutions in the early part of the twentieth century.
Growth was initially hindered by the diversity of members'
backgrounds and the geographical and linguistic heterogeneity
of Canada.   When these factors were overcome and the different
synagogues fused into what could legitimately be called a
community it was only under the prevailing influence of a
modern and systematically organized Reform tradition in the
neighboring United States.

0554   Calley, Malcolm J.C.   *God's People: West Indian Pentecostal Sects in England.*   London: Oxford University Press, 1965.

Calley contributes useful data to sociological wisdom on the dynamics of sect formation, fission, organization and control. The work is rich in raw data and Calley interprets the rituals and ecstasies he surveys as satisfactions for individuals who perceive themselves to be as rejected by the world as they are world-rejecting.   The work is illustrated with photographs of such rituals as foot-washing and there are statistical returns on the sizes of the black pentecostal sects in Britain, the largest of which are the New Testament Church of God and the Church of God of Prophecy.   Calley's figures are now, of course, out of date as the groups he studies have greatly expanded. See also the work of Clifford Hill (0579-0582) and Pryce (0614).

0555   Centre National des Hautes Études Juives. *La Vie Juive dans l'Europe Contemporaine.*   Brussels: Editions de l'Institut de Sociologie de l'Université Libre de Bruxelles, 1962.

This volume is a collection of conference papers on aspects of Jewish life in contemporary Europe.   The main problem addressed is that of sources and methods for the acquisition of demographic statistics on Jews in the continent of Europe, with rather less attention being given to theoretical issues.   Government and non-government sources are investigated and there are several tabulations.   Eminent contributors include Abraham Miles and Max Gottschalk.   Neher's "La Crise Spirituelle" is separately annotated in this bibliography (0607).

0556   Clements, Kevin.   "The Religious Variable: Dependent, Independent or Interdependent." *A Sociological Yearbook of Religion in Britain*   4 (1971): 36-45.

In the literature of the subject the religious variable is assumed to be dependent upon other variables, exerting no or only marginal influence in human life and merely legitimizing the status quo.   On the basis of a study of the social and political history of New Zealand, it is argued that religion can exert considerable influence and can be measured as an independent variable.   In the first of three successive periods in the 1930s, socio-religious ideology was dependent on non-religious definitions of the situation; in the second it acted interdependently; and in the third, following riots in 1932, religious institutions came to be established and effective on an independent basis.

0557   Collins, Daniel F.   "Black Conversion to Catholicism: Its Implications for the Negro Church." *Journal for the Scientific Study of Religion*   10 (1971): 208-218.

A study of the sources of the southern Black's conversion to Catholicism.   Collins indicates the breakdown of the traditional Negro Church with its social, political and economic roles as well as its religious concerns.   At the individual level he observes a change from communal forms of religious expression to personal initiative and responsibility.

0558 Constantinides, Pamela. "The Greek Cypriots: Factors in
the Maintenance of Ethnic Identity." In *Between Two Cultures:
Migrants and Minorities in Britain,* edited by James L.Watson,
pp. 269-300. Oxford: Blackwell, 1977.

The Greek Orthodox Church has had variable successes in its
endeavors to focus ethnic identity for the different migrant
groups it serves. One of the problems for Greek Cypriots in
Britain is that the church organization comes under that
of mainland Greece and not of the island of Cyprus to which
cultural identity naturally relates. In 1974 there was a
Greek Orthodox convent and a monastery in Britain and some
fifty churches, nearly half of them in London. But there
persisted within the Church a tension between Cypriots and
mainland Greeks.

0559 Corm, Georges G. *Contributions à l'Etude des Sociétés Multi-
confessionnelles.* Paris: Pichon and Durand-Auzias, 1971.

Corm makes a study of the social, legal and political effects
of religious pluralism. He adopts synchronic and diachronic
perspectives, examining the problem both in ancient societies
and in non-western civilizations such as the Islamic world.
Cases observed range from Egyptian monarchies to Jewish
communities of the diaspora. Within modern western societies
the problems addressed are matters of social organization,
religious dogma and mission, inter-faith dialogue and functions
of the Christian conception of "the world".

0560 Dassetto, Felice and Bastenier, Albert. "Éthique, Pratique
Religieuse et Socialisation des Fils d'Immigrés Italiens en
Belgique." *Social Compass* 25 (1979): 125-143.

Dassetto provides a study of the religious socialization of a
group of sons of Italian migrants to Belgium, showing religious
practices and moral convictions and the functions of these
among members of a marginal group.

0561 Davis, Moshe, ed. *World Jewry and the State of Israel.*
Jerusalem: Institute of Contemporary Jewry, 1977.

An international panel of leading Jewish thinkers is convened
by Moshe Davis to discuss three of the basic issues occupying
the Jewish people in modern times. These include the study of
manifestations of hostility against Jews throughout the world,
the nature of Jewish identity and identification, the
centrality of Israel and interaction among world Jewish
communities.

0562 Davis, Moshe, ed. *Zionism in Transition.* Jerusalem:
Institute of Contemporary Jewry, 1980.

The transitions that Zionism has undergone in modern Jewish
history include those from messianism to political activism

and thence to a virtually complete identification with the
aspirations and vicissitudes of the State of Israel.   Certain
ideologies survived the course of these transformations.   The
diagnosis of this work adopts an historicist perspective; its
prescription is a reformulation of Zionist ideology and
practice.   This volume is useful as a source-book on the
development and contemporary circumstances of Zionism in
various countries.

0563   Denhardt, Robert B. and Salomone, Jerome J.   "Race,
Inauthenticity and Religious Cynicism."   *Phylon*   33 (1972):
120-131.

The effect of the research reported in this article is to measure
the salience of the Roman Catholic Church in issues relating to
race against skin color as a determinant of attitudes expressed.
Black and white Catholics participated in the inquiry which was
held in the period following the death of a nationally known
advocate of racial segregation and white dominance, Judge
Leander Perez.   It was found that black respondents are
generally cynical of the official position of the Roman Catholic
Church and that their own orientation is rooted more in ethnic
identity than in denominational allegiance.

0564   Ediger, Marlow.   "Other Minorities: Old Order Amish and
Hutterites."   *Social Studies*   68 (1977): 172-174.

This is a basically documentary introduction and a call for
further research.   The author is concerned with the Amish and
Hutterian brethren as exemplars of ethnic religious minorities.
There are substantial studies of these two communitarian sects
by Hostetler (0391, 0392); see also Stoltzfus (0442) on the
Amish and for the Hutterites see Bennett (0363), Frideres
(0376) and Peter (0417).

0565   Elazar, Daniel J. and Monson, Rela Geffen.   "The Synagogue
Havurah: An Experiment in Restoring Adult Fellowship to the Jewish
Community."   *Jewish Journal of Sociology*   21 (1979): 67-80.

The *havurah* is an innovative concept of fellowship in which
individuals and families come together for mutual social
support and to pursue self-directed programs such as Jewish
education and community service.   The institution has been
widely welcomed in North American Jewry and the authors
document the distribution of *havurot* across the traditions.
Many rabbis, however, are ambivalent over the *havurot* and the
authors analyze resistance to them.

0566   Farago, Uri.   "The Ethnic Identity of Russian Students in
Israel."   *Jewish Journal of Sociology*   20 (1978): 115-127.

There were some 120,000 Soviet Jews who migrated to Israel
between 1970 and 1977, many of them young persons.   This
article includes a wealth of statistical data on the
potency of Russian and Jewish identities in a sample of

450 respondents.   The Russian group is in many ways distinctive but declares itself to be well satisfied and to feel at home.

0567 Favero, Luigi and Tassello, Graziano. "La Religiosité de l'Émigré Italien: Enquête en Allemagne, Suisse et Grande-Bretagne." *Social Compass* 26 (1979): 99-123.

This article represents a synthesis of investigations into the religiosity of the Italian migrant carried out between 1970 and 1976 in Germany, Switzerland and Great Britain.   The authors consider social factors bearing upon the religious behavior of the Italian migrant settled in these countries and then explore four dimensions of religiosity; these are acquaintance with the religious institution, doctrinal conformity, consistency in ethical practice and religious practice.   Discussion is centered upon the role of the ethnic church in expressing and pursuing the aspirations of the migrant faithful.

0568 Fishman, Aryei. "Judaism and Modernization: The Case of the Religious Kibbutzim." *Social Forces* 62 (1983): 9-31.

The Potential of Judaism for modernization has been diversely assessed by Werner Sombart and Max Weber; and Fishman's paper follows their work.   His focus is the orthodox kibbutz in Israel and he argues on the basis of empirical observation that the impulse to modernize Judaism is energized primarily by the political elite.

0569 Glazer, Nathan N. "The Jewish Family and Humanistic Values." *Journal of Jewish Communal Service* 5 (1969): 269-273.

Glazer conducts an apologetic analysis of the stable norm of Jewish family life.   Such a family is characterized by Glazer as patriarchal, extended across three generations, devoted to the welfare of its members, regulated by festivals and sabbaths and according to historically based formulae.

0570 Gottlieb, David and Sibbison, Virginia. "Ethnicity and Religiosity: Some Selective Explorations among College Seniors." *International Migration Review* 8 (1974): 43-58.

In a survey of 1800 college seniors, results pointed to the importance of religio-ethnic identity in the socialization process.   Subjects were tested for attitudes relating to work and lifestyle.

0571 Gould, S.J. "American Jewry: Some Social Trends." *Jewish Journal of Sociology* 3 (1961): 55-75.

Gould finds in American Jewry a process of secularization comparable with that observable in other religious traditions in the United States.   However, there is a recognizable return of American Jews to synagogue attendance and this is analyzed as the function of suburban migration.

0572 Grizzard, Nigel and Raisman, Paula. "Inner City Jews in Leeds." *Jewish Journal of Sociology* 22 (1980): 21-33.

Leeds is a large town in the north of England with 18,000 Jews: the authors are particularly interested in the 450 strong Jewish community in Chapeltown. In contrast to other Jewish groups in Leeds, that at Chapeltown suffers the lack of integrating institutions and the authors categorize it as a "sub-population" rather than a "sub-community".

0573 Guizzardi, Gustavo. "Sécularisation et Idéologie Ecclésiale: Hypothèse de Travail." *Social Compass* 24 (1977): 383-405.

Guizzardi conducts a discussion of theories of secularization as related to the social conditions in which they are generated, drawing upon insights from the sociology of knowledge.

0574 Guttmann, Allen. "The Conversions of the Jews." In *The Ghetto and Beyond: Essays on Jewish Life in America,* edited by Peter Rose, pp.433-448. New York: Random House, 1969.

From the time of the first generations of Jewish settlers in the United States the pressures to assimilate have persisted. Secular and other religious ideologies have often prevailed in the dominant culture and even within Judaism the Reformed tradition has had its appeal to Jews of a more conservative orientation. The author notes with some approval the resilience of traditional Judaism and argues that it is unlikely to yield in the future, not least because it provides community values and structures that are not available in American society at large.

0575 Gutwirth, Jacques. "Les Communautés Hassidiques, Sources et Trésors pour le Sociologie Religieuse de la Judaïcité." *Social Compass* 18 (1971): 385-397.

The genesis of the Hassidic community in the Ukraine was a faction of opposition to established Judaism; now, however, social changes without have rendered it a bastion of orthodoxy and the contemporary Hassidic community appeals to the sociologist of religion for instructive comparative study. The conservative talmudism of the Hassidim legitimizes archaic economic relations and structures such as ancient occupational groupings.

0576 Hames, Constant. "Islam et Structures Sociales chez les Immigrés Soninké en France." *Social Compass* 26 (1979): 87-98.

France accommodates a large Moslem minority as a consequence of migration from Africa. This article reports research on the Soninké community from Mauritius, in which wisdom resides with a group called the *moodi*. Hames considers two dimensions of religious practice among the Soninké: the first is that of orthodox Islamic teaching as dispensed by the *moodi* and the other a looser system of practices purported by its exponents

to be founded in Islam.   The role of the *moodi* survives in the
Soninké community and all religious practices except the fast
of *ramadan* appear to be on the increase.

0577 Heilman, Samuel C. *Synagogue Life: A Study of Symbolic
Interaction*. Chicago: University Press, 1976.

The community of a modern Orthodox Jewish Synagogue provides
the setting for this study of social interaction among its
members.

0578 Heller, Celia Stopachka and Pinkney, Alphonso. "The
Attitudes of Negroes toward Jews." *Social Forces* 43 (1965):
364-369.

An analysis of *Newsweek* poll data reveals that in general
Negroes had a favorable view of the behavior of Jews toward
their cause in respect of civil rights. See also Houtart
and Lemercinier (0584).

0579 Hill, Clifford. *Black and White in Harmony*. London: Hodder
and Stoughton, 1958.

At the time of writing Clifford Hill was the minister of a
London church.   Here he gives a first hand documentary account
of aspects of cultural adaptation and cultural maintenance
among West Indians joining London churches.   These include
continuities in style of worship and the inhibition of this in
white majority communities, the celebration of passage rites
and the tension between assimilation and pluralism. See also
Calley (0554) and Hill (0580-0582).

0580 Hill, Clifford. "Some Aspects of Race and Religion in
Britain." *A Sociological Yearbook of Religion in Britain* 3
(1970): 30-44.

Clifford Hill draws attention to several significant features
of the situation in Britain.   There is no homogeneous immigrant community here.   The pattern of immigrant settlement
has been uneven.   The environment is hostile and prejudice
is, he suggests, deeply entrenched.   At the time of his
writing, over half of all immigrants from the New Commonwealth has come from Christian backgrounds.   He draws
attention to a general weakness on the part of the churches in
areas of immigrant settlement but notes some enterprising
exceptions in, for example, the sphere of social work.   The
essay includes some particular comments on West Indians and
the English churches.   See also Calley (0554) and Hill
(0579, 0581, 0582).

0581 Hill, Clifford. "From Church to Sect: West Indian Religious
Sect Development in Britain." *Journal for the Scientific Study
of Religion* 10 (1971): 114-123.

Migration from the West Indies to England involves an abandonment of traditional church affiliations and a new association

with the (mainly) pentecostal churches which are strongly
millennialist and major on themes of ethnic and status deprivation.
The reversion to sectarian ethos is demonstrated by case study of
the largest of the West Indian pentecostal churches in Britain,
the New Testament Church of God. See also Calley (0554) and
other works by Hill (0579, 0580, 0582).

0582 Hill, Clifford. "Immigrant Sect Development in Britain: A
Case of Status Deprivation?" *Social Compass* 18 (1971): 231-236.

Hill finds a link between the measure of deprivation generated by
prejudice and active membership of the all-black sects.   He
predicts that among first generation immigrants at least, sect
membership will continue to increase as long as race relations
continue to deteriorate.   The causal relationship is mutual:
if the second generation follows the first in joining the
racially exclusive sects, the social distance between black and
white will further increase. See also Hill (0579-0581) and
Calley (0554).

0583 Hooper, Rachel. *Act Now*. London: Church Missionary Society,
1970.

A survey was conducted in August and September 1969 on race
relations in Britain and this report takes up particularly the
response of the Church of England and the Church Missionary
Society.   The situation was then rapidly changing and the author
endeavors to draw conclusions that will help the Church and C.M.S.
adapt to need. For example, it is recommended that C.M.S.
missioners returning from overseas service could usefully be
employed by the Church in parts of Britain where there are
concentrations of ethnic minorities.

0584 Houtart, François and Lemercinier, Geneviève. "Catechesis
and Anti-Semitism: A Research Work into the Transmission of
Religious Codes." *Social Compass* 18 (1971): 427-443.

A student sample from Catholic schools in Brussels was used to
monitor the effects upon perceptions of Jews resulting from
catechetical elements asserting the superiority of Christian
beliefs and degrading Jews and Judaism.   The author is
interested in the eradication of these elements and the
consequences for more positive dispositions by Catholics
toward Jews.   See also Heller (0578).

0585 Hunt, Larry L. and Hunt Janet G. "A Religious Factor in
Secular Achievement among Blacks: The Case of Catholicism."
Social Forces 53 (1975): 595-605.

The authors select results from a more general survey of urban
blacks to highlight Protestant-Catholic differences in respect
of black identity and aspirations in the secular domain.   It
emerges that except in the lower-class sections of the sample
Catholic subjects had higher aspirations of career and social
status and this appeared to be enhanced with greater commitment

and participation in the religious sphere.   Likewise, black
identity diminished or was less asserted within the Catholic
sample.

0586 Johnson, Walton R. *Worship and Freedom: The Black American
Church in Zambia.* London: International African Institute, 1977.

The African Methodist Episcopal Church originated and is based
in the United States.   Its membership exceeds one and a half
millions and it has a professional ministry approaching six
thousands.   As well as a developed presence in the Caribbean,
the A.M.E. church has settled in fifteen countries in Africa.
This book gives a thorough account of its organization in
Zambia from the moment of entry and there are precise data
on membership, beliefs, local activities, finance, religious
practice and the benefits of affiliation.

0587 Kayal, Philip M. "Religion and Assimilation: Catholic
'Syrians' in America." *International Migration Review* 7 (1973):
409-425.

Kayal offers an examination of the Lebanese/Syrian community
in the United States and the strain involved in the maintenance
of its national culture.   Attention is particularly drawn to
the problem of transmitting that culture to second, third and
subsequent generations and the disintegrating effect of
residence and intermarriage in a pluralistic society.   One of
the consequences for religious organization is that the Eastern
Churches which had depended on affiliation by the ethnic
community are now developing conversionist strategies.

0588 Kiernan, Jim P. "Where Zionists Draw the Line: A Study of
Religious Exclusiveness in an African Township." *African Studies*
33 (1974): 79-90.

Sectarian exclusiveness of the world is ritualized among Zulu
Zionists in the closing of windows and doors against outsiders.
Separateness is achieved by taboos familiar in western sects
such as prohibitions upon social drinking; and Zionists favor
occupational styles that afford isolation from non-Zionists.
Kiernan's observations were conducted in a township outside
Durban, South Africa, and signify that the divisions celebrated
are not between black and white but within the black community.
This finding has implications for the supposition common in
the sociology of African religion that the independent African
churches represent a reaction against white domination and
exclusiveness.   It might be necessary to modify this interpretation to suggest that patterns of exclusion within the
independent churches emulate the model experienced in the white
churches.   See also Kiernan (0399).

0589 Kitzinger, Sheila. "Protest and Mysticism: The Rastafari
Cult of Jamaica." *Journal for the Scientific Study of Religion*
8 (1969): 240-262.

The Rastafari cult is studied in detail as a male-oriented
politico-religious protest movement involving the messianic
worship of Emperor Haille Salassie of Ethiopia.   Kitzinger
identifies the basis of the cult as a self-renewing and self-
justifying system of belief and practice.   See also Barrett
(0545).

0590 Kolig, Erich. *The Silent Revolution.* Oxford: Clio, 1981.

A study of the effects of modernization upon Australian
aboriginal religion, sociological interest in which was first
excited in the work of Emile Durkheim. See also Stanner
(0086).

0591 Kosmin, Barry A., and Grizzard, Nigel. *Jews in an Inner
London Borough.* London: Board of Deputies of British Jews, 1975.

A study of the predominantly working-class Jewish population of
the London borough of Hackney based on the official census of
1971 which provided a series of demographic measures.   Some
assessment is made of Jewish community life in Hackney,
including affiliation to its forty-four synagogues, Jewish
welfare and religious education.

0592 Krausz, Ernest. *Ethnic Minorities in Britain.* London:
McGibbon and Kee, 1971.

Cases of minority communities having strong religious bases which
are studied in this general account include the Poles, Jews, the
Irish, Indians and Pakistanis.   Statistical and historical data
are used to amplify each example and there are breakdowns by age,
sex, fertility, population projections and geographical
distribution.

0593 Krausz, Ernest. "The Religious Factor in Jewish
Identification." *International Social Science Journal* 29 (1977):
250-260.

The religious dimension in Jewish identity is problematic.
Judaism is an important but not an exclusive reference, operating
alongside secular formulations of ethnicity, nationalism and
community.   The author draws from studies in the United States,
Britain and Israel to illuminate this relationship.

0594 Lalive d'Épinay, Christian. "Les Églises du Transplant:
Le Protestantisme d'Immigration en Argentine." *Social Compass* 18
(1971): 213-229.

This is the report of a study of eleven protestant "immigrant"
churches in the republic of Argentina.   The author takes up and
rejects interpretations which attribute the rise of such churches
to the social and economic status of the immigrant; his
explanation refers instead to the ecclesiastical traditions which
predominated before migration.   The ethnic church is examined
here for its origins, conditions of development and orientations,
whether toward assimilation or toward social divisiveness.

0595 Lambroza, Shlomo. "Jewish Self-defence during the Russian
Pogroms of 1903-1906." *Jewish Journal of Sociology* 23 (1981):
123-134.

The period studied is one of political turmoil and, for Jews,
of intensive persecution resulting in accelerated emigration.
Jewish vigilante groups were involved in bloodshed but also
had a certain deterrent effect.

0596 Lampe, Philip E. "The Acculturation of Mexican Americans
in Public and Parochial Schools." *Social Analysis* 36 (1975):
57-66.

This is a study which points to the importance of the school
above other agencies of acculturation. The research is done
by the administration of questionnaires among nearly 400
eighth-graders of ethnic origin, the sample being divided
between public and parochial schools and other factors being
controlled in the analysis.

0597 Lasker, Arnold A. "Motivations for Attending High Holy Day
Services." *Journal for the Scientific Study of Religion* (1981):
241-248.

Groups of Conservative and Orthodox Jews were sampled in the
course of this inquiry into their purpose in attending High Holy
Day services. The most important motivation was the realization of Jewish identity among Conservative respondents.
Attendance was seen as an opportunity to "lobby" God and to
relate to the Jewish community.

0598 Lavender, Abraham D. "Studies of Jewish College Students:
A Review and a Replication." *Jewish Social Studies* 39 (1977):
37-52.

Following Irving Greenberg's 1949 study of Jewish students at
the University of Maryland, Lavender undertook a similar study
in the same place in 1971 to give comparative findings across
two generations. On conventional measures of religiosity,
students proved to be less observant than their parents in
both cases. Conservative Judaism was more salient among
parents in 1971 than in 1949 and Orthodox Judaism less so:
and, predictably, the socioeconomic status of the 1971 cohort
was higher.

0599 Lazerwitz, Bernard. "Religious Identification and its Ethnic
Correlates: A Multivariate Model." *Social Forces* 52 (1973):
204-220.

For protestants and Jews separately, Lazerwitz applies an
individual developmental model of religious socialization from
the primary agency of the family through religious education
to religious participation within the ethnic community and
parental concern for the religious socialization of the young.
In verification of an hypothesis proposed by Lenski it is found
that activity within the ethnic community is for Protestants

independent of religious activity; but for Jews the two spheres
of action are interdependent, albeit less so among Jews of higher
socioeconomic status.

0600   Leman, Johan.   "Jehovah's Witnesses and Immigration in
Continental Western Europe." *Social Compass* 26 (1979): 41-72.

The relative success   of Jehovah's Witnesses among certain
migrant groups such as Polish mineworkers in northern France
prompts Leman to enquire whether this is attributable to the
Witnesses' deliberate strategy or to tendencies operating within
the migrant group.   A case study of Caltanisanta, Sicily,
features in the meticulous investigation which is reported in
this article.

0601   Lewis, Herbert S.   "Yemenite Ethnicity in Israel." *Jewish
Journal of Sociology*   26 (1984): 5-24.

Yemeni Judaism is a stable and distinctive tradition.   This
study of its transposition to Israel becomes of necessity an
examination of policy.   It is suggested that the cognizance of
ethnic revivals during the 1960s in the western world and of
"the realities of the ethnic mosaic in Israel" has served to
grant to the Yemeni community what Weber calls "status honor".
In this it is distinguished from the Libyan and Moroccan
minorities.

0602   Martin, Bernard.   *Movements and Issues in American Judaism.*
Westport: Greenwood, 1978.

A collection of fourteen essays from different experts,between
them covering most aspects of the development of Jewish life
in America since 1945.   The volume includes reports of much
research and useful statistical tables.   See also Mayer
(0603).

0603   Mayer, Egon.   "Jewish Orthodoxy in America: Towards the
Sociology of a Residual Category." *Jewish Journal of Sociology*
15 (1973): 151-165.

The author schematizes the problem of second and third generation
assimilation in respect of Orthodox Jews.   The immigrant
generation, it is said, took refuge in the ghetto and there found
comfort in an insulated context for culture maintenance: this
insulation was sustained by ideological disapproval of the host
culture.   The second generation was more open-minded about the
world outside and the third generation was even attracted to
join it.   Mayer questions this model on the basis of its
assumption of cognitive dissonance between the minority and
majority cultures.   See also Martin (0602).

0604   Mol, Hans.   "Theory and Data on the Religious Behaviour of
Migrants." *Social Compass* 26 (1979): 31-39.

The author explores and commends the identity theory as
illuminating the religious behavior of migrants.   This theory

directs attention to the important area of boundary maintenance, provides an explanatory model for varying levels of church participation and has universal applications, whether to castes in India or to the totems of Australian aborigines.

0605 Moles, Abraham A. and Grunewald, Tamar. "Altérité et Identité Vues par le Psycho-sociologue." *Social Compass* 18 (1971): 357-373.

Moles reports a cross-cultural study of Jews and non-Jews using the Semantic Differential Technique in order to measure expressed attitudes and in particular covert attitudes.   Other dependent variables are isolated in order to measure the Judaicity factor in attitude differences.

0606 Morrish, Ivor. *The Background of Immigrant Children*. London: Allen and Unwin, 1971.

Morrish conducts a systematic documentary study of the cultures and traditions of the principal ethnic minorities represented in contemporary Britain.   His unique contribution is to establish the importance of the religious factor in cultural identity; religion is much more fully treated than in comparable texts.   The inevitable hazard of presenting stereotypes of minority cultures is not fully overcome; for example, there is little sense of liberal and orthodox variations of adherence to religious traditions.   See also Open University (0610).

0607 Neher, André. "La Crise Spirituelle." In *La Vie Juive dans l'Europe Contemporaine*, Proceedings of the Centre National des Hautes Études Juives, pp. 163-188. Brussels: Editions de l'Institut de Sociologie de l'Université Libre de Bruxelles (0555).

It is the author's view that the dramatic events of the Second World War, notably Auschwitz and Hiroshima, turned about the character of the crisis experienced by religions in the western world.   Formerly, the problem was one of atheism and materialism; but since 1945 there has been a new yearning for spiritual meaning and to this the Catholic and Protestant churches responded.   So too, Neher contends, should Judaism. To this end he sets out a three-dimensional program for the renewal of Judaism in the cultural life of contemporary Europe.

0608 Nimbark, Ashakant. "Status Conflicts within a Hindu Caste." *Social Forces* 43 (1964): 50-57.

The constituency is the Sadhu, a low-status marginal caste in western India, and it is here researched by the content analysis of over four hundred items from its journals.   It transpires that the caste is undergoing social changes which the author relates to the sociopolitical context.   In the endeavor to achieve an enhanced social status some of its older members are rejecting traditional symbols and adopting new ones.

0609   Oliver, Paul. *Songsters and Saints: Vocal Traditions on Race
Records*. Cambridge University Press, 1984.

Oliver conducts an exercise in the sociology of music which fully
documents and interprets the religious traditions of the blues and
other contemporary musical forms: the sacred vocal traditions
from the song-sermons of the Baptists and the Sanctified preachers
to the gospel songs of the church congregations and the "jack-leg"
preachers and street evangelists.   The work includes a useful
index of seven hundred song titles.

0610   Open University. *Minority Experience*. Milton Keynes: Open
University Press, 1982.

The book comprises material designed for the Open University course
"Ethnic minorities and community relations"; the style is
documentary and there are illustrations.   Minorities studied
include South Asians, West Indians, the Irish, and Jews.   In
each case the account includes the historical circumstances of
migration and settlement, culture patterns and culture maintenance in which the religious organizations have functions which
vary from one case to another.   See also Morrish (0606).

0611   Parker, James H. "The Integration of Negroes and Whites in an
Integrated Church Setting." *Social Forces* 46 (1967): 359-366.

Research by participant observation in an American Baptist
Convention revealed conflicting tendencies of which the author
offers an interpretation.   On the one hand seating patterns
showed a considerable degree of segregation, but on the other
choice of conversation partners evidenced a low level of
discriminatory behavior.

0612   Patterson, Sheila. "The Poles: An Exile Community in Britain."
In *Between Two Cultures: Migrants and Minorities in Britain,* edited
by James L.Watson, pp. 215-241. Oxford: Blackwell, 1977.

Poles migrated to Britain in large numbers during the Second
World War and by 1948 there were over 100,000 of them who had
settled for the most part in a small number of centers such as
Birmingham, Bradford and Ealing in west London.   Of these some
eighty-six per cent were Roman Catholic, the others being largely
Orthodox and Protestant.   Only two per cent of the migrants
were Jewish, compared with ten per cent of the population in
Poland.   In London there had been a Polish Catholic Mission
since 1894 and this served the new migrants as a center of
religious organization to be succeeded in the years after the war
by Polish Catholic Churches in each of the areas of settlement.
The author refers to problems of defection by the young
intelligentsia and among working-class Poles and detects an
anglicization of Polish Catholicism that is not evidenced among
Polish communities in the United States.

0613 Poll, Solomon. "The Persistence of Tradition: Orthodoxy in America." In *The Ghetto and Beyond: Essays on Jewish Life in America*, edited by Peter Rose, pp. 118-149. New York: Random House, 1969.

While there are significant common features among American Jews, the tendency to homogenization has been resisted by certain conservative groups, of whom the Ashkenazim and the Hasidim are given particular examination in this paper. Poll studies the ideological and historical foundations of separatism within American Jewry and treats of religious rituals and educational systems characterizing the Orthodox. In conclusion he speculates about the future of Orthodox Judaism and suggests that the notion of struggle for existence is likely to continue to legitimize separate practice and taboos such as inter-marriage; Orthodox Judaism, he suggests, will remain intact as a link between the past and the future.

0614 Pryce, Ken. *Endless Pressure.* Harmondsworth, England: Penguin, 1979.

Pryce makes a study of West Indian lifestyles in Bristol, England. Within what the author calls "the expressive-disreputable orientation" he examines the world of hustlers, teenyboppers and social alienation. Of greater interest to the sociologist of religion is the second part of the book which deals with "the stable law abiding dimension". Chapter 18 entitled "Saints" is a study of pentecostal life in Bristol achieved by covert participant observation. Pryce went as far as being baptized within the pentecostal church in order to disguise his scientific purpose. In common with previous studies of pentecost, Pryce has an interest in the social and moral teachings such as sexual taboos and he also explores the social and economic security which the oppressed find in religious organization; the effect is to render saints increasingly dependent upon each other and independent of outsiders. See also Calley (0554).

0615 Rabi, W. "Modes et Indices d'Identification Juive." *Social Compass* 18 (1971): 337-356.

Jewish identity is diversely perceived as a social condition, a religious faith and an historic destiny. These dimensions are empirically investigated in a number of - chiefly Anglo-Saxon - countries. The author observes an evolution of the Jewish identity from religious belief to external signs in behavior to a secularized form.

0616 Raphael, Freddy. "Le Juif et le Diable dans la Civilisation de l'Occident." *Social Compass* 19 (1972): 549-566.

Over the centuries the Jew has been tainted by a mythical association with the Devil. Freddy Raphael attempts to account for the survival of this myth in changing political, economic, social and cultural situations. He finds that the myth accords with the stereotypical Jewish role in economic affairs and with a politically subversive role attributed to the Jews under Hitler.

0617   Raphael, Freddy. "La Représentation de la Mort chez les
Juifs d'Alsace."   *Archives de Sciences Sociales des Religions*   39
(1975): 101-117.

The Jews of Alsace have over time introduced certain elements
and symbols derived from native Alsatian and Rhenish cultures.
This paper is an examination of the management of death, of the
procedures for the support of the dying and of the religious
principles which have the function of distance for the bereaved
community.

0618   Rock, Kenneth W. "The Colorado Germans from Russia Study
Project." *Social Science Journal* 13 (1976): 119-126.

The group concerned migrated from Russia to Germany in the
eighteenth century and thence to Colorado in the nineteenth.
There are German Lutheran, Mennonite and Catholic accretions
within the community which, in Rock's plea, warrants more
serious research than it has hitherto been accorded.

0619   Rose, Peter, ed. *The Ghetto and Beyond: Essays on Jewish
Life in America.* New York: Random House, 1969.

The essays range across problems of Jewish urban life, community
relations and culture maintenance.   Particular reference is
made to the functions of the religious organization and the
persistence of religious values and practices.   Papers on
religious aspects annotated in this bibliography are those by
Sklare (0632), Poll (0613), Stern (0635), Guttmann (0574), and
the symposium by Irving Greenberg and others (0854).

0620   Rosenstein, Carolyn. "The Liability of Ethnicity in Israel."
Social Forces 59 (1981): 667-686.

This study complements those that appear from time to time in
the *Jewish Journal of Sociology* for it documents and analyzes
differential opportunity and achievement patterns between
migrant groups in Israel, and in this case offers a comparison
with discrimination against blacks in the United States.   The
differences which constitute the concern of this paper are
those of the attainments of Oriental Sephardic Jews and
Askenazi Jews in the early 1960s.

0621   Roskin, Michael and Edleson, Jeffrey, L. "A Research Note
on the Emotional Health of English-speaking Immigrants in Israel."
Jewish Journal of Sociology 26 (1984): 139-144.

An investigation of the emotional health of immigrants in Israel
reveals that those from North America are less healthy than
those from Britain and South Africa.   This article discusses
the implications of that finding and makes a proper plea for
further research to isolate the critical variable against
previous health record and differential expectations in
migration.

0622   Rosoli, Gianfausto.   "Chiesa e Comunita Italiane Negli Stati
Uniti 1880-1940."   *Studium*   (Italy) 75 (1979): 25-47.

This is a study of the relationship of church and community among
Italians in the United States.   The sixty year period surveyed
was one in which the Roman Catholic Church was effective in the
celebration and maintenance of ethnic identity.

0623   Rotenberg, Mordechai.   *Dialogue with Deviance: The Hasidic
Ethic and the Theory of Social Contraction.* Oxford: Clio, 1983.

This is a systematic endeavor to assess the relationships between
Jewish ethics and contemporary society, with a focus upon the
exclusive Hasidim.   Comparative reference may be made to the
work of Solomon Poll (0613) and Shaffir (0629).

0624   Saloutos, Theodore.   "The Greek Orthodox Church in the United
States and Assimilation."   *International Migration Review*   7 (1973):
395-407.

Saloutos makes a study of the vicissitudes of the Greek Orthodox
Church in the United States in its role as custodian of Greek
national identity.   During periods of accelerated immigration
national culture and religion were effectively sustained but the
Church has more recently conceded to the forces of assimilation.
Since 1945 there has been a fated endeavor to maintain Greek
language schools but the process of assimilation has been
advanced first by the identity of the second generation as
Greek-Americans and second by the recognition of the Greek
Orthodox Church in the United States as an indigenous church.

0625   Schaefer, Richard T.   *Racial and Ethnic Groups.*   Boston:
Little Brown, 1972.

Of particular interest to the sociologist of religion is the
sixth chapter of this work which examines the problematic
relationship of religion and ethnicity in contemporary American
life.   Religious pluralism affords the rediscovery of
ethnicity.   The author assesses the extent of religious
diversity within American Catholicism and within Protestantism.

0626   Schlesinger, Benjamin.   "The Jewish Family and Religion."
Journal of Comparative Family Studies   5, 2 (1974): 27-36.

Schlesinger explains the functions and responsibilities of
the Jewish family and its members as enshrined in the Talmud.
The religious regulation of these functions operates through
the celebration of festivals and the enactment of rites of
passage.

0627   Schutte, A.G.   "Dual Religious Orientation in an Urban
African Church."   *African Studies*   33 (1974): 113-120.

This study informs us of the (limited) importance of denominational criteria in the choice of a religious community to
which to affiliate.   Interviews of over half the members of a

Dutch Reformed congregation in Soweto, South Africa, showed that
kinship ties were particularly important and that individuals
had a need to affiliate to a church but were less concerned
which it should be.   By the same token belief and doctrine are
considered relatively unimportant and the author relates these
observations to his previous findings that members were able
to operate and confess to two potentially contradictory sets of
religious beliefs.

0628   Scult, Melvin.   "English Missions to the Jews - Conversion in
the Age of Emancipation." *Jewish Social Studies* 35 (1973):
3-4.

The London Society for the Promotion of Christianity among the
Jews was founded in 1809 and is still in existence.   It
represents a major effort in a series of programs to convert
the Jews, upon which enormous energy and material resources
have been expended with little or no visible results.   In terms
of efficiency, it is a history of abject failure.   From its
resources of wealth the London Society bought off a few poor
Jews but that was all.   The finances accrued testify to the
desire of the wealthy English classes to assimilate the Jewish
presence.   The author does not elaborate an analysis of the
capacity of Jews to resist such missions.

0629   Shaffir, William.   "Hassidic Jews and Quebec Politics."
Jewish Journal of Sociology 25 (1983): 105-118.

Mainstream Montreal Jewry viewed Quebec's *francization* laws
with apprehension but the Tasher Hassidim and the Lubaritcher
sects were relatively indifferent.   The author's interpretation is that mainstream Jewry feared alienation whereas the
two Hassidic groups had always sought insulation and were
therefore accustomed to it, whatever the dominant national
culture.   See also Poll (0613) and Rotenberg (0623).

0630   Sharot, Stephen.   "The Three-generations Thesis and the
American Jews." *British Journal of Sociology* 24 (1973):
151-164.

The thesis examined is drawn from Herberg's *Protestant-
Catholic-Jew* (0067) in which an attempt was made to relate
certain quantifiable changes in religious practice to identify
within a sequence of three generations from the immigrant first
generation of the 1880s to the third generation which was
marked by a "return to religion" in the post-war period.
The thesis is not borne out by Sharot's evidence from American
Jews, however.   The first generation of Jews, he suggests,
were not traditionally religious, the second did not revolt
against religion and the third did not return to it in a
deep sense, although Sharot recognized an increase in
synagogue attendance.

0631   Sharot, Stephen.   "Native Jewry and the Religious Anglicization of Immigrants in London: 1870-1905." *Jewish Journal of
Sociology* 16 (1974): 39-56.

The period studied is marked at its outset by the large-scale
migration to London of Jews taking refuge from the *pogroms*.
Exiles were not welcomed by Jews already resident in London
who attempted a strategy of assimilation, dispersing them from
existing Jewish centers and putting on English language
evening classes.   Sharot studies the character of Samuel
Montagu, a rich native Jew who was both Orthodox and
anglicized, and of the United Synagogue which operated a
systematic program of anglicization.

0632 Sklare, Marshall. "The Ethnic Church and the Desire for
Survival." In *The Ghetto and Beyond: Essays on Jewish Life in
America*, edited by Peter Rose, pp.101-117. New York: Random
House, 1969.

It is hypothesized that the degree of acculturation experienced
by an ethnic minority relates directly to the rate of its
social mobility.   Comparisons are made with the ethnic church
in the United States and a special study is made of Congregation-
alism.   This comparison affords an analysis of the will to
survive which persists through several generations against
common expectations that the ethnic group would assimilate
values and practices of the host culture.

0633 Sklare, Marshall. "The Sociology of the American Synagogue."
Social Compass 18 (1971): 375-384.

The emergence and development within American Jewry of the
"synagogue center" represents an institutional innovation
designed to enhance the chances of survival in an open society
in which the future of the ethnic group is not secure.

0634 Smith, Anthony D. "Nationalism and Religion: The Role
of Religious Reform in the Genesis of Arab and Jewish Nationalism."
Archives de Sciences Sociales des Religions 35 (1973): 23-43.

This is an empirical and theoretical inquiry based around the
proposition that nationalism arises out of reform within ethnic
religion although essentially religion and nationalism are
opposed.

0635 Stern, Kenneth. "Is Religion Necessary?" In *The Ghetto and
Beyond: Essays on Jewish Life in America*, edited by Peter Rose,
pp.190-200. New York: Random House, 1969.

Being a Jew is often considered to be a matter of birthright
membership of an ethnic group with a strong sense of community
and a characteristic set of religious beliefs.   Stern takes up
the questionable inclusion of a religious factor in this
characterization.   The demise of Judaism, he suggests, is an
indicator in the decline of a separateness identity and he
happens to approve such a trend if it is to promote a more
united society.

0636   Ward, Robin H.   "Some Aspects of Religious Life in an
Immigrant Area in Manchester."   *A Sociological Yearbook of
Religion in Britain*   3 (1970): 12-29.

The study concerns the Moss Side district of Manchester in the
north of England which has a cosmopolitan population; there is
a close and predictable relationship between country of origin
and religious affiliation, the Irish and Poles being
predominantly Roman Catholic, Asians were mainly Moslem but
for a few Sikhs and the West Indians were variously Anglican,
Methodist, Roman Catholic, Adventist or Pentecostal.   Special
attention is given to the recently arrived West Indians and
their absorption into a common immigrant class.   At the time of
the study the conventional churches were failing to integrate
these immigrants into their new environment.

0637   Wierzbicki, Zbigniew T.   "The Polish Schism in the United
States of America."   *Polish Sociological Bulletin*   4 (1979):
47-56.

At the end of the nineteenth century a faction broke from the
Roman Catholic Church and formed the Polish National Catholic
Church which survives in the present day.   Wierzbicki
analyzes the reasons for this schism, distinguishing those
that were official at the time from the actual causes.   He
examines the process of metamorphosis from faction to church.
In matters of representation there was dominance of Poles by
Irish and German Catholics and they were not able to nominate
a Polish bishop.   Whereas the Irish regarded themselves and
were regarded by others as permanent settlers, Poles were
perceived as temporary residents not warranting institutionalized provision.   See also 0176.

0638   Wood, James R. and Zald, Mayer N.   "Aspects of Racial
Integration in the Methodist Church: Sources of Resistance to
Organizational Policy."   *Social Forces*   45 (1966): 255-265.

Wood and Zald make a study of the problems of policy initiation
in a voluntary organization in which the leadership at national
and local levels can depend upon a low level of lay consensus
and few if any sanctions at its own disposal.   The congregations,
for their part, had the sanction of economic support and this
they variously withheld or diminished.   The authors relate
resistance to policies of racial integration to the proportions
of black membership in the respective congregations.

O. SECULARIZATION

0639   Archer, Margaret Scotford and Vaughan, Michalina.   "Education,
Secularization, Desecularization and Resecularization."
A Sociological Yearbook of Religion in Britain   3 (1970): 130-145.

The institutional integration of education is inseparable from
the decline and ultimate exclusion of its former integration

with religion.   This argument is variously expressed in three
complementary arguments - that secularization is inevitable,
that desecularization is improbable, that resecularization is
unavoidable.   These propositions are explored in respect of
three theory types, the idealist, the structuralist and the
dialectical, in all of which, the authors conclude, the
religious variable has been consistently neglected.

0640 Berger, Peter L. *A Rumour of Angels*. New York: Doubleday,
1969.

So studious have sociologists and others been of the process of
secularization that there is a tendency to regard religion as a
phenomenon that is disappearing rather than as one that is
merely transforming.   Berger's contribution is to identify and
explore the contemporary transformations of religious belief
and the non-organized forms in which religion persists.   The
alleged demise of the supernatural is questioned by Berger.
"We are," Berger concludes, "whether we like it or not, in a
situation in which transcendence has been reduced to a rumour."

0641 Berkes, Niyazi. "Religious and Secular Institutions in
Comparative Perspective." *Archives de Sociologie des Religions*
16 (1963): 65-72.

This is a study of the political transformation of Islamic
society in Turkey.   Berkes defies the assertions of Muslim
modernists and some western scholars that it is not possible
to apply conventional models of secularization to non-western
societies.

0642 Carroll, John. *Puritan, Paranoid, Remissive: A Sociology of
Modern Culture*. London: Routledge and Kegan Paul, 1977.

Carroll disentangles religious and secular themes in contemporary
culture and identifies types characterizing each.   He engages
the decline of individual authority as a major feature of
cultural change and reviews what he calls "the remissive prospect".

0643 Cipriani, Roberto. "Il Concreto Sociologico di
Secularizzazione." *Sociologia* 7 (1973): 117-143.

This provides an examination of the concept of secularization
as deployed by sociologists and draws attention to confused and
very different uses of the concepts of the sacred and the secular.
Those whose usages are juxtaposed include Howard Becker, Robert
N.Bellah, Luke Ebersole and Talcott Parsons.

0644 Decker, Raymond. "The Secularization of Anglo-American Law,
1800-1970." *Thought* 49 (1974): 280-298.

This article is concerned with legislation of various kinds -
domestic, criminal and constitutional.   The elimination of
explicitly religious values in the expression and legitimation
of law comes about not so much as a consequence of the decline

in religious values but as a strategy of achieving consensus
in a society marked by an increasing measure of religious
pluralism.

0645 Delumeau, Jean. "Dechristianisation ou Nouveau Modèle de
Christianism?" *Archives de Sciences Sociales des Religions* 40
(1975): 3-20.

Here is an endeavor to locate the moments and conditions of
christianization and dechristianization. Delumeau provides
an overview of recent work on this problem in which few
interpreters have pointed to the modern period, the sixteenth
to eighteenth centuries, and not to the mediaeval period as
that which witnessed the burgeoning of the western Church.
He speaks of it practising a pedagogy of fear in alliance with
the State.

0646 De Neve, André. "Secularisation in Russian Sociology of
Religion." *Social Compass* 20 (1973): 593-601.

Russian sociologists treating of secularization remain true to
the thrust of their own and their predecessors' writings before
the introduction of this concept. Whereas in western
scholarship, studies regard religion to be a diminishing factor
in public life, their Russian counterparts have as their
starting point the view that religion is a form of self-
consciousness which has already become obsolete: their studies
of secularization only prove the official theory.

0647 Deshen, Shlomo A. "The Varieties of the Abandonment of
Religious Symbols." *Journal for the Scientific Study of Religion*
11 (1972): 33-41.

This is a study of secularization in the tradition of Weber and
the author distinguishes two elements of the process of abandonment, eradication and effacement. The first dimension refers
to the cessation of religious rituals, the second to a loss of
belief, and each is related to specific social conditions.
The author undertakes a comparison of a Lele ritual and
symbolic changes in a Djerban synagogue in Israel. See also
Deshen (0830).

0648 Dobbelaere, Karel; Lauwers, Jan; and Ghesquiere-Waelkens,
Mieke. "Sécularisation et Humanisation dans les Institutions
Hospitalières Chrétiennes." *Social Compass* 20 (1973): 553-568.

This article is the report of a good example of consultancy in
that a group of sociologists is commissioned to explore the
meaning of being a Catholic for the benefit of the Belgian
Federation of Catholic Nursing Institutions. They resolve
the problem by the exploration of a number of subsidiary
questions of sociological import; these include the
structuration of being Catholic within certain institutional
contexts, and the Catholic character of Catholic hospitals as
defined by their sponsors or managers. The report details what

the authors perceive as a program of humanization as defined
by various elements within the institution.

0649 Fenn, Richard K. "The Process of Secularization: A Post-
Parsonian View." *Journal for the Scientific Study of Religion*
9 (1970): 117-136.

Fenn provides a theoretical paper which picks up Talcott Parsons'
model of a religiously based moral order with congruent cultural,
structural and personality levels in the social system.   Fenn
adopts the Parsonian model and endeavors to sketch in some of
the norms of contemporary secular society.   He comes to the
inescapable conclusion that the model of a religiously based
moral order depending on congruence does not work for the highly
differentiated society of America.

0650 Glasner, Peter E.   "'Idealization' and the Social Myth of
Secularization." *A Sociological Yearbook of Religion in Britain* 8
(1975): 7-14.

The notion of secularization as religious decline supposes an
historic period in which religious observance and influence were
stronger than they are seen to be in the present time.   Glasner
adduces evidence to suggest that perceptions of the past have
been distorted by an ideology of progress that underlies historical
sense and that the Tudor and Stuart periods of English history
have been idealized.   The process of idealization has been
instrumental in the propagation of what Glasner calls "the social
myth of secularization in England".

0651 Glasner, Peter E. *The Sociology of Secularisation: A Critique
of a Concept.* London: Routledge and Kegan Paul, 1977.

While secularization is the thematic focus of this study, the
exposure of the paucity of theory in the sociology of religion
is its motive.   Glasner reckoned that at the time of writing
there had developed no adequate scientific theory of the
secularization process and that research done was at best
systematic empiricism.

0652 Goodridge, R.Martin. "The Ages of Faith." *Sociological
Review* 23 (1975): 381-396.

This is a bubble-bursting exercise, the bubble being the
assumption general in sociological accounts that there was an
age of faith in the Middle Ages which suffered a decline with or
before industrialization.   The author points to Germany in which
there was massive abstention from the rites of the Church for
marriage and churchgoing was the behavior pattern of the élite.
He suggests that the extent of participation and faith in the
Middle Ages has possibly been exaggerated and that a decline
of popular faith has not been proven.   See also Greeley
(0653).

0653 Greeley, Andrew M. *The Persistence of Religion*. London:
S.C.M. Press, 1973.

This has been noted as a resourceful and challenging work in which
one amassed powerful and plausible arguments that conflict with
the general tenor of much sociological research.   Greeley
contradicts the orthodox views that secularization is progressive and irreversible and he contends that the degree of secularization in western societies has been conventionally overstated.
Such a position is also adopted by Goodridge (0652).

0654 Hartel, Bradley R. and Nelsen, Hart M. "Are We Entering a
Post-Christian Era? Religious Belief and Attendance in America,
1957-1968." *Journal for the Scientific Study of Religion* 13
(1974): 409-419.

This is not a genuine longitudinal study but a comparison of the
results of two Gallup Polls.   The later poll shows no appreciable
decline in basic beliefs such as the devil and life after death,
although there is an increase in explicit disbelief in life after
death.   The prospect of an imminent post-Christian era is
affirmed by the finding that church attendance has declined among
believers and the church is losing its primacy as an agency of
consolation in times of personal crisis.   Whether two sets of
poll data spaced over eleven years provide evidence of a trend
is of course arguable.

0655 Herberg, Will. "Religion and Culture in Present-day America."
In *Roman Catholicism and the American Way of Life*, edited by Thomas
T.McAvoy. Notre Dame: University of Notre Dame Press, 1960.

The three categories for which Herberg is celebrated - Protestant,
Catholic, and Jew (0067) - are, he here argues, alternative modes
of being American and of self-identity within American society.
This identity goes beyond the dimension of religiosity and is
secular in its quality.   Herberg cites Dwight D.Eisenhower's
appreciative recognition of the moral and spiritual values of
democracy and offers a sociological interpretation of the manifestation of religious tenors in the secular and political domain.
His purpose is to illustrate the Americanization of religion in
the United States and thereby its "thorough-going secularization".
See also Bellah (0883).

0656 Isambert, François-André. "La Secularisation Interne du
Christianisme." *Revue Française de Sociologie* 17 (1976):
573-589.

Secularization is commonly approached as the diminishing influence
of the sacred within the domain of the secular, but Isambert
brings into focus the internal transformations of the Christian
religion.   These include the demythologizing of Scripture,
desacralization and deritualization of the liturgy.   The
distinctly sacred expressions of the Christian faith are
articulated in a secular language.

0657 Kerševan, Marko. "Les Traitements des Morts dans la Société Socialiste." *Social Compass* 29 (1982): 153-165.

This is an essay in the state secularization of Slovenia, the predominantly Catholic north-western province of Yugoslavia. The article treats of two potentially religious institutions, the funeral and "All Dead People's Day", the latter having been formed by a secular merger of the traditional holy days, All Saints Day and All Souls Day. In respect of both institutions the author points to three ideological domains, the civil, the Church and the family.

0658 Krausz, Ernest. "Religion and Secularization: A Matter of Definitions." *Social Compass* 18 (1971): 203-212.

Krausz pleads for conceptual clarification in the course of which he raises the problem of boundary definition between the religious and the secular. The author's own inclination is to adopt a definition of religion that emphasizes its institutional character and the transcendance of the basis of its belief system; such a definition enables the distinction between two further categories often confused, religious beliefs and ideological beliefs.

0659 Kubiak, Hieronim. *Religijność a Środowisko Społeczne*. Wroclaw: Zaklad Narodowy Imienia Ossolińskica, 1972.

This Polish work on religiosity and social milieu has as its focus the effects upon religious practice of migration from the countryside to the town.   These effects are radical and diverse. Religious attitudes become heterogeneous.   The range of religious concerns that are tolerated, however, is more narrow and certain political involvements are not approved.   There is a tendency to privatize problems related to religion and so to reduce the possibility of religious conflict.   In all categories of respondent, religious doubt was a concomitant of urbanization and religion was not thought a necessary habit for the decent citizen.

0660 Lalive d'Épinay, Christian and Bassand, Michel. "Vie Religieuse et Sécularisation: Éléments Théoriques et Application à une Ville Moyenne Suisse." *Schweizerische Zeitschrift für Soziologie* 2 (1976): 83-117.

The authors study religious life in a Swiss town with particular reference to the problem of secularization.   In the typology they develop, distinctions are made between the areligious, the nonpractising heterodox, the churchless heterodox, the modernist, the churchless orthodox and the practising faithful.   This typology is chiefly useful in identifying types of secularism and in recognizing religious patterns among the unchurched.   The model is then operated with a sample of 300 respondents in the town of Delémont, Switzerland.

0661 Lauwers, Jan. "Les Théories Sociologiques Conçernant le
Sécularisation - Typologie et Critique." *Social Compass* 20
(1973): 523-533).

Lauwers discusses theories of secularization respectively
emphasizing pluralization (Herberg and Yinger), individualization
(Luckmann and Berger) and rationalization (Weber and Bryan Wilson).
All of these theories assume that it is possible to distinguish
between essence and accident, and all assume the separability of
religious and non-religious.   Lastly, Lauwers considers the
dialectical relationship of ideology and social reality:
not only is secularization an ideology but it can by a program
of action become a social reality.

0662 MacIntyre, Alasdair. *Secularization and Moral Change*. London:
Oxford University Press, 1967.

The argument is centered upon the separate religious histories
of the English middle and working classes since 1800.   The
urbanization and industrialization of the working class represents
its detachment from a community governed by universal God-given
norms.   MacIntyre views religious decline and moral disintegration as the two sides of a single process, but neither as cause
and neither as effect.   To the extent that the rejection of
Christianity by the English working class was voluntaristic,
it related to the paternalistic view of society which the Church
was perceived to enshrine.

0663 Maduro, Otto.   "Avertissements Épistemologico-politiques pour
une Sociologie Latino-américaine des Religions." *Social Compass*
26 (1979): 179-194.

The author proposes a new Latin-American sociology of religion
that would be constructed in accordance with his identification
of themes appropriate to the tensions and aspirations in which
religious agencies share in that part of the world.   The problems
he enumerates include totality, objectivity, human interest,
values, usefulness, politics and language.   With the offering of
this agenda Maduro makes some exhortations to be heeded by
sociologists of religion in general.

0664 Martin, David. *The Religious and the Secular: Studies in
Secularization*. London: Routledge & Kegan Paul, 1969.

This is a collection of essays, some of them previously published,
which offer an exploration of secularization at the conceptual
level and study its manifestations in various milieux such as
music and secular theology and in two contrasting national
cultures, England and Bulgaria.   The volume includes Martin
(0667) and Martin (0668)   and anticipates Martin's *General
Theory* (0665).

0665 Martin, David. *A General Theory of Secularization*. Oxford:
Blackwell, 1978.

David Martin's theory is not an explanatory model but an empirical typology of the relationships of political and religious forms throughout post-war Christendom.   It is an undertaking disting- uished by its magnitude and the work brings together insights from the sociology of religion and from political sociology.   In the endeavor to identify the conditions under which religious institutions become less powerful and religious beliefs less acceptable, there emerge basic patterns of religious and political dominance and equivalence, monopoly and pluralism, cases of which are studied by reference to a vast literature.

0666 Martin, David. "Towards Eliminating the Concept of Secularization." In *Penguin Survey of the Social Sciences*, edited by Julius Gould. Harmondsworth: Penguin, 1965.

Martin here condemns the concept of secularization and proposes that the word "be erased from the sociological dictionary" on the grounds that its meaning has become subject to ideological distortion and that its very use obfuscates examination of, say, the impact of geographic and social mobility on religious practice. The real intention of this essay was not to banish a word but to open a debate (he says in 0665) and arguably he succeeded. It is reprinted in Martin (0664) and the publication of Martin's *General Theory* (0665) has done more than anything to ensure the rehabilitation of the concept.

0667 Martin, David. "Some Utopian Aspects of the Concept of Secularization." *Internationales Jahrbuch für Religionssoziologie* 2 (1966): 87-96.

Martin looks to utopian metaphysics and traces in the idea of an ultimate harmony achievable by the unveiling of truth the roots of two popular conceptions of secularization - the growth of scientific thinking and the alienation of the proletariat. These metaphysical systems attempt to resolve the dualisms of Christianity - of God and man, Church and State, heaven and earth; secularization is seen as the utopian transposition of theology in the Judaeo-Christian tradition.   Reprinted in Martin (0664).

0668 Martin, David. "The Secularisation Process in England and Wales." In *Religion in a Technological Society*, edited by Gerald Walters. Bath: Bath University Press, 1968.

The constituencies with which this essay is concerned are more general than the title suggests: for while there are frequent references to trends within the United Kingdom, the purpose is to propose patterns characteristic of Protestant and Catholic societies (individual striving and class antagonism respectively), to distinguish sub-varieties such as pluralist and monopolist and to explore the consequences of the dominance of one society by another.   The theses adumbrated here recognizably anticipate the more expansive *General Theory* (0665).   Reprinted as "The Secularization Pattern in England" in Martin (0664): 114-130.

0669 Martin, David. "Institutionalism and Community." *Actes de la 12ième Conférence Internationale de la Sociologie Religieuse* (1973).

This paper synthesizes some thirty contributions to the biennial session of the C.I.S.R. It detects among these a fear of bureaucratization and institutionalization and a nostalgia and romantic vision of community: they suggest that the individual is progressively repressed, excluded and confined. The pervasiveness of bureaucracy in the religious domain is exemplified by modern cults such as Scientology and Christian Science. With special reference to the Roman Catholic Church there is a review of the reformulation of the relationship between clergy and laity: the theory of secularization bears upon the process of social differentiation currently affecting the position of the clergy. The Weberian theme of bureaucratization has many exemplifications in religious organization and is traced also into civil religion and public rituals. Reprinted in *The Month* (December 1973) and in Martin (0035).

0670 Martin, David. "The Secularization Question." *Theology* 76 (1973): 81-87.

The formula of secularization as a straightforward process of decline in religious belief and influence is, David Martin suggests, altogether too simple. Certainly the Church was formerly dominant, and before the Reformation it enjoyed a monopoly power; but the one-time unity of religions and civic cultures has always been underlain by a common substratum of folklore and even disbelief which persists to the present day. And some current sentiments, such as reverence for religious buildings, were not at all characteristic of earlier centuries.

0671 Parsons, Talcott. "Religion in Postindustrial America: The Problem of Secularization." *Social Research* 41 (1974): 193-225.

Parsons surveys developments in religious formation from the Middle Ages to the present day and speculates about the future of current trends. He points to the sacraments as quasi-magical ordinances and thereby attaches historical significance to the attenuation of sacramental religion by the Protestant Reformation. He indicates two major trends of the post-Reformation period of universal significance, secularization and ecumenicalism. And he considers two cases that are not easily accommodated by his scheme, civil religion and Marxist socialism.

0672 Pfautz, Harold W. "The Sociology of Secularization: Religious Groups." *American Journal of Sociology* 61 (1955): 121-128.

The cult transforms to a sect, the sect either to an institutionalized sect, to a church or to a denomination. Each of the three stages represents an increasing degree of secularization. Pfautz reports the transformation of Christian Science to an institutionalized sect.

0673 Pickering, William S.F. "The Secularized Sabbath: Formerly Sunday; Now the Weekend." *A Sociological Yearbook of Religion in Britain* 5 (1972): 33-47.

Pickering picks up the nineteenth century model of Sunday as a day of rest set aside by the middle class for worship, guaranteed by the Factory Act of 1847 but used by the working class of Victorian times for recreation and sundry domestic tasks (see Homan, 0198). He notes a decline in the religious use of Sunday for church and Sunday School attendance, and a particular decline in evening attendance. Within the "socio-religious component" of Sunday, he records various trends, responding not least to the availability of television as entertainment; in place of a single day set apart, Sunday is now the second of a pair of days, the weekend, and is distinguished as a time of pleasure, relaxation and mobility (by automobile). This changed attitude, it is suggested is current among church members as well as non-members and it is noticed that churches have in recent years made morning worship the principal Sunday Service.

0674 Raphael, Freddy. "Judaism and Secularization." *Social Compass* 18 (1971): 399-412.

It is proposed that as far as Judaism is concerned the only authentic religious attitude is that of the prophet and of eschatology (that is, the hope for the future rather than the experience of disaster). Such a conclusion emerges from a study of the sociological implications of the theological perspective and of Jewish nationalism as a form of secularization.

0675 Rendtorff, Trutz. "Zur Säkularisierungsproblematik: Über die Weiterenwicklung der Kirchensoziologie zur Religionssoziologie." *International Jahrbuch für Religionssoziologie* 2 (1966): 51-70.

The author explores a fundamental ambivalence in the application of the category of secularization as displayed in the work of Lübbe and Blumenberg. In a concluding section Rendtorff develops the notion of secularization as the emancipation of religious behavior from the church system.

0676 Rigby, Andrew and Turner, Bryan S. "Communes, Hippies et Religion Secularisées." *Social Compass* 20 (1973): 5-18.

One of the anomalies of secularization is that the decline of institutional religion is accompanied by a proliferation of new religious movements of which Rigby and Turner here study some manifestations from the late 1960s. Hippie culture represents both a rejection of traditional belief and ritual and a search for a new belief and practice outside the established order. The authors are struck first by the diversity of alternative culture and second by its appeal to middle-class and intellectual youth, a constituency not historically engaged by established religion. The authors conduct their observations

in two communes in Britain.   For comparison see research on
the Nichiren by Oh (0415).

0677 Robertson, Roland. "Sociologists and Secularization."
Sociology 5 (1971): 297-312.

This paper takes stock of secularization as the principal theme
occupying sociologists of religion in recent years.   It
ventures into mapping new routes within critical sociology and
the sociology of the possible and examines the explanations of
secularization offered by sociologists and by theologians
informed by the social sciences.

0678 Sarikwal, R.C. "Industrialisation and Religious Organisation -
A Sociological Analysis." *Indian Journal of Social Research* 13
(1972): 127-130.

Sarikwal provides a brief analysis of the effects of social
change upon religious organization in India and his article
constitutes a useful document for the comparative study of
secularization.   Secular tendencies are discerned in belief
and faith and the cult is identified as a religious phenomenon
engendered by industrialization.

0679 Shiner, Larry E. "The Concept of Secularization in Empirical
Research." *Journal for the Scientific Study of Religion* 6 (1976):
207-220.

Shiner surveys the usage and meaning of the concept of secularization across a broad literature, both sociological and theological.
He discovers a situation of confusion and misunderstanding. Of
two proposals he makes, that with the unlikeliest future is the
declaration of a moratorium on the use of the term in favor
of more specific, neutral and commonly understood terms such
as "differentiation" and "transposition".   But these are more
particular elements of the general process which, along with
desacralization, might be embraced by an agreed usage of the term
"secularization".   Shiner's more confident proposal is therefore
the suggestion of such an agreement.   Reprinted with editorial
comment by William M.Newman (0040): 304-324.

0680 Tomka, Miklos. "Les Rites de Passage dans les Pays
Socialistes de l'Europe de l'Est." *Social Compass* 29 (1982):
135-152.

Throughout eastern Europe state and social organizations have
initiated secular variants to the religious ceremonies and
anniversaries which have traditionally been within the domain
of the Church.   Tomka points to the spread of these "socialist
ceremonies in the family".   The question that then arises is
whether these rites and anniversaries are to be considered as
a religious phenomenon.

0681 Weigert, Andrew J. and Thomas, Darwin L. "Secularization and Religiosity: A Cross-national Study of Catholic Adolescents in Five Societies." *Sociological Analysis* 35 (1974): 1-23.

This is an attempt to illuminate the process of secularization by comparing the religious beliefs of adolescents in rural and urban communities; it is supposed that traditional religiosity will diminish with urbanization whereas religious knowledge will increase. The analysis is based on findings of a survey conducted in American, German, Spanish and Puerto Rican high schools. The authors' expectation is confirmed in broad terms.

0682 Winter, Gibson. *The New Creation as Metropolis.* New York: Macmillan, 1963.

Gibson Winter turns to the fact of a secularized world and by means of a sociological perspective explores a new role for the Church based on the biblical paradigms of prophet and servant. The organizational forms within which such a role is likely to be enacted are also adumbrated; these include residential and evangelical centers.

P. RELIGIOUS PROFESSIONALS; CLERGY; MINISTRY; RELIGIOUS COMMUNITIES AND RELIGIOUS ORDERS; MISSION

0683 Abell, Aaron Ignatius. *The Urban Impact on American Protestantism 1865-1900.* Hamden: Archon, 1962.

The urban environment invites a peculiar response from the churches. Poverty has spiritual as well as material dimensions and the urban poor lack a sense of social purpose. Yet the churches of the city are distinguished by their sectarianism. The Christian humanitarian response is often undenominational in its organization and projected at a particular social sector or occupational group. The concept of Christian social service which operates in the early part of the period is later replaced by that of social Christianity which has its heyday in the last two decades of the century.

0684 Absalom, Francis. "The Anglo-Catholic Priest: Aspects of Role Conflict." *Sociological Yearbook of Religion in Britain* 4 (1971): 46-61.

Absalom identifies two ideal-types of priestly role current in Anglo-Catholicism. The traditional priest is an authoritarian paternalist, socially distant, commanding the deference of his faithful, and highly committed to the observance of a routine of rituals. For the second type, which has only burgeoned since the 1950s, structural status has not been available; the new type of Anglo-Catholic priest is less committed to the performance of traditional rituals and more vulnerable to liberal theology, sociology and

ecumenism.   Absalom argues that "the role of priestly leadership is more unstable than ever before."

0685 Allchin, A.M. *The Silent Rebellion: Anglican Religious
Communities 1845-1900*. London: S.C.M. Press, 1958.

The historical period studied was one of considerable social
change for the place of the religious within the Church of
England, for the role of women and for the social programs of
the established church under the impact of the Oxford Movement.
The style of this work is documentary and its perspective
historical but the material between its covers is of certain
sociological significance.

0686 Bentley, James. "The Bishops, 1860-1960: An Élite in
Decline." *A Sociological Yearbook of Religion in Britain* 5 (1972):
161-183.

Bentley documents a decline in the quality of bishops whose
visions did not extend beyond their own class alignments and
who saw in God the ultimate sanction for national interests
and institutions.   Whereas some other professions, such as the
British civil service, broadened the class bases of their
highest ranking personnel, the hierarchy of the Church of
England was persistently of noble birth, exclusive schooling
and conservative view.

0687 Bibby, Reginald W. and Mauss, Armand L. "Skidders and their
Servants: Variable Goals and Functions of the Skid Road Rescue
Mission." *Journal for the Scientific Study of Religion* 13 (1974):
421-436.

The thesis of this article is an intriguing one which might
reward application to various kinds of religious organization.
The skid road missions are benevolent institutions in Seattle.
It is suggested that the manifest functions of these missions
are not fulfilled but they continue to exist because they
serve a purpose not for their intended clients but for those
who administer them.   The approach to this subject adopted by
the authors was in substantial measure anticipated by Rooney
(0746).

0688 Blaikie, Norman W.H. "Altruism in the Professions: The Case
of the Clergy." *Australian and New Zealand Journal of Sociology*
10 (1974): 84-89.

A postal survey of Australian parish clergy is used to pick up
perceptions of the professional role and the extent to which
altruistic definitions exceed formal obligations.   A high
valuation of the pastoral role is general among respondents.
Two models of perception emerge, the one emphasizing recruitment and spiritual dimensions and the other giving priority
to social reform.   Clergy whose theological views stress
transcendance adopt the first of these role perceptions,
while those of a secularist orientation favor the second.

0689 Bodart, Josianne. "Modernité et Néo-clercs: Á Partir de
l'Image de Soi du Travailleur Social." *Social Compass* 29 (1982):
283-295.

The profession of social work is analyzed in comparison with
the priesthood. Both have a vocational element; both involve
a devotion and the economic support system is also comparable.
In this article the social worker is termed "the neo-cleric" and
problems of role uncertainty and organizational affiliation are
shown to manifest ambivalences involving strain for the
professional.

0690 Bourdillon, M.F.C. "Freedom and Constraint among Shona
Spirit Mediums." In *Religious Organization and Religious Experience*,
edited by J.Davis, pp.181-194. London: Academic Press, 1982
(0013).

There is a recognition in the literature that the authority of
spirit mediums among the northern Shona is of a bureaucratic
type whereas that of the counterparts among the central Shona
is charismatic. Bourdillon's paper is a careful disputation
of this assumption and the problem of who is what will be of
limited interest to the general sociologist. What is more
interesting is the application of Weberian types to this
constituency and the possibility of local variations between types.

9691 Bryman, Alan. "Sociology of Religion and Sociology of Elites:
Elite and Sous-élite in the Church of England." *Archives de Sciences
Sociales des Religions* 38 (1974): 109-121.

Bryman adduces evidence to demonstrate elite structures and
continuities among the clergy of the established Church of England.
Tabulated data show family background, education, career patterns
and membership of prestigious "clubs". Bryman then reprimands
sociologists for having failed to locate religion within a
framework of the sociology of elites.

0692 Burchard, Waldo W. "Role Conflicts of Military Chaplains."
American Sociological Review 19 (1954): 528-535.

This is a study of ideological dilemmas inherent in the role of
a little-studied category of religious professional. It is
found that conflicts are reconciled either by rationalization
or by the compartmentalization of role behaviors. The chaplain
has a function, too, in resolving the dilemmas of individual
servicemen by interpreting the values of the military organization. Reprinted in Yinger (0070): 587-599.

0693 Campbell, Keith E. and Greenberg, Donald. "Religiosity and
Attitude Toward the Vietnam War: A Research Note Using National
Samples." *Sociological Analysis* 40 (1979): 254-256.

The authors use national samples to assess the character of the
relationship, positive or negative, between attitudes to the

Vietnam war and religiosity; they discover no significant relationship of either kind.

0694   Collard, E.;   Dellepoort, J.;   Labbens, J.;   Le Bras, G.; and
Leclercq, J.   *Vocation de la Sociologie Religieuse: Sociologie des
Vocations*.   Paris: Conférence Internationale de Sociologie
Religieuse, 1958.

This is a collection of papers exemplifying the practice of
religious sociology and considering its place among cognate
disciplines.   These papers are the proceedings of the fifth
meeting of the Conférence Internationale, nowadays published as
the *Actes*.   They demonstrate the practice of sociology in the
service of the Catholic Church, a relationship celebrated by the
formal granting of the *Nihil Obstat et Imprimatur*.   The second
part of the collection, representing the special theme of the
conference, is devoted to the sociology of religious vocations
and includes papers on the clergy, female vocations and problems
of recruitment.

0695   Cope, Gilbert, ed.   *Christian Ministry in New Towns*.
Birmingham, England: Institute for the Study of Worship and Religious
Architecture, 1967.

New towns are residential areas established and planned to
accommodate the overspill population from larger cities such as
the metropolis of London.   Physical rehabilitation is attended
by respective spiritual problems and this collection of papers
is concerned with the various dimensions of ministry in the new
towns; these include the pastoral role and pastoral planning, the
liturgy and new prospects and perspectives.

0696   Coxon, Anthony P.M.   "Patterns of Occupational Recruitment:
The Anglican Ministry."   *Sociology* 1 (1967): 73-79.

Recruitment of the Anglican ministry is examined as a process
of withdrawal from the general population of an increasingly
homogeneous group.   Coxon takes an historical view and
distinguishes the current pattern of recruitment as an amalgam
of two distinct groups and processes, a declining group electing
the ministry as first occupational choice, and a growing group
making the choice late and as a second option.   The trend toward
the second pattern is recognizable in other religious ministries
and may be related to a general loss of prestige.   See also
Paul (0739).

0697   Curcione, Nicholas R.   "The Family Influence on Commitment to
the Priesthood: A Study of Altar Boys."   *Social Analysis* 34 (1975):
265-280.

The author adopts a developmental approach to the factors which
solidify in some altar boys the commitment to seek ordination
while others of their peers remain uncommitted.   The title of the
paper preempts its conclusion, in which it is suggested that the
major factor is the stability of support by the aspirant's family.

0698   Daniel, Michael.   "Catholic, Evangelical and Liberal in the
Anglican Priesthood." *A Sociological Yearbook of Religion in Britain*
1 (1968): 115-123.

Clergy of the Church of England differentiate themselves on the
basis of churchmanship: there are two distinctive groups,
Catholic and evangelical, each characterized by its own cluster
of beliefs and interpretations.   Both groups have their orthodox
or conservative and their liberal members.   This article reports
a study of ninety-five London clergymen, a third of whom thought
themselves theologically liberal: the author points out the
ideological overtones of this description as a correlate of
progressive but notices that some *soi disant* liberals do not
greatly differ in views from their conservative counterparts.

0699   Deconchy, Jean-Pierre.   "L'Orthodoxie Enseignée par
Renforcement du Réglage de l'Appartenance." *Archives de Sciences
Sociales des Religions* 38 (1974): 91-108.

This is the report of an experiment conducted among Catholic
seminaries and clergy, the purpose of which is to illuminate
the conformity of their individual beliefs to orthodoxy as
controlled by the system of authority.   See also Deconchy
(1001).

0700   Dempsey, Kenneth C.   "Conflict in Minister/Lay Relations."
A Sociological Yearbook of Religion in Britain 2 (1969): 58-74.

A study conducted in a congregation of the Australian Methodist
Church, from which emerge certain tentative hypotheses wanting
confirmation from comparable contexts.   It is suggested that
the minister's role and status are ill-defined, giving rise to
the assertion of charismatic authority in which some ministers
are not naturally competent: in their cases conflict arises.
In rural areas (in Australia) where ministers are isolated
from their peers and there is a high level of extra-church
interaction between members, many conflicts are relatively likely
to be resolved in the laity's favor.

0701   Dubach, Alfred T.   "Entre la Resistance et l'Adaptation:
Situation Professionelle du Prêtre en Suisse." *Social Compass* 19
(1972): 291-299.

Dubach's concern is with ambiguities in the professional posture
of the priest in Switzerland.   The role is perceived by its
actors as an uncertain one and several factors conspire to
engender the feeling of malaise.   These factors include the
pressure of work, and the inevitable diversion from primary
commitments to secondary activities; poor co-operative relationships in the wider context than the parish; the mismatch of
what the church is willing to provide and what the people are
perceived to want; inadequate training and preparation for the
task; and the necessity of accommodating a managerial role.
The effect of changes in the priest's role is to align his
vocation with the secular professions from which skills and
styles are being imported.

0702   Dunstan, G.R.   "The Sacred Ministry as a Learned Profession."
Theology   70 (1967): 431-442.

The challenge of the Paul Report (0739) and the comment upon it
by Bryan R.Wilson (0772) are here taken up by a theologian
disturbed by the possibility that even in its pastoral role the
clerical profession has lost influence.   He considers seriously
the thesis that ecumenism, clinical theology, amateur sociology
and liturgical reform are outlets for clergy seeking to recover
lost influence.

0703   Estivill, Jordi and Barbat, Gustau.   "Anticléricalisme
Populaire en Catalogne au Début du Siècle."   *Social Compass*   27
(1980): 215-230.

This article arises from research on working-class conditions
in Barcelona at the beginning of the century.   The tendency
toward rebellion shown by the working classes there was
expressed in anticlericalism.   This leads to a discussion of
the role of the contemporary Catholic Church in general.

0704   Fay, Leo F.   "Differential Anomie Responses in a Religious
Community."   *Sociological Analysis*   39 (1978): 62-76.

The disruption of an organizational system in a closed religious
community engenders a condition akin to that which Durkheim
identifies as structural anomie.   The case studied in this
paper is a community of Roman Catholic nuns.   The author
operates the Anomie Scale of McClosky and Scharf and finds
significant measures of psychological anomie among authoritarian and traditionalist respondents.

0705   Gannon, Thomas M.   "The Impact of Structural Difference on
the Catholic Clergy."   *Journal for the Scientific Study of Religion*
18 (1979): 350-362.

This paper is an examination of the perceptions of religious
and secular priests and of the extent to which these are
affected by lifestyle and career structure.   The study is
based in the United States and data may be compared with those
collected from the Anglican clergy by Paul (0739).   See also
Goldner (0709).

0706   Garrett, William B.   "Politicized Clergy: A Sociological
Interpretation of the 'New Breed'."   *Journal for the Scientific
Study of Religion*   12 (1973): 383-399.

The 1960s saw the radicalizing of substantial sections of the
American clergy.   Garrett finds characteristics among the
clergy that portend a burgeoning social reform movement and
the prospect of a major impact on national religious life.

0707   Gernet, Jacques.   "La Politique de Conversion de Matteo
Ricci en Chine."   *Archives de Sciences Sociales des Religions*
36 (1978): 71-89.

Gernet provides an essay on the political strategy of Matteo
Ricci, a Christian missionary to China whose Jesuit forerunners
had encountered a hostility following piracy by the
Portuguese, poor indigenous religiosity and other factors.
Ricci's course was to secure legitimacy as a priority and this
he achieved partly by virtue of the science which he taught.

0708 Glenn, Norval D. and Gotard, Erin. "The Religion of Blacks
in the United States: Some Recent Trends and Current Characteristics." *American Journal of Sociology* 83 (1977): 443-451.

The authors point to a decline in religious vocations among
blacks in the last two decades which continues against the
general trend of black religiosity and without the accompani-
ment of the anti-clericalism observable in some white churches.

0709 Goldner, Fred H.; Ference, Thomas P.; and Ritti, Richard R.
"Priests and Laity: A Profession in Transition." *Sociological
Review Monographs* 20 (1973): 119-137.

This is a sociological inspection of the crisis of recruitment
to the Catholic priesthood, conducted over a three year period
in a major American diocese with the cooperation of its bishop.
Findings point to the bearing of plausibility structure,
intraprofessional conflict and the perceived irrelevance of
the work to much of everyday life. Among other factors,
increased lay participation in the liturgy has usurped what
was formerly a distinctively priestly role. See also Gannon
(0705).

0710 Gombrich, Richard. "Le Clergé Bouddhiste d'une
Circonscription Kandienne et les Élections Générales de 1965."
Social Compass 20 (1973): 257-266.

The author infers that the religious factor in Singhalese
politics has been overestimated. Analyzing results of a
questionnaire conducted among Buddhist monks, the author
recognizes an involvement of his subjects with political
issues and voting in elections. Caste membership, self-
interest and opposition to communism weigh heavily and in that
order in their voting behavior. But they are not opinion
leaders in political affairs: their place is to reflect
politics rather than to initiate.

0711 Greenwold, Stephen Michael. "Buddhist Brahmans." *Archives
Européennes de Sociologie* 15 (1974): 101-123.

A study of Newar Buddhism in which celibacy, asceticism and
vows of renunciation are no longer required of the priesthood. The symbols and rituals of the old dispensation,
however, survive; these signify a purity that is notionally
achievable within an ordinary life, and it is the principle
of purity that legitimizes the persistence of a caste system
of which the Brahmins are the custodians and from which
pariah groups are excluded.

0712   Gustavus, William T.   "The Ministerial Student: A Study in the Contradictions of a Marginal Role."   *Review of Religious Research* 14 (1973): 187-193.

Some four hundred students, half of them in ministerial training, were surveyed and the rate of response was less than fifty per cent.   Respondents indicate approval or disapproval of certain social practices.   It is hypothesized that ministerial students are more marginal than their peers but findings on this survey are inconclusive and contradictory.   It is suggested that the role of the ministerial student is in a state of flux.

0713   Hadden, Jeffrey K. and Rymph, Raymond C.   "Social Structure and Civil Rights Involvement: A Case Study of Protestant Ministers." *Social Forces*   45 (1966): 51-61.

Over forty ministers from seven Protestant denominations attending a joint training program were given the opportunity to participate in a civil rights demonstration.   Most availed themselves of this and the authors characterize the twenty-five who "chose to be arrested"; these tended to be younger ministers not account- able to all-white congregations.

0714   Hadzimichali, Nectaire.   "L'Église Orthodoxe Grècque et le Messianisme en Afrique."   *Social Compass*   22 (1975): 85-95.

The Greek Orthodox presence in Africa dates from a mission to Kenya in 1912.   In years of depression in the homeland the African mission was a welcome source of distraction and optimism. As Orthodoxy spread to Uganda and the Belgian Congo its characteristic support of national consciousness was found to be in accord with burgeoning nationalist and messianic movements in those countries.   Orthodox missionaries have supported independence movements in the African states, and in a predictive note Hadzimichali supposes that Orthodoxy is likely to be regarded with favor in the independent states.

0715   Haig, Alan.   *The Victorian Clergy*.   London: Croom Helm, 1984.

The clergy of the Church of England constitute a professional organization which is largely but not exclusively an inheritance of the nineteenth century.   Other studies show that it has since lost prestige and invariably make comparison with its antecedents (Russell, 0747).   Alan Haig accumulates a wealth of statistical material   and exemplars, and traces the professionalization of the clergy in Victorian times; he analyzes the structure of this occupational group and treats of its marginal elements as well as its aspirants to higher status.

0716   Hammond, Phillip E.;   Gedicks, Albert;   Lawler, Edward; Turner, Allen;   and Allen, Louise.   "Clergy Authority and Friendship with Parishioners."   *Pacific Sociological Review*   15 (1972): 185-201.

The enquiry was conducted by postal survey among 350 responding
Wisconsin clergy in Baptist, Episcopal, Lutheran and pentecostal
denominations.   In testing the hypothesis that those in
authority seldom seek friends among those whom they control, the
authors investigate factors such as the high church - low church
variable, desire, freedom and the puritanism factor, and find
that their hypothesis is complicated by the effects of these.

0717   Hertel, Bradley R.   "Church, Sect and Congregation in
Hinduism: An Examination of Social Structure and Religious Authority."
Journal for the Scientific Study of Religion   16 (1977): 15-26.

The social class basis of church-sect differentiation is here
adapted and applied to the case of Hinduism in which the "church"
is constituted by the superior castes and the "sect" by the
lower castes.   The fieldwork represented here was conducted
in Uttar Pradesh.   The author challenges the stereotype that
the priestly caste, the Brahmins, enjoys a purely hereditary
power: in his assessment there is a measure of accountability
that renders the congregation a powerful force if priestly
status is to be sustained.

0718   Higgins, Edward.   "Les Rôles Religieux dans le Contexte
Multi-racial Sud-africain: Le Profil du Ministère dans le
Calvinisme et le Catholicisme."   *Social Compass*   19 (1972): 29-47.

Higgins offers a comment on the role of Calvinism and Catholicism in South Africa and their impact upon the social and cultural
system.   This article brings together work by Kiernan on the
role of the Catholic priest and by Alant on the role of the
pastor in the Dutch Reformed Church (Nederduitse Gereformeerde
Kerk).   Both functionaries are reported to have their roles
privatized, sanctified and thereby diverted from political
involvement.

0719   Holm, Nils G.   "Revivals and Society in the Nordic Countries."
Actes de C.I.S.R.   17 (1983): 243-251.

This paper takes into account religious revivals in Scandinavia
over a period of three centuries up to and including the 1970s.
Among the more interesting movements detailed is Laestadianism
which spread in the early nineteenth century.   Holm relates
a number of cases to the type of social change accompanying
revival movements and suggests that those of the 1970s cannot
be understood on the same basis as others.

0720   Jeffries, Vincent and Tygart, Clarence E.   "The Influence of
Theology, Denomination, and Values upon the Positions of Clergy on
Social Issues."   *Journal for the Scientific Study of Religion*   13
(1974): 309-324.

A cross-denominational sample of over three hundred Los Angeles
clergy is surveyed in an endeavor to assess the dependence or
independence of political and theological orientations.   Their
views are monitored on a cluster of social issues including
welfare aid, civil rights, commitment to the Vietnam war and

penal law.   The authors want to know whether clergy views on
these issues are determined by theological considerations or
by values introduced from outside the religious sphere.
Results of the questionnaire survey suggest that theological
orientations are the more powerful influence upon the formation of views on social issues.   It may well be, however,
that clergy are influenced more than they suppose by secular
values but that they turn to theology to legitimize the
positions they adopt.

0721   Jioultsis, Basil.   "Religious Brotherhoods: A Sociological
View."   *Social Compass*   22 (1975): 67-83.

The brotherhoods which are the subject of this article are a
Greek phenomenon and arise out of private missions addressed
to the spiritual needs of the Greek people during the nineteenth
century.   The manifest functions of these brotherhoods of
monks and nuns are spiritual, devotional and catechetical but
they have also identified with a political position in critique
of the administration and finance of the Greek Church.   The
brotherhoods have also been active in liturgical reform and
in recent years have been accompanied by similar movements of
the laity, such as *Zoi* and *Stavros*, which are documented in
this account.

0722   Keith, Pat M.   "Perceptions of Needs of the Aged by Ministers
and the Elderly."   *Review of Religious Research*   18 (1977):
278-282.

The elderly constitute large contingents of churchgoers and
this study is an endeavor to assess the awareness of their
needs by the religious professionals who minister to them.
Responses of ministers and the elderly are compared to yield an
indication of consensus and disagreement.   They were asked to
evaluate services such as training courses and housing services
and social and counseling activities.   The elderly gave
priority to supportive services against participatory
activities whereas ministers tended to favor the latter.

0723   Laloux, Joseph.   "Une Enquête sur une Congrégation Religieuse."
Social Compass   18 (1971): 142-144.

Some 1,250 nuns in Europe, Africa, North America and Latin
America were questioned on aspects of religious life, work,
community and the apostolate.   The results concern the
structures and values by which the religious life is sustained.
In comparing responses from younger and older sections of the
sample, it is observed that the younger tend toward a more
personalized conception of the religious life.

0724   Leat, Diana.   "Putting God over: The Faithful Counsellors."
Sociological Review   21 (1973): 561-572.

This is an examination of some aspects of secularization
effecting a response in the professional behavior of the clergy

who turn to a secular and scientific skill, counseling, in
order to adapt to the perceived needs of a changing world.
See also Maddock et al. (0729).

0725 Levesque, Bendit. "L'Orde Religieux comme Projet Rêvé:
Utopie et/ou Secte?" *Archives de Sciences Sociales des Religions*
44 (1976): 77-108.

Levesque analyzes the religious order against two models of
comparison, Utopia and the religious sect.   The case chosen
for study is the community of the Clerics of Saint Victor,
founded about 1812 near Lyons.   The data analyzed are drawn
from early writings including the biography of the Trappist
reformer Augustin de Lestrange.

0726 Lienhardt, Godfrey. "The Dinka and Catholicism." In
Religious Organization and Religious Experience, edited by J.Davis,
pp.81-95. London: Academic Press, 1982 (0013).

The mission of the Verona Fathers in 1858 to the Dinka tribe
on the White Nile was an accidental affair in that they were
sailing up the river when their boat was grounded. So the
seed of Catholicism was sown among them.   Lienhardt studies
the christianization of the Dinka as a process of thought
reform, of the revision of traditional myths and practices
and the adjustment of existing rites and concepts: for example,
the symbolic use of water in baptism was made comprehensible
by the existence in Dinka belief of the concept of *doc piu
nhialic*, "blessed with God's water".

0727 Longino, Charles F. and Hadden, Jeffrey K. "Dimensionality
of Belief among Mainstream Protestant Clergy." *Social Forces* 55
(1976): 30-42.

This reports an extensive survey of over 7,000 clergy in six
of the main Protestant denominations.   Subjects were questioned
in a range of sixteen areas of theological content.   In the
analysis of their responses, Longino and Hadden point out the
unidimensionality of belief patterns; there is a variation
from fundamentalist belief to a more liberal position and all
other beliefs are clustered around a locus on this continuum.

0728 McSweeney, B. "Priesthood in Sociological Theory." *Social
Compass* 21 (1974): 5-23.

Through discussion of Weber on priesthood and an account of
the history and legitimation of priestly authority, there
emerges a model of a power system of three interrelated
components - ritual, myth and discipline.   It is suggested
that the system of priestly power in the church is analogous to
the maintenance of white supremacy in South Africa by means of
the rule of apartheid: common attributes include the solidarity
of fellow-clergy and the creation of a mystique around the
power group which sustains beliefs in the superiority of its
members.

0729 Maddock, Richard; Kenny, Charles T.; and Middleton, Morris M.
"Preference for Personality versus Role-activity in the Choice of
a Pastor." *Journal for the Scientific Study of Religion* 12 (1973):
449-452.

Active lay members of Episcopal churches were given a range of
personality attributes and role characteristics and asked to
signify which they considered most important in a potential
minister.   Respondents of all types favored the personality
characteristics and it is suggested that this finding might have
implications for the training of clergy so that more emphasis is
given to affective programs.   See also Leat (0724).

0730 Malalgoda, Kitsiri. "The Buddhist-Christian Confrontation
in Ceylon, 1800-1880." *Social Compass* 20 (1973): 171-200.

The period surveyed was one of ascendancy for the British missions
to Ceylon and of internal reform for native Buddhism.   The
British missions enjoyed an advantage in their control of the
educational system so that Buddhists were obliged to pass through
Christian schools in order to acquire any formal education.   The
Buddhists in turn defended their faith with organization along the
lines of the missionary society model.

0731 Mantzaridis, George. "New Statistical Data Concerning the
Monks of Mount Athos." *Social Compass* 22 (1975): 97-106.

Mantzaridis presents population figures of the various monasteries,
of details of composition and of changes over seven censuses from
1959 to 1974.   Numbers are broken down by monastic status, age
and educational level of the inhabitants.   Mainly useful as raw
data.

0732 Murphy, Steven E. "A Note on Clergy-Laity Differences Among
Lutherans." *Journal for the Scientific Study of Religion* 11
(1972): 177-179.

Differences of belief between clergy and laity provide one of
the indicators of belief conformity within a church and its
efficiency in religious socialization.   Here Murphy studies lay
and clerical members of the Lutheran Church in northern Illinois
and finds significant deviations of belief in social and
political issues.   The constituency is a relatively conservative
one in which political activism would be a disturbing factor,
but the author suggests that ministers with deviant political
views within his sample tended to keep them in low profile and
they were not allowed to damage pastoral relationships.

0733 Nauss, Allen. "Problems in Measuring Ministerial Effectiveness." *Journal for the Scientific Study of Religion* 11 (1972):
141-151.

The investigation of effectiveness in the clerical profession
has been thwarted by a variety of obstacles ranging from the
problem of delineating objectives of the ministry to a history
of non-collaboration between clergy and between clergy and

people.   Nauss surveys these impediments and suggests strategies
for their resolution, such as the adoption of primary rather than
secondary definitions of the ministerial function.   See also
Nauss (0734).

0734 Nauss, Allen. "The Relation of Pastoral Mobility to Effectiveness." *Review of Religious Research* 15 (1974): 80-86.

Pastoral mobility is operationalized as the rate at which ministers
change from one pastorate to another, and the number and duration
of pastorates held are the basis of quantification.   Mobility is
not here a geographical concept, nor is account taken of variations
in specialized roles.   Among older ministers high effectiveness
ratings correlate with long pastorates but this is not necessarily
so among those of less than six years' experience.   Nauss discusses
denominational policy as a factor in the assessment of effectiveness.   For discussion of the problem of measuring ministerial
effectiveness see Nauss (0733).

0735 Neal, Marie Augusta. "A Theoretical Analysis of Renewal in
Religious Orders in the U.S.A." *Social Compass* 18 (1971): 7-25.

The situational context of the renewal movement is diagnosed by
the author in sociological terms: she speaks of anomie and a loss
of cohesion within the religious orders.   The response to this
is a renewed resolution to eradicate misery in the world.   The
renewal movement has a prophetic rather than a priestly function
within the Church and is exemplified in this article by the
Sister Formation Movement which is engaged in social and
educational work.   There is a shift of emphasis from personal
vows and communal living to mission and engagement in the world.

0736 Nebreda, Julian. "La Crisis Vocacional del Instituto Marista
y su Futuro en Andalucia." *Cuadernos de Realidades Sociales* 6
(1975): 59-107.

The Maris Brothers constitute a teaching order with a worldwide
membership of nearly 8,000.   The subject of this article is
the current crisis of sacred vocations as it affects the order.
In an attempt to analyze this crisis attention is given to
political, historical and spiritual factors.   The author
assesses contemporary conditions inhibiting the election of a
sacred vocation and notes variable rates of vocation in the
provinces of Spain.   This affords some speculation on future
trends.

0737 Nelsen, Hart M.; Yokley, Ratha L.; and Madron, Thomas W.
"Ministerial Roles and Social Actionist Stance: Protestant Clergy
and Protest in the Sixties." *American Sociological Review* 37
(1973): 375-386.

The authors report the results of a questionnaire mailed to
Protestant clergy in a number of major American cities.   Their
purpose is not to measure the degree of overall protest during
a decade in which progressive political objectives were actively
pursued but rather to analyze the role sets of clergy and to

establish the relationship of component elements.   It transpires
that liberalism in political and theological beliefs and the
commitment to the solution of community problems are positively
related whereas conservatism relates, as might be expected, to
a more traditional interpretation of the clerical role and an
aversion to political involvement.

0738 Nelsen, Hart M. and Maguire, Mary Ann. "The Two Worlds of
Clergy and Congregation: Dilemma for Mainline Denominations."
Sociological Analysis 41 (1980): 74-80.

The authors analyze the crisis experienced by clergy ministering
to congregations of dissonant religious beliefs and ideologies.
The responsibility of giving sermons on matters of personal
morality is eschewed by liberal clergy addressing conservative
congregations, especially by clergy of nonfarm backgrounds.
Conflicts arise in the ministerial role in respect of
congregations characterized as local against cosmopolitan and
traditional against liberal.

0739 Paul, Leslie. *The Deployment and Payment of the Clergy*.
Westminster: Church Information Office, 1964.

The Paul Report, as it has come to be widely known, was commissioned by and within the Church of England to provide information
on the Anglican clergy at a time when the profession was declining
in social prestige and the problem of recruitment was causing
alarm - as it has continued to do. Paul's survey charted
dimensions of decline within the Church against a social background characterized by expansion. He examined the structure,
scope, entrance procedures and membership of the ordained
ministry. Tables of statistical data are presented at every
opportunity. In the fashion of a government report Paul makes
recommendations on the development of a lay ministry, on re-
organizing the parochial system, sabbatical terms for clergy,
a clearly delineated career structure, changes in the system of
patronage and the establishment of a research unit. Few of
Paul's recommendations have been implemented in the forms
envisaged, but in the spirit of Paul there has been the extensive
development of a non-stipendiary ministry, lay involvement in
synodical government and the setting up of advisory units at
national and diocesan levels on such issues as education and
social responsibility. See also the comment by Wilson (0772)
and the work of Coxon (0696) and Russell (0747).

0740 Peterson, Robert W. and Schoenherr, Richard A. "Organizational Status Attainment of Religious Professionals." *Social Forces*
56 (1978): 794-822.

This is an analysis of survey data from a sample of 3,000
Catholic priests and bishops in eighty-five dioceses. It
transpires the social origins of a priest constitute a relatively weak determinant of the status he attains. High status is
associated rather with important professional responsibilities
in the passage of the career, the attendance of élite seminaries,

the acquisition of higher degrees and, most of all, seniority in priesthood.

0741 Pickering, William S.F. "Hutterites and Problems of Persistence and Social Control in Religious Communities." *Archives de Sciences Sociales des Religions* 44 (1977): 75-92.

The Hutterite *Bruderhof* is remarkable for its historical persistence. This is an analysis of the control mechanisms developed within the Hutterite community and the peculiar problems that attend them. For further work on Hutterites see Bennett (0363), Frideres (0376), Hostetler (0392), Peter (0417) and Ediger (0564).

0742 Potter, Sarah. "The Making of Missionaries in the Nineteenth Century: Conversion and Convention." *A Sociological Yearbook of Religion in Britain* 8 (1975): 103-124.

The article offers two main types of missionary recruitment in the nineteenth century. The first, which is current in the early part of the century, comprises orthodox evangelican conversion in adolescence issuing in pioneer missionary work. The second, belonging to the latter part of the century, relies upon an education insulated from adolescent temptations and leads to missionary work as a respectable career.

0743 Poulat, Émile. "The Future of the Worker Priests." *The Modern Churchman,* June 1959: 191-199.

The analytical quality of this article is poor and its conclusions are barely sociological; but it is useful at the documentary level as a case study of a phenomenon initiated in the Church of Rome in 1943 and terminated in 1954. The article traces the context of this ill-fated scheme and is made the more pertinent by the revival in recent years of a comparable "non-stipendiary ministry", notably within the Church of England. It emerges that the Roman Catholic worker-priests of the late 1940s proved less pliable than their bishops desired and debate over their existence quickly polarized.

0744 Quinley, Harold E. "The Dilemma of an Activist Church: Protestant Religion in the Sixties and Seventies." *Journal for the Scientific Study of Religion* 13 (1974): 1-21.

The social and political ferment of the late 1960s provided an arena which clergy were differentially inclined to enter. Quinley's survey of protestant clergy in California reveals a polarization of clergy with respect to political activism. There is also evidence of a division between laity and clergy, with members of congregations falling away from religious leaders known to be politically active. The author anticipates the persistence within liberal churches of an ambivalence concerning political involvements.

0745 Reidy, M.T.V. and White, L.C. "The Measurement of Tradition-alism among Roman Catholic Priests: An Explanatory Study." *British Journal of Sociology* 28 (1977): 226-241.

Responses from Roman Catholic priests questioned in New Zealand are compared with findings in North America and other societies in the western world. The purpose is to assess their respons-iveness to rapid social change and in particular the variables which relate most closely to this. It is found that age and age related characteristics are the most reliable indicators of priests' locations on a scale of traditionalism and adaptivity.

0746 Rooney, James F. "Organizational Success through Program Failure: Skid Row Rescue Missions." *Social Forces* 58 (1980): 904-924.

Like many welfare institutions the rescue missions exist on the basis of a social need which it is their manifest function to eliminate: if successful, they would cease to be. This produces a moral and professional dilemma for mission staff who would be redundant were they more effective. In fact there is never a risk of their achieving the stated aim of converting to the Christian faith the most marginal and rejected members of the communities to which they minister. Such a fatalist perception of the function of the mission, however, is inappropriate in the appeals made by missioners for financial sponsorship: there are therefore both pessimistic and optimistic themes in the self-perception of mission staff. See also Bibby and Mauss (0687).

0747 Russell, Anthony. *The Clerical Profession*. London: S.P.C.K., 1980.

By means of detailed historical analysis of the professionaliz-ation of the clergyman's role in the Church of England, the author comes to an examination of that role in the present and some speculation regarding its future. Problems documented include the loss of status and prestige and a decline in academic prowess; the clergyman's contemporary estate, it is argued, is one of profound crisis. See also Coxon (0696) and Paul (0739).

0748 Séguy, Jean. "Charisme, Sacerdoce, Fondation: Autour de L.M. Grignion de Montfort." *Social Compass* 29 (1982): 5-24.

Séguy tests Weber's theory of charisma by its application to religious orders, the personalities of their founders and the process of their foundation. The case around which this paper is based is the founder of the Missionaries of the Society of Mary (Montfortian Fathers), St.Louis-Marie Grignion de Montfort (1673-1716).

0749 Sharot, Stephen. "Religious Change in Native Orthodoxy in London, 1870-1914: Rabbinate and Clergy." *Jewish Journal of Sociology* 15 (1973): 167-187.

The period surveyed was one in which the English rabbinical system underwent extensive changes in a departure from continental models. In role delineation and economic arrangements the office of Chief Rabbi was elevated above that of the clergy who were merely cantors in the ritual.   In the course of these changes the role of Principal Rabbi which had operated in each synagogue was displaced and the author examines the tensions and partisan interests generated thereby.

0750 Sharot, Stephen. "The British and American Rabbinate: A Comparison of Authority Structures, Role Definitions and Role Conflicts." *A Sociological Yearbook of Religion in Britain* 8 (1975): 139-158.

This essay traces shifts in emphasis in the role of rabbi from piety and scholarship to congregational ministry.   American rabbis are reported to have adjusted with relative ease to the role as now defined whereas British rabbis have experienced more acutely feelings of deprivation of status, income and authority.   The tendency in Britain to sustain traditional role definitions is partly accountable to the cultural origins of the British group in traditionalist communities in Europe.   Sharot further attributes this difference to the general abandonment of religion by the English middle class, a phenomenon which has no close parallel in the United States.

0751 Sharot, Stephen. "Instrumental and Expressive Élites in a Religious Organization." *Archives de Sciences Sociales des Religions* 43 (1977): 141-155.

Sharot adopts Etzioni's typology of the culture of religious organizations and applies this to that of the United Synagogue in London.   The case studied shows a synthesis of expressive and instrumental dimensions and provides an exception to Etzioni's rule.

0752 Shupe, Anson D. and Wood, James R. "Sources of Leadership Ideology in Dissident Clergy." *Sociological Analysis* 34 (1973): 185-201.

The dissonance of clergy and people, often as a function of the latter's conservation, is a frequent incidental theme of theoretical discussions of the relationships of sociology and theology (0858-0881). This article, however, offers an empirical study of that tension and suggests coping strategies to which dissident clergy resort; in particular, clergy look to theology and views of church polity in order to sustain commitments to social action in the face of lay opposition.

0753 Simpson, George Eaton. "The Rastafari Movement in Jamaica: A Study of Race and Class Conflict." *Social Forces* 34 (1955): 167-170.

Simpson makes an early study of a messianic cult burgeoning among the socially and economically disprivileged, and providing a case for the comparative study of movements that are more explicitly religious in belief and terminology.   Reprinted in Yinger (0070): 507-514.   See also Barrett (0545) and Kitzinger (0589).

0754   Spruit, Leo.   "Conceptions Ecclésiales et Modèles Pastoraux." *Social Compass*   20 (1983): 441-456.

Starting from the work of Johann Baptist Metz, the author operates and elaborates three ecclesial models: these are the popular church *(Volkskirche)*, the service-institution (bourgeois church) and the grassroots church *(Basiskirche)*.   These models provide a typology of pastoral practice, the empirical data for which are collected in the Netherlands.   See also Van Hemert (0762).

0755   Stark, Werner.   *The Sociology of Religion: A Study of Christendom*   4.   *Types of Religious Man.*   London: Routledge and Kegan Paul, 1969.

This is not, as might be expected, a typology of religiosity according to variables of belief and practice, but of roles and vocations.   So Stark treats of the founder of Christianity and his successors, of Saint, priest, prophet, monk and predicant. Examples studied are as diverse - in view of sociologists if not of the faithful - as St.Peter and Brigham Young.

0756   Sterk, J.G.M.   "Priesterbeeld en Godsdienstig-Kerkelijke Orientatie."   *Sociologische Gids*   15 (1968): 239-246.

After a background history and literature review of perceptions of the priesthood, the author explores the problem of its social status.   The profession of priest ranked low aside that of doctor, teacher in high school, company director and social worker, and the vocation was found to be unattractive to respondents in various Catholic groups surveyed.   The attitude shown towards priests as persons was, however, positive and they enjoyed a measure of respect apparently by the very virtue of their low status.

0757   Stryckman, Paul.   "Les Défis Occupationnels du Clergé." *Recherches Sociographiques*   19 (1978): 223-250.

This article is one of a series of studies undertaken both sides of the Atlantic and concerned with the consequences of a decline in vocations to the ministry.   This article reports extensive interviewing of Roman Catholic priests in Quebec.   Quantitative data are meticulously presented and it is suggested that the effect of decline is to bring about a systematic reappraisal of the professional role.

0758   Suaud, Charles.   "L'Imposition de la Vocation Sacerdotale." *Actes de la Recherche en Sciences Sociales*   3 (1975): 2-17.

This paper effectively demythologizes the notion of "vocation" as literally interpreted.   It is a study of recruitment to the Catholic priesthood in the Vendée region of France over the period 1920-1970.   While the sense of a call underlies the career choice of boys electing the Church, the most powerful determinants are social and economic.   In the extreme interpretation of the author's analysis, boys are inclined to the priesthood by the social and economic conditions of their families, which together with the recruiting agencies of the Church reinforce the boys' commitment.

0759   Towler, Robert.   "The Changing Status of the Ministry." *Crucible*, May 1968: 73-78.

This is an examination of the loss of social prestige and status by the English clergyman of the twentieth century attended by the shrinkage of the ministry and the role uncertainty of the clergy. Towler suggests three strategies for stabilizing the ministry: clergy could become efficient religious organizers and administrators, they could accept and become reconciled to their diminished and anomalous social status, or the full-time ministry could be run down and replaced by lay leadership. Reproduced in an amended form in Robertson (0049).   See also Towler (0760).

0760   Towler, Robert.   "Puritan and Antipuritan: Types of Vocation to the Ordained Ministry."   *A Sociological Yearbook of Religion in Britain*   2 (1969): 109-122.

This is a study based on the periodic interviewing of eighty ordinands in five Anglican theological colleges.   Two types of vocation emerge.   The puritan type is characterized by a high level of religious interest, a clearly defined faith and rigid beliefs, and a low level of aesthetic interest; Towler suggests that the puritan is a familiar type among Anglican ordinands. Less familiar is the antipuritan type, whose level of religious interest is not greatly above that of the population as a whole, who is flexible in belief and scores high in aesthetic interest. The two types account for about sixty per cent of Towler's sample.   See also Towler (0759).

0761   Traina, Frank J.   "Catholic Clergy on Abortion: Preliminary Findings of a New York State Survey."   *Family Planning Perspectives* 6 (1974): 151-156.

This reports a survey of a cross-section of Catholic clergy in New York State, the focus of which is the conformity of priests to the traditional teachings of the Church on the abortion issue. Results are broken down by age, education and other variables and it transpires that hospital chaplains are inclined to support the Church's position whereas greatest disagreements are found among the younger priests in the sample and those with the longest formal education.   One third of the sample had reservations of varying intensity over the Church's teaching on abortion.

0762   Van Hemert, Martien.   "La Pratique dans le Cadre des Modèles
Pastoraux."   *Social Compass*   30 (1983) : 457-475.

Three pastoral models elaborated by Leo Spruit (0754) are used
in four research enquiries conducted in Roman Catholic parishes
and reported here.   The enquiries were based on the initiation
rites of baptism, first communion and confirmation.   Interesting variable factors emerge and the author offers in conclusion
a typology for use in further work.

0763   Vázquez, Jesús María.   "Los Religiosos Españoles Hoy: Síntesis
de Conclusiones."   *Cuadernos de Realidades Sociales*   4 (1974):
133-159.

This offers a general sociological assessment of the religious
in contemporary Spain.   The article includes statistical data
on the number, morphology and demography of religious
institutions and their memberships, political relationships
with the Catholic hierarchy and the circumstances affecting a
defection from religious communities in the late 1960s.

0764   Verdonk, A.L.T.   "Réorientation ou Désintégration?   Une
Enquête Sociologique sur une Congrégation Religieuse Masculine
aux Pays-Bas."   *Social Compass*   18 (1971): 123-141.

Verdonk conducts an inquiry within a missionary religious order
in the Netherlands in 1967; the focus is upon members' orientations toward change or pattern maintenance.   It was
hypothesized that subjects' perspectives toward change would
vary according to age and their formal status within the order.
In the event, change orientation was found to be greater among
the younger respondents and among novices and status quo
orientation greater among the older respondents and those of
higher rank.

0765   Verryn, Trevor David.   "Anglican and Roman Catholic Priests
in South Africa."   *Social Compass*   19 (1972): 93-99.

Verryn reports a questionnaire survey conducted in 1970-1971
which covered a range of factors including church affiliation,
celibacy and social awareness.   The results give a familiar
picture of role uncertainty and lack of professional cohesion.

0766   Walker, Andrew G. and Atherton, James.   "An Easter
Pentecostal Convention: The Successful Management of a 'Time of
Blessing'."   *The Sociological Review*   19 (1971): 367-387.

Walker and Atherton report an observational study of a four-day
convention of pentecostals in the north of England.   They show
that there are recognized formulae for the conduct of such
occasions, adherence to which ensures that participation will
judge the occasion as successful.   While subjects perceived
the blessing to be an experience in God's control, stage
management is the focus of the sociologists who observe them.

0767   Webb, Sam C. and Hultgren, Dayton D.   "Differentiation of
Clergy Subgroups on the Basis of Vocational Interests." *Journal
for the Scientific Study of Religion* 12 (1973): 311-324.

Webb and Hultgren report and analyze a study of 3,617 Protestant
clergymen, grouped according to occupational expertise.
Findings show an association of such expertise with corresponding clergy roles and it is suggested that the basis of
differentiation used in this study be recognized by the
counselors of clergy.

0768   Weigert, Andrew J.   "An Emerging Intellectual Group Within
a Religious Organization: An Exploratory Study of Change."
Social Compass 18 (1971): 101-115.

The Society of Jesus represents a traditional order of a
relatively conservative kind within a changing Catholic Church.
The focus of this paper is the emergence of a new intellectual
grouping within the Jesuits and the author studies the psychological and organizational implications for the Order as a whole.
The author was formerly a member of the Order and he claims
his experience within it as "participant observation" and
"hundreds of informal interviews".

0769   White, Gavin.   "Ideals in Urban Mission: Episcopalians in
Twentieth-Century Glasgow." In *The Church in Town and Countryside*,
edited by Derek Baker, pp.441-448. Oxford: Blackwell, 1979.

In Scotland Episcopalians are a disestablished minority tending
toward Catholic theology and liturgy.   At the beginning of the
century they perceived missionary potential in the large city
of Glasgow but over the next forty years their zeal diminished.
This paper applies the benefit of hindsight to a reflection
upon strategies deployed.

0770   Wiebe, Paul D.   "Protestant Missions in India: A Sociological
Review." *Journal of Asian and African Studies* 5 (1970):293-301.

Wiebe conducts a literature review and analysis to interpret
the social system of India in a way that is almost geological,
with castes and sub-castes representing the strata and
differentially resisting the impact of Christianization by the
Protestant missions.   Success in recruitment has followed caste
lines, and this is to be expected on account of the powerful
economic and cultural cleavages which the caste system
represents.

0771   Wilson, Bryan R.   "The Pentecostalist Minister: Role Conflicts
and Contradictions of Status." *American Journal of Sociology* 64
(1959): 494-504.

One of the features of the partial denominalization of
pentecostal groups in Great Britain has been the acceptance of
permanent, paid ministers whose consequent guardianship of a
distinctively sectarian ethic has tended to conflict with their
own denominational tendencies.   This is a perceptive survey of

conflicts and contradictions of status peculiar to the role of the pentecostal minister.

0772 Wilson, Bryan R. "The Paul Report Examined." *Theology* 68 (1965): 89-103.

Wilson offers a sociological review of the Paul report of 1964 (0739) which highlights the limitations of the methods of investigation deployed and the inferences drawn from data. Wilson criticizes the report for treating "Anglicanism as if it were the only available religious affiliation in England" because the activities of other denominations inpinge in various ways, not recognized by Paul, on the operations of the Anglican clergy. He questions Paul's preoccupation with organization as the major factor of decline and expects the recommendations of the report, if implemented, to result in a lowering of clerical status and an increase in ecclesiastical bureaucracy.

0773 Wimberley, Ronald C.; Hood, Thomas C.; Lipsey, C.M.; Clelland, Donald A.; and Hay, Marguerite. "Conversion in a Billy Graham Crusade: Spontaneous Event or Ritual Performance?" *Sociological Quarterly* 16 (1975): 162-170.

This article discloses aspects of the dynamic and organization of Billy Graham revivalism that have become fairly well-known over the ten years since its publication but it survives as an instructive document.   In particular it makes an informed comment on the provenance of Dr.Graham's audience and shows how participation in the crusade functions to solidify existing religious allegiances.   There is an elaboration of the ritualization of conversion in the crusade.   See also Clellend et al. (0186) and Altheide (0776).

0774 Winter, Gibson. *The Suburban Captivity of the Churches: An Analysis of Protestant Responsibility in the Expanding Metropolis.* New York: Doubleday, 1961.

Gibson Winter's work as represented in this volume has been widely noticed and few general works in the sociology of religion fail to draw upon it.   It deals with the migration of the faithful from the urban center to the suburbs and their identification there with the middle class and its character-istic religious expressions.   A new religious style comes into being which has implications for congregational integrity, ministerial roles and missionary capacity.   However, intro-versionist sectarianism persists in its place and Winter notes the cases of the Negro churches and the ethnic churches. Whereas the church of the inner city is inclusive of its local population, the suburban church draws upon a nonresident community of the faithful and this difference is of fundamental significance.

Q. MEMBERSHIP; RECRUITMENT; SOCIALIZATION

0775 Ahtik, Miroslav. "Uticaj Religioznih Seoskih Pozodica U Srbiji na Formiranje Religioznith Uverenja kod Polomstva." *Sociologija Sela* 9 (1971): 31-32.

This is a study based in Serbia on the effect of the peasant family upon the religious beliefs of its young. Whereas many western investigations point to the primacy of the family as a socializing agency, this paper suggests that parents have little influence and that religious beliefs are formed in the context of the local community. The farm environment to which the author refers is, of course, a special phenomenon which perhaps does not have close parallels in the western world.

0776 Altheide, David L. and Johnson, John M. "Counting Souls: A Study of Evangelical Crusades." *Pacific Sociological Review* 20 (1977): 323-348.

Researchers attended a Billy Graham crusade in Phoenix, Arizona, and responded to his invitation to go forward to the platform. This enabled them to observe as participants the practice of the crusade counselors and the application of purposely trained skills in discerning the behavior of the respondent. The counselor operates a number of procedures and referrals according to contingency and the authors suggest that the arrangements for counseling accord with a bureaucratic model of organization. See also Clelland et al. (0186) and Wimberley et al. (0773).

0777 Archer, Antony. "Remaining in the State in Which God Has Called You: An Evangelical Revival." *Archives de Sciences Sociales des Religions* 40 (1975): 67-78.

A study of the Message Revival group which became active in the late 1960s in the Methodist Church in England. Archer analyzes the methods deployed and the message conveyed and finds close parallels with other Methodist revival movements.

0778 Babchuk, Nicholas and Crockett, Harry J. "Changes in Religious Affiliation and Family Stability." *Social Forces* 45 (1967): 551-555.

In a survey of married women support is found for the hypothetical stabilizing function of religious affiliation. Changes by married couples between denominations are usually to the affiliation of the better educated spouse.

0779 Barker, Eileen. *The Making of a Moonie: Brainwashing or Choice?* Oxford: Blackwell, 1984.

This is possibly the most thorough ethnological study of the Unification Church to date and represents extensive research by a wide range of empirical methods - observation, attendance of recruitment workshops, in-depth interviews and questionnaires. Dr. Barker's sensibilities are always sociological but she

proves herself theologically literate in analyzing belief
systems.   The problematic areas which are given special
attention in this work include the recalcitrance of some recruits,
methods of induction, social characteristics of converts, the
daily and family lives of Moonies, the effects of agencies of
socialization before recruitment and the themes which have been
or moral concern both in popular and in scientific reports of
Moonies, those of coercion and free will.

0780 Bibby, Reginald W. and Brinkerhoff, Merlin B. "Sources of
Religious Involvement: Issues for Future Empirical Investigation."
Review of Religious Research 15 (1974): 71-79.

The effect of this useful article is to broaden the focus of
the study of recruitment to religious organizations. In a
survey of over four hundred recruits to a number of churches in
Canada it is found that socialization is the major determinant
factor in recruitment; deprivation and the prospect of
compensation within sectarian religion, which together have
most occupied the attentions of sociologists, emerge from this
study as the least important.

0781 Billette, André. "Se Raconter une Histoire... Pour une
Analyse Revisée de la Conversion. *Social Compass* 23 (1976):
47-56.

This started as a piece of research on the phenomenon of
religious conversion based on the accounts of converts.   It
yields useful and cautionary insights on the method adopted,
stressing the retroactive dimension of autobiographical accounts
and verifying this by means of the analysis of speech patterns.
Accounts accord with received formulae for conversion narrative.
They are, the author suggests, not only reproductive but even
"productive".

0782 Blaikie, Norman W.H. "What Motivates Church Participation?
Review, Replication and Theoretical Reorientation in New Zealand."
Sociological Review 20 (1972): 39-58.

On the basis of a literature review and an interview survey of
householders in Christchurch, New Zealand, the author questions
the course taken by previous researchers into reasons for church
attendance.   He suggests that religious participation has been
understated as an expression of a world-view and overestimated
as a dimension of community identity.

0783 Bouma, Gary D. "Keeping the Faithful: Patterns of Membership Retention in the Christian Reformed Church." *Sociological
Analysis* 41 (1980): 259-264.

To the author at least, a conservative Calvinist denomination
is a relatively unattractive prospect in a modern world offering
many more congenial alternatives.   In a survey of members past
and present he finds that the principal factors for defection
are the C.R.C.'s reported intolerance and excessive demands
and constraints: those who stayed cited the truth for them

of conservative theology and worship and positive features of the church community.

0784 Carrier, Hervé. *Psycho-sociologie de l'Appartenance Religieuse*. Rome: Presses de l'Université Grégorienne, 1961.

Hervé Carrier unravels the various strands of the phenomenon of religious affiliation, of which he provides an empirical survey from the perspectives of sociology and social psychology.   He interprets religious belonging as an attitude related to behavior and examines the formation of this attitude through the individual's conversion, integration and religious instruction.   The differentation of the attitude is by means of types of socioreligious cohesion and communal participation. Carrier's work is useful not for the quantitative measures of religious belonging which he collects but for its careful attention to the rituals which mark the process of internalization.   Published in English as *The Sociology of Religious Belonging*. London: Darton, Longman & Todd, 1965.

0785 Davidson, James D. and Knudsen, Dean D. "A New Approach to Religious Commitment." *Sociological Focus* 10 (1977): 151-173.

The authors operate a definition of religious commitment that includes elements of both belief and participation and question some 570 fresher students with tendencies toward certain Protestant denominations.   They consider individual orientations in doctrine, determinants of religious commitment such as the affiliations of parents and, after Glock, the consequences of religious commitment such as participation in social and political organizations.

0786 Dericquebourg, Régis. "Les Témoins de Jehovah dans le Nord de la France: Implantation et Expansion." *Social Compass* 24 (1977): 71-82.

The mining basin in northern France has been the scene of remarkable success in recruiting within the Watch Tower movement, the appeal of which has been to French workers and, to an even greater extent, Polish migrants.   The social and cultural factors to which Dericquebourg relates this expansion include a legitimacy crisis in Catholicism, the inadequacy of political leadership, the non-fulfilment of economic aspirations and the possible identity of the Watch Tower movement as a surrogate motherland for émigré Poles.

0787 Fichter, Joseph H. "The Marginal Catholic: An Institutional Approach." *Social Forces* 32 (1953): 167-173.

Most typologies in the sociology of religion are developed at the level of organization: this basically descriptive paper - however interesting is its general applicability - is a contribution to the typology of religious participants. Reprinted in Yinger (0070):423-433.

0788 Filsinger, Erik E.; Faulkner, Joseph E.; and Warland, Rex H. "Empirical Taxonomy of Religious Individuals: An Investigation Among College Students." *Sociological Analysis* 40 (1979): 136-146.

A questionnaire is administered to 220 college students and responses are sorted to provide seven groups by type of religious individual, each group signifying a distinctive approach to religious belief and practice. The authors name the emergent types as Conservative, Culturally Religious, Marginally Religious, Modern Religious, Orthodox, Outsiders and Rejectors. As these names suggest the principle of conformity is dominant among the researchers' criteria of classification.

0789 Finney, John M. "A Theory of Religious Commitment." *Sociological Analysis* 39 (1978): 19-35.

Finney is interested in conformity to group norms and identifies five dimensions in the process of religious commitment. These are, in rank order, ritual practice, knowledge, experience, belief and devotional practice. This is tested in the course of a telephone survey with five hundred subjects which confirms the importance of the place of collective ritual behavior.

0790 Fukuyama, Yoshio. "The Major Dimensions of Church Membership." *Review of Religious Research* 2 (1961): 154-161.

The author reviews the literature with particular reference to the dimensions of religiosity elaborated by Glock (0122). He analyzes returns from some 4,095 Congregationalist respondents in terms of four religious orientations, (the cognitive, the cultic, the creedal (sic) and the devotional, thereby neglecting Glock's distinctive "consequential" dimension). Within each of these orientations respondents are rated as low, moderate and high and these ratings are related to other variables such as gender, age and socioeconomic status. While Fukuyama's purpose is to confirm the usefulness of the dimensions of religion he chooses to operate, there are other incidental findings that are worth attention. For example, only 28 per cent of his Congregationalist sample scored high on doctrinal conformity and this complements other studies of degrees of orthodoxy within various denominations (Bouma, 0783). Reprinted in William M.Newman with an editorial comment (0040): 19-28.

0791 Glock, Charles Y., ed. *Religion in Sociological Perspective: Essays in the Empirical Study of Religion.* Belmont, Ca.: Wadsworth, 1973.

Glock invites others to join him in a collection of papers on the process of religious affiliation and the dimensions of religious commitment with which Glock's name is usually associated. Further groups of papers concern the effects of religion, conformity and deviance among religious professionals, the origins and evolution of religious groups and the future of religion. It is an excellent and coherent set of papers; previous research is consolidated and new perspectives are also

explored.   Contributors include the editor, Rodney Stark,
Stephen Steinberg, John Lofland, Gary T.Marx and Armand L.Mauss.

0792 Glock, Charles Y.;   Ringer, Benjamin B.;   and Rabbie, Earl R.
To Comfort and to Challenge: A Dilemma of the Contemporary Church.
Berkeley: University of California Press, 1967.

This volume is the source of the "comfort thesis" in which it
is argued that church involvement is sought by marginal groups
as a refuge from dull and empty lives.   The authors argue that
this is affirmed by the preponderance in church life of the
elderly and the widowed and the relative absence of families.
Though the pattern is found to obtain in some constituencies,
Hobart adduces evidence of the involvement in denominational
life of the young and married and his paper constitutes a
challenge of the comfort thesis (0797).

0793 Goussidis, Alexandre.   "Analyse Statistique et Sociographique
des Ordinations deans l'Église de Grèce entre 1950 et 1969."
Social Compass 22 (1975): 197-147.

This analysis of the developing pattern of ordinations in the
Church of Greece between 1950 and 1969 is an endeavor to test
the hypothesis that the rate of ordinations is inversely related
to modernization, the latter being measured here by rural rather
than urban population settlement, lower educational levels and
greater age.   In confirmation of this hypothesis, it transpires
that ordinations are most frequent in the lower and less
educated classes.

0794 Harrison, Michael I.   "Preparation for Life in the Spirit:
The Process of Initial Commitment to a Religious Movement." *Urban
Life and Culture* 2 (1974): 387-414.

Harrison analyzes the elements of the management of initiation
among Catholic pentecostals and he points out a system of
immediate rewards and reinforcements legitimized in the appeal
to an absolute authority.   Baptism in the Spirit, recognized
to be manifest in the speaking in tongues, is regarded as the
proof of conversion.   Non-charismatics are often unaware of
this phenomenon and its significance.   Further, converts are
not required to sever friendships with non-converts or to
pursue an orientation that is dissonant with their wider social
milieu.   Catholic pentecostals are therefore of a different
type to converts in the traditional sects.   See also Harrison
(0795).

0795 Harrison, Michael I.   "Sources of Recruitment to Catholic
Pentecostalism." *Journal for the Scientific Study of Religion*
13 (1974): 49-64.

This article reports a questionnaire survey conducted among
Catholic prayer-groups in Michigan during the early period of
the growth of the charismatic movement within the Roman
Catholic Church.   It was found that those drawn into this
movement tended to be middle-class, young, often students and

that many clergy had become attracted.   See also Harrison
(0794).

0796 Himmelfarb, Harold S.   "Measuring Religious Involvement."
Social Forces   53 (1975): 606-618.

The author adumbrates inadequacies of existing schemes of
typifying religious involvement and offers what he regards to
be an improved typology comprising four dimensions; these are
the supernatural, the communal, the cultural and the interpersonal.   He explains and applies this typology in reference
to the research project in which it was developed, being a
study of the religious factor relating Chicago Jews to school
education.

0797 Hobart, Charles W.   "Church Involvement and the Comfort
Thesis in Alberta." *Journal for the Scientific Study of Religion*
13 (1974): 463-470.

The article reports themes of an extensive survey of leisure
activities of over 4,000 adults in Alberta, Canada.   The
findings are used to confute the thesis of Charles Y.Glock
et al. (0792) that church involvement offers a comfortable
activity and security for those whose secular lives are
disprivileged and that church participants are self-conscious
refugees.   Although Anglican, sect and cult members showed
higher levels of involvement among elderly/widowed groups than
in families, this tendency was not apparent in the
denominations.

0798 Homan, Roger and Youngman, Jane.   "School and Church as
Agencies of Religious Socialization." *British Journal of Religious
Education* 5 (1982): 22-27.

Children aged twelve in three schools in England were tested
for religious knowledge, orthodoxy of Christian belief and
frequency of contact with school or Sunday School.   The
partnership of home and church/Sunday School emerged as the
dominant socializing agency, with school making relatively
little impact on knowledge and belief.

0799 Ifeka-Møller, Caroline.   "White Power: Social-structural
Factors in Conversion to Christianity, Eastern Nigeria 1921-1926."
Revue Canadienne des Études Africaines 8 (1974): 55-72.

This article examines the hypothesis of "monolatry" developed
by Robin Horton and challenges this on the basis of evidence
from eastern Nigeria.   The author of this article rejects
intellectualist accounts and favors explanations that relate
rates of conversion to Christianity to contemporary economic
and social conditions.   The central palm-oil region of Nigeria
with strong trade links to Britain was significantly the region
in which the Christian missions achieved their greatest
successes.

0800   Jitodai, Ted T.   "Migrant Status and Church Attendance."
Social Forces   43 (1964): 241-248.

In a sample of over 3,000 respondents rates of church attendance
were compared for native residents on the one hand and migrants,
both urban and rural, on the other.   Differential attendance
behavior was thereby exposed and the author interprets the
higher rate of attendance among recent migrants to signify the
role of the urban church as a mechanism of integration and
settlement.

0801   Kanter, Rosabeth Moss.   "Commitment and Social Organization:
A Study of Commitment Mechanisms in Utopian Communities." *American
Sociological Review*   33 (1968): 499-517.

The author typifies three kinds of adhesion by which personalities are bound to social systems, each type having a
respective function in the consolidation and maintenance of
the community.   She then sets out the organizational strategies
deployed in American utopian communities to secure adhesion in
the long term.

0802   Kertzer, David I.   "Participation of Italian Communists in
Catholic Rituals: A Case Study." *Journal for the Scientific Study
of Religion*   14 (1975): 1-11.

In some parts of eastern Europe the Communist Party explicitly
regulates against the participation of its members in religious
rituals: a contrary model is current in Italy and elsewhere
and regards Communist activism and Catholic participation as
utterly compatible.   These being the theoretical models,
Kertzer undertook in 1971-1972 an empirical study in a working-
class district in the heartland of Italian communism, Bologna,
using methods of interview and participant observation at mass.
The conclusion is that neither of the simple models of exclusion
and synthesis is adequate for the situation observed in Bologna;
communists continue to look to the Catholic church for rites of
passage but in the sphere of community rituals such as festivals
the Church is giving way to the Party.

0803   Lopez de Ceballos, Paloma.   "Conversions à Singapour:
Contribution à une Sociologie de la Mutation Socio-religieuse."
Social Compass   23 (1976): 23-46.

The economic, social and cultural development of Singapore is
in many ways unique within the Asian world.   This article
reports research conducted there in 1966-1967 on the nature of
conversion to the Catholic Church.   Converts and conversions
are respectively analyzed.   The article is purported to be a
contribution to the sociology of socio-religious mutations.

0804   Mendz-Dominguez, Alfredo.   "Family Structure and Religious
Symbolization among Guatemalans." *Journal of Comparative Family
Studies*   5, ii (1974): 55-70.

Groups of Indian and non-Indian adolescents in Guatemala are sampled and tested on beliefs in God, the Devil and the Virgin Mary.   In the analysis their responses are related to the subjects' positions in their family structures.

0805 Mol, Hans, ed. *Identity and Religion: International Cross-cultural Approaches*. Beverly Hills: Sage Studies in International Sociology, 1978.

This is a collection of papers on identity and religious socialization, integration or pluralism, alienation and identity crisis, commitment and identity maintenance.   Each paper presents a different case arranged alphabetically; these are Australia, Canada, England, (West) Germany, Ghana, India, Indonesia, Netherlands, New Zealand, South Africa and the United States.

0806 Mol, Hans. "The Sacralization of the Family with Special Reference to Australia." *Journal of Comparative Family Studies* 5, ii (1974): 98-108.

The 1971 survey *Religion in Australia* (0956) demonstrated a relative independence of child and parent attendance patterns within religious organizations.   This prompts Mol to investigate the integration of religious phenomena within the family, covering the salience of religion during passage rites and in respect of divorce, mixed marriages, reproduction and so on. While focused upon the Australian situation this article takes account also of India, China and ancient Rome.

0807 Muller, Jean-Claude. "Old Wine in New Wineskins: Tradition-alists and Christians among the Rukuba." *Archives de Sciences Sociales des Religions* 38 (1974): 49-62.

A study based in Rukuba, Nigeria, where converts to Christian-ity co-exist with adherents of the traditional religions, both groups having ideological reasons legitimized in traditional dogma for their religious affiliation.   Muller investigates perceptions of one group by the other and converts' own justifications of their apostasy.   In the light of findings the author discusses a theory of conversion in West Africa advanced by Horton.

0808 Munters, Quirinus J. "Recruitment as a Vocation: The Case of Jehovah's Witnesses." *Sociologia Neerlandica* 7 (1971): 88-100.

WatchTower evangelism is a systematic and effective enterprise involving high-level organization and the heavy commitment of time by its functionaries.   It is as a sophisticated managerial structure that the author treats his subject.   He examines missionary goals and missionary motives.   After an examination of the expansion of Jehovah's Witnesses as a proletarian movement, the author closely studies strategies of recruitment.   Reporting a survey conducted in Utrecht, converts are characterized by sex, age, marital status,

occupational group and birthplace: it transpires that the average
recruit is middle-aged and is newly resident in Utrecht.
However, the author observes a wide discrepancy between the
actual recruitment level of Jehovah's Witnesses and·that which
they express as the ideal.   See also Munters (0809).

0809 Munters, Quirinus J.   "Recrutement et Candidats en Puissance."
Social Compass 24 (1977): 59-69.

The research reported and analyzed in this article was conducted
among Jehovah's Witnesses in the Netherlands.   Its particular
concern is the duty of recruitment, for the effective exercise
of which Witnesses discern potential candidates for admission
from those who show little promise.   Munters investigates
particularly the class of "promising outsiders".   See also
Munters (0808).

0810 Nash, Dennison.   "A Little Child Shall Lead Them: A
Statistical Test of an Hypothesis that Children Were the Source of
the American 'Religious Revival'." *Journal for the Scientific Study
of Religion* 7 (1968): 238-240.

Nash gives a quantitative analysis of the enlargement of the
American churches in the period since 1950.   It is found that
the presence of children and activities for children is the
factor which inclines parents to join churches and that Sunday
Schools and comparable institutions have had a major effect upon
the American "religious revival" in this period.

0811 Neal, Marie Augusta.   "Women in Religion: A Sociological
Perspective." *Sociological Inquiry* 45 (1975): 33-39.

Women in sociology have with notable exceptions tended in recent
years to occupy themselves in women's studies.   As a consequence
they are underrepresented in the sociology of religion.   Although
the issue of the ordination of women is live in many mainstream
churches, it has been neglected as a subject of sociological
import.   This article is therefore an object with some rarity
value.   It is much concerned with proportions of representation
in various spheres of church life.

0812 Nelsen, Hart M.   "Religious Transmission Versus Religious
Formation: Pre-adolescent-Parent Interaction." *Sociological
Quarterly* 21 (1980): 207-218.

The study of political socialization is widely informed by studies
of the role of parents.   Not so the study of religious socialization and this paper is therefore a useful contribution.
Nelsen's survey covered 2,724 Minnesota adolescents and confirmed
the expectation that in pre-adolescence there is a strong
correlation between the religious orientations of the young and
that of their parents.   A more interesting investigation might
have covered the older age group in which the relative
independence of leisure time activity might correlate with dis-
sociative religious orientations.

0813 Newport, Frank. "The Religious Switcher in the United States."
American Sociological Review 44 (1979): 528-552.

This instructive paper takes in a comprehensive range of religious
organizations in America and examines movement between them and in
and out of them.   The Baptist and Roman Catholic Churches are
among those to suffer losses by defection and both high and low
status denominations enjoy gains at their expense.   The
incidence of defection is higher in youth than in middle and old
age.   Factors inclining individuals to switch allegiance include
gravitation to religious communities of like socioeconomic status
and to the allegiance of husbands and wives.

0814 O'Connell, John J.   "The Integration and Alienation of
Religions to Religious Orders." *Social Compass* 18 (1971): 65-84.

Studies of religious orders as bureaucratic organizations have
been preoccupied with the relationship of individual and
community, often negatively defined in terms of alienation.
O'Connell argues that system maintenance, of which he recognizes
the importance, does not reside in the alienation of the
individual, or in the inhibition of personal development.

0815 Pickering, William S.F. "Who Goes to Church?" In *The Social
Sciences and the Churches* edited by C.L.Mitton, pp.181-197.
Edinburgh: T. and T.Clark, 1972 (0875).

Pickering asks this simple question in respect of religion in
England and finds that the answer is not straightforward.
The evidence of research is fragmentary although the prevailing
view in 1972 was that churches were attended by one person in
ten.   The individual least likely to attend church, it is
suggested, is a male between twenty-five and forty-five years
of age who is of unskilled occupation and lives in a large urban
area such as London or Birmingham.

0816 Scott, William A. *Values and Organizations: A Study of
Fraternities and Sororities.* Chicago: Rand McNally, 1965.

This is a study of the individual within a social group and of
the functions performed by the values held by both.   Twelve
measures of values were tested on a constituency of students at
the University of Colorado, who were pledged to ten sororities
and fraternities.   By comparative study with a non-pledging
control group, an attempt was made to distinguish the values
that differentiated fraternity and non-fraternity members and
those which signified successful membership.   In this way
fraternities and sororities are analyzed as agencies of
socialization and the study provides an insight of moral
development to complement that of Piaget et alia.

0817 Shaffir, William. "The Recruitment of *Baalei Tshuvah* in
a Jerusalem Yeshiva." *Jewish Journal of Sociology* 25 (1983):
33-46.

In the context of a widespread concern that many secular Jews
are attracted to non-Jewish sects, the author evaluates the
endeavor of Jerusalem rabbis to secure the fidelity of those
who briefly visit from overseas.   In most cases their
influence is short-lived and few of the young men to whom they
appeal sustain orthodox belief and practice.

0818   Shapiro, Howard M. and Dashefsky, Arnold.   "Religious
Education and Ethnic Identification: Implications for Ethnic
Pluralism."   *Review of Religious Research*   15 (1974): 93-102.

The study was conducted by questionnaire survey of Jewish males
in Minnesota.   The effect of Jewish education is found to be
slight but durable in the determination of ethnic identity,
other primary and secondary agencies of religious socialization
notwithstanding.   It is found that secular education in adult
life only reinforces the ethnic identity derived from prior
Jewish education.

0819   Thomas, L.Eugene.   "Generational Discontinuity in Beliefs:
An Exploration of the Generation Gap."   *Journal of Social Issues*
30, 3 (1974): 1-22.

The author is concerned with cross-generational differences
on measures of beliefs, attitudes and value orientations.
He draws from the literature of political socialization to
show higher agreements between parents and children on
partisan attitudes than on value orientations.   Conclusions
about generation gaps depend on whether the evidence relates
to attitudes or value orientations.

0820   Van Kemenade, J.A.   "Typen van Religieus-Kerkelijke
Binding."   *Sociologische Gids*   15 (1968): 222-250.

This is a typology of religious bonds between individuals and
churches.   The author opens up dimensions of such bonds of
which research inquiries should take account in addition to
the favored line of inquiry respecting attendance.   Devotion
and subscription to a church's beliefs and values are also
relevant variables to the strength of individual allegiance.
A project measuring acceptance at several levels including
hierarchy and rules was conducted with a Catholic sample in
1968 and it is cited in detail to illustrate the dimensionality
of religious bonds.

0821   Wallis, Roy.   "Recruiting Christian Manpower."   *Society*   15
(1978): 72-74.

The new religious movements and their antecedents have engaged
lively popular interest and controversy and sociologists have
sometimes preferred to restrict their researches to innocuous
themes.   Not so Roy Wallis, however, who in this useful
contribution touches upon the use of sexual enticement as a
strategy of recruitment to the Children of God whose
organization is communal.

0822 Wieting, Stephen G. "An Examination of Integenerational
Patterns of Religious Belief and Practice." *Sociological Analysis*
36 (1975): 137-149.

The correlation of religious behavior and belief between parents
and children is here assessed for a number of key variables.
Children showed a pronounced disaffection from the religious
organization of their parents but there were relative
continuities in belief and in the interpretation of religious
symbols.

0823 Wieting, Stephen G. "Measuring Integenerational Religious
Behavior Patterns: A Comment on Alternative Representational
Strategies." *Review of Religious Research* 16 (1975): 111-123.

The author investigates general confusion in the scientific
study of religious behavior and diagnoses a lack of conceptual
clarity at the empirical level. He elaborates and considers
four representational theories as the basis of such study:
these are structuralism, psychometric theory, phenomenology
and ethnoscience.

0824 Zimmerman, Carle C. "Family Influence upon Religion."
Journal of Comparative Family Studies 5, 2 (1974): 1-16.

This is a useful attempt to rectify the dearth of socialization
studies available to sociologists of religion.   The approach is
theoretical rather than empirical and it is not Zimmerman's
purpose to measure the effectiveness of the family in the
orientation of its children.   Rather he surveys the role of the
family as a socializing agency and a sanctified network of
relationships as variously conceived within the major religious
traditions of the world.   There are conflicts of allegiance to
family and religious tradition and both institutions undergo
strain in the modern world.

R.   LITURGY AND RITUAL

0825 Andrieux, Francis. "L'Image de la Mort dans les Liturgies des
Églises Protestantes." *Archives de Sciences Sociales des Religions*
39 (1975): 119-126.

Factors affecting transformations in the religious representation
of death include theological ones, such as a recent emphasis upon
resurrection, and psychological, such as an emphasis upon
comfort for the living derived from the science of the caring
profession.   Andrieux finds expressions of these shifts in
Protestant liturgies recently devised or revised for funeral
purposes.   He observes an adaptation of the significance
attached by the Church to death to that attached to it by
contemporary society.

0826 Billington, Raymond J. *The Liturgical Movement and Methodism*.
London: Epworth, 1969.

The liturgical movement of recent decades has affected many
Christian denominations; Billington's essay takes stock of change
and looks at implications for English Methodism.   The expressed
desirability of "relevance" in modern worship, for example, has
palpably sociological implications both in the engagement of
"the world" and in the ecumenical alignment of the religious
practice of Methodism to that of other Christian denominations.

0827 Bloch, Maurice. "Symbols, Song, Dance and Features of
Articulation: Is Religion an Extreme Form of Traditional Authority?"
Archives Européennes de Sociologie 15 (1974): 53-81.

This is a linguistic analysis of utterances pronounced over the
religious ritual of circumcision among the Merina of Madagascar.
The style is characterized as formal and related to political
discourse.   The author draws upon Weber's typology of authority
to typify the conduct of the religious functionaries.

0828 Centre Régional d'Études Socio-religieuses. "Sermon ou
Homélie: Le Fonction de la Prédication." *Social Compass* 27
(1980): 363-373.

The study reports and analyzes some twenty-seven addresses
delivered in the area of Lille, France. The purpose of the
research was to investigate the place of preaching, and it is
found that this activity has a stronger association with the
ethical dimension than with the doctrinal or ritual.   The
preference of preachers for the term "homily" rather than
"sermon" reflects a shift from a didactic approach to an
inductive.   See also Dassetto (0829) and Rousseau and
Dassetto (0846).

0829 Dassetto, Felice. "La Production Homilétique Catholique."
Social Compass 27 (1980): 375-396.

A discussion of the ambiguities involved in the production of
the sermon.   The process is bound on one hand by orthodox
standards and on the other by the needs and demands of
potential audiences.   The author is interested also in the
use of the vocabulary of Judaism within the Catholic liturgy.
See also Centre Régional d'Études Socio-religieuses (0828)
and Rousseau and Dassetto (0846).

0830 Deshen, Shlomo A. "Ethnicity and Citizenship in the Ritual
of an Israeli Synagogue." *Southwestern Journal of Anthropology*
28 (1972): 69-82.

The study is based in an ethnic synagogue in Israel to which
some sixty families have recently migrated from north Africa.
The arrival of this contingent has implications for the tension
that exists between the celebration of ethnic identity and of
Israeli citizenship.   In the ritual new symbols are introduced

to express ethnicity while old symbols are translated or adapted to new emphases.   See also Deshen (0647).

0831   Fenn, Richard K. *Liturgies and Trials: The Secularization of Religious Language.* Oxford: Blackwell, 1982.

The concerns of this book range from the political context of liturgical change and its relationship to secularization on the one hand to an analysis of speech-acts in sacred and secular settings on the other.   The author distinguishes "eventful" speech observable in liturgy and "uneventful" speech typified in seminar discourse.   The thrust of this book is to demonstrate and elaborate the tension between what the author calls liturgical spirit and the literalism of the law.

0832   Flanagan, Kieran.   "Competitive Assemblies of God: Lies and Mistakes in Liturgy." *Research Bulletin* of the Institute for the Study of Worship and Religious Architecture (University of Birmingham, England)   (1981): 20-69.

The outcome of liturgical reform has been a gaggle of competitive assemblies seeking less to change the world than to cope with their liturgical rivals in the same church.   Pluralism of liturgical reform has evolved into a democratic virtue.   But this plurality has eroded the central worshipping identity of church membership.   Increasingly people "shop around" for a form of service that meets individual needs of age, gender, orthodoxy and non-orthodoxy.   Compartmentalized by simple or complex styles of liturgy and taste, rites also vary in their affirmation of vertical or horizontal dimensions of encounters with the sacred.   This pattern of diversity and conflict is explored in the light of Vatican II and there is a careful analysis of the regulation of liturgical lies and deceptions with reference to the Roman Catholic Church.   As ever with Dr. Flanagan's work, the footnotes are extensive and highly readable in themselves.

0833   Flanagan, Kieran.   "Liturgy, Ambiguity and Silence: The Ritual Management of Real Absence." *British Journal of Sociology*   36 (1985): 193-223.

This is a substantial sociological analysis of aspects of liturgy with particular study of the place and use of silence in the ritual act.   The author draws attention to certain convenient ambiguities which are manageable if apprehended at the level of the numinous but problematic if registered within the domain of social reality.   He introduces and explains the notion of the "apophatic" as an essential concept in the understanding of liturgy.

0834   Hamnett, Ian.   "Idolatry and Docetism."   In *Liturgy and Change,* edited by Denise Newton, pp.21-37.   University of Birmingham: Centre for the Study of Worship and Religious Architecture, 1983.

The author proceeds to a sceptical and minimalist assessment
of the place of sociology in Christian religious practice. He
argues that the Christian religion, if not other religions, rules
out the formal theory of ritual or liturgy as idolatrous.
While "idolatry" in such a sense besets the Catholic tradition,
the Reformed falls into the heresy of Docetism.

0835 Hesser, Garry, and Weigert, Andrew J. "Comparative Dimensions
of Liturgy: A Conceptual Framework and Feasibility Application."
Sociological Analysis 41 (1980): 215-229.

An exploratory endeavor to develop and test (on fifty-one diverse
congregations) single instruments for the collection of data.
Factor analysis yielded empiricist groupings - High Church, urban
black, pentecostal, etc. - and selected social variables were
related to language, dress, gestures and so on.

0836 Homan, Roger. "Church Membership and the Liturgy." *Faith and
Worship* 9 (1980): 19-24.

This reports a survey of electoral roll memberships in 1975 and
1980 in the archdeaconry of Chichester, England. It was found
that parishes changing to the modern liturgy "Series 3" during
that period suffered the greatest net losses (-14.9 per cent)
whereas those which maintained a traditional liturgy throughout
the period enjoyed net increases (+3.7 per cent in parishes
using the Book of Common Prayer and +19.4 per cent in parishes
adhering to "Series 2").

0837 Homan, Roger. "Liturgical Change and the Clerisy in Crisis."
Faith and Worship 13 (1982): 10-17.

The encounter of professionals and laity within the Church of
England is characterized within four types of zone - the "altar",
"pulpit", "vestry" and "vicarage".   Each of these zones provides
sanctuary for the clergy in moments of crisis, as do dimensions
of the clerical hegemony, providing institutionalized
opportunities for assertion, dominance and mystification.

0838 Isambert, François André. "Les Transformations du Rituel
Catholique des Mourants." *Archives de Sciences Sociales des
Religions* 39 (1975): 89-100.

This paper is concerned with the introduction of new rites for
the dying to succeed those that have stood in the Catholic Church
since 1914.   Among other changes, the name "Extreme Unction" is
replaced by "Unction for the Sick".   The change of name
signifies a change of emphasis.   Isambert speculates upon this
shift and asks whether the Catholic Church is desacralizing
death and sacramentalizing sickness.   The issue is discussed in
respect of cultural correlates in the secular world.

0839 Lawson, E.Thomas. "Ritual as Language." *Religion* 6 (1976):
123-139.

This is a highly analytical and theoretical paper which is an endeavor to develop an explanatory interpretation of religious ritual.   The particular example detailed by way of illustration is that of baptism in the Episcopal Church of the United States.

0840   Lazar, Morty M.   "The Role of Women in Synagogue Ritual in Canadian Conservative Congregations." *Jewish Journal of Sociology* 20 (1978): 165-171.

The author adduces evidence of differentials in ritual particip-ation between gender groups after the Bar Mitzvah ceremony.   Of the available explanations for this, one of the most plausible, it is suggested, is that there is a residue of the Orthodox belief that women are unclean during menstruation and this has implications for participation in the ritual.   This and other possibilities are discussed in this article.

0841   MacAloon, John J. ed. *Rite, Drama, Festival, Spectacle: Rehearsals Toward a Theory of Cultural Performance*. Oxford: Clio, 1984.

Based on the belief that cultural performances are "more than entertainment, didactic formulations, or cathartic indulgences", this collection examines performance events with an eye to their cross-cultural significance.   Victor Turner's concept of "social drama" as well as the contributions of Dell Hymes, Milton Singer, Kenneth Burke and Erving Goffman are here applied to a wide variety of forms and events, ranging from exorcisms to stage plays and from carnivals to athletic competitions.

0842   Martin, David. *The Breaking of the Image: A Sociology of Christian Theory and Practice*. Oxford: Blackwell, 1980.

This is a sociological study of Christian symbolism, particularly of that which is important in Christian worship and derives from its meaning in the secular world an essential and significant ambiguity.   Professor Martin treats of communion and communicat-ion, of the symbols of blood and brotherhood, of profane habit and sacred usage.

0843   "The Negation of Holy Charity: A Parochial Case Study." *Faith and Worship* 18 (1985): 8-16.

Machiavellian tactics are not expected to be found in the conduct of church government at local level: it is supposed that Christians will have scruples about such things.   However, this very precise documentary study of parish management in the matter of choosing liturgical forms to be used in worship evidences practice on the part of the clergy quite as sharp as what might be found in the secular world.   In taking on board modern managerial skills the Church adjusts to an autocratic style in the guise of democracy and consultation.   Although the laity have rights in the matter of liturgy which are enshrined in the statutes of the Church of England, the evidence here is that these rights are in practice ignored.

0844 Remy, Jean; Servais, Émile; and Hiernaux, Pierre. "Formes Liturgiques et Symboliques Sociales." *Social Compass* 22 (1975): 175-192.

This is an analysis of liturgical forms in a context of social symbols and social realities. The development of technological society is a model and a factor in the evolution of liturgical forms, on the way in which ministers are established and upon the religious organization.

0845 Riegelhaupt, Joyce F. "Festas and Padres: The Organization of Religious Action in a Portuguese Parish." *American Anthropologist* 75 (1973): 835-850.

The *festa* is a social as well as a religious phenomenon and this article examines its social and religious significance from the eighteenth century up to the present day. It is seen as a territorial rite and its celebration has to do with the dynamics of the Portuguese village, while within the religious domain it contributes to a tension between the clergy and the laity on what religion is about.

0846 Rousseau, André and Dassetto, Felice. "Discours Religieux et Métamorphose des Pratiques Sociales." *Social Compass* 20 (1973): 389-403.

Here is a sociological analysis of the sermon as delivered in the Catholic liturgy. It is studied as an utterance that conforms to certain concrete conditions including the speech-community to which it is addressed and the legitimacy enjoyed by the preacher. See also Centre Régional d'Études Socio-religieuses (0828) and Dassetto (0829).

0847 Segalen, Martine. "Rituels Funéraires en Normandie et Attitudes vis-à-vis de la Mort." *Archives de Sciences Sociales des Religions* 39 (1975): 79-88.

The case studied is a highly developed cult of the dead in Normandy, France, in the Eure district of which the ritualiz-ation of death survives under the custody of Confraternities of Charity which have responsibilities for burial.

0848 Volpe, Rainer. "La Liturgie en tant que Comportement Social: Réflexions en Vue de l'Élaboration de Méthodes Empiriques de Recherches." *Social Compass* 22 (1975): 157-174.

This is an analysis of the problems arising from endeavors to improve the effectiveness of the liturgy. The author notes that new liturgies are increasingly verbal and deficient in participation and meditation. Further, the effect of a new emphasis upon the communal character of the mass is to marginalize small groups not embraced by prescriptive formulae.

0849 Wilmeth, Marlyn Walton and Wilmeth, J. Richard. "Theatrical
Elements in Voodoo: The Case for Diffusion." *Journal for the
Scientific Study of Religion* 16 (1976): 27-37.

This article treats of syncretistic features of voodoo and creole
religions and the theatrical elements of voodoo rituals
including the use of props and costumes. Voodoo is considered
both in its African context and in respect of its manifestations
elsewhere in the world.

0850 Wilson, Stephen. "Religious and Social Attutudes in *Hymns
Ancient and Modern*." *Social Compass* 22 (1975): 211-236.

The object of analysis is a hymnal published in 1889 and much
used in the Church of England. The article contributes to the
sociology of liturgy and explores, for example, the function of
religion as legitimation of an existing social order. The
author finds that against a background of contemporary hymnody,
"A and M" represents a departure for moderation: it sanctions
war and signifies a defensive position against secularization,
but the hymns present a loving God and adopt a less threatening
and more conciliatory attitude toward the individual.

S. ECUMENISM

0851 Bryman, Alan and Hinings, C. Robin. "Participation, Reform
and Ecumenism: The Views of Laity and Clergy." *A Sociological
Yearbook of Religion in Britain* 7 (1974): 13-25.

This is a survey of lay and clerical opinion in the Church of
England, the results of which are more interesting for what
they reveal about participation. For all that the laity in
the sample were constitutionally involved in church government,
their participation in decisions over ecumenical schemes is
marginal. There is an alignment of clerical opinion on church
reform and organization with the official view of the Church;
the laity is comparatively conservative but powerless, contrary
to the spirit of corporate ministry and synodical government.

0852 Clark, David B. *Survey of Anglicans and Methodists in Four
Towns*. London: Epworth Press and Church Information Office, 1965.

The four English towns in which Anglicans and Methodists were
surveyed were Bromley, Trowbridge, Ellesmere Port and Rugby.
There was operated a battery of questions on social attitudes
and views about the church. Subjects were asked their views
on sporting activities on a Sunday, on dancing in church, on
total abstinence, on the place of laypersons in worship and so
on. Overall results disguise local differences: for example,
7 per cent of Ellesmere Port Anglicans approved the regular
preaching of laypersons, against 26 per cent of those in Bromley.
There were marked general agreements between Anglicans and
Methodists on social, political and educational aspects of the
minister's role but the major disagreements, which were to be

taken as impediments to Anglican-Methodist unity, included the place of Holy Communion and proximity to the Roman Catholic church. See also Clark (0884) and Clark (0917).

0853 Gephart, Jerry C.; Siegel, Martin A.; and Fletcher, James E. "A Note on Liberalism and Alienation in Jewish Life." *Jewish Social Studies* 36 (1974): 327-329.

It is often in the face of conflict and domination that disparate religious traditions are brought to lesser or greater reconcil- iation.   This short paper points to the Jewish community of Salt Lake City, the theological divisions of which were subordinated in the cause of a union of the Reform and Conservative synagogues. See also Greenberg et al. (0854).

0854 Greenberg, Irving; Kaplan, Mordechai M.; Petuchowski, Jakob J.; and Siegel, Seymour. "Toward Jewish Unity: A Symposium." In *The Ghetto and Beyond: Essays on Jewish Life in America,* edited by Peter Rose, pp. 150-172. New York: Random House, 1969.

Judaism in America is heterogeneous. There are separate conservative and liberal traditions, the adherents of which are often subject to taboos upon social and personal relations with each other.   Transcending these practical arrangements, however, there is a common commitment to the people of Israel, albeit expressed in different forms and degrees.   Each of the four contributors to this symposium attempts to assess the movement toward a united American Judaism on the evidence of past experience and in the light of present circumstances.   See also Gephart et al. (0853).

0855 Mantzaridis, George. "La Naissance du Dogme Relatif à l'Unité de l'Église." *Social Compass* 22 (1975): 19-32.

A notional sociology of Christian dogma is provided by Weber and Troeltsch and provides the starting point of this article.   The regulatory process of Church unity is seen to develop through the study of the functions of the ecclesiastical cult and of notions of the alliance of Church and episcopacy.

0856 Turner, Bryan S. "The Sociological Explanation of Ecumenicalism."   In *The Social Sciences and the Churches,* edited by C.L.Mitton, pp.233-245. Edinburgh: T. and T. Clark, 1972 (0875).

Turner considers ecumenicalism at various levels and endeavors to offer an explanation.   He submits that secularization, bureaucratization and homogenization are sufficient conditions for what Berger has called "friendly collaboration" but not for amalgamation.   This essay was originally published in *The Expository Times* and makes particular reference to Methodism.

0857 West, M.E. "Independence and Unity: Problems of Cooperation between Independent Church Leaders in Soweto." *African Studies* 33 (1974): 121-129.

The protestant churches in South Africa are highly fissiparous and there are some three thousand church organizations in all. Leadership is normally charismatic and often competitive and so the relationships between leaders are the key to union as well as to division.   West makes a particular study of the largest organization remaining intact, the African Independent Churches' Association, and he analyzes bids for its leadership in the period of five years before 1974.   The discussion is set within the context of the social and political divisions of South Africa and of the tensions between races.

T.   SOCIOLOGY AND THEOLOGY

0858   Bruce, Steve.   "A Sociological Account of Liberal Protestant-ism." *Religious Studies* 20 (1984): 401-415.

This is an interpretation of the rise of liberalism and the response to it of the protestant churches in the west. Particular themes occupying the author include the self-images of the sects and denominations and sociability.   The chronology of liberal protestantism is traced to its fall.

0859   Comblin, José.   *The Church and the National Security State.* New York: Orbis, 1979.

This is an analysis of the insecurity of the state in the countries of Latin America and of the role of the Catholic Church in those conditions.   At one level this is what is dubbed "liberation theology": at another, it demonstrates the integration of sociological insight with moral and theological awareness, as though *sociologie religieuse* went into a tunnel in the 1960s and has now come out in a new light.

0860   Compton, H.   "Limitations of the Sociological Approach." In *Sociology, Theology and Conflict,* edited by D.E.H.Whiteley and R.Martin, pp.153-167.   Oxford: Blackwell, 1969 (0880).

This paper concludes a compilation of varied contributions on the common concerns and applications of theology and sociology. Compton's tailpiece conveys a challenge for the sociologist in that he points to the inadequacies of sociology as an explanatory model and its tendency to be exclusive of other disciplines.

0861   Friedrichs, Robert W.   "Social Research and Theology: End of the Detente." *Review of Religious Research* 15 (1974): 113-127.

After generations of concord between theology and the social and behavioral sciences, the author observes with concern the threat to peace constituted by B.H.Skinner's critique of the place of religion in society and the publication of the Humanist Manifesto.   He affirms the importance of scientific

inquiry.   In the years that have elapsed since Friedrichs
took fright, however, there has been a normalization of the
relationship and in retrospect his anxiety looks like undue
panic.

0862 Gill, Robin. *The Social Context of Theology: A Methodological
Enquiry.* London: Mowbray, 1975.

Gill's is an important work which prepares for a relationship
between theology and sociology that is more mutually informed
than hitherto.   He urges sociologists of religion to study
theological content more closely and reminds theologians of
the empirical basis of much of their work, to which sociology
can make a pertinent contribution.

0863 Gill, Robin. *Theology and Social Structure.* London:
Mowbray, 1977.

Dr. Gill uses insights from the sociology of knowledge to
suggest dimensions of the interaction of theology and society.
Cases examined include Christian attitudes to war and to
abortion and the reaction in its day to John Robinson's *Honest
to God.* And the book goes on to explore the contribution of
sociological methods to the conduct of applied theology.

0864 Gill, Robin. "British Theology as a Sociological Variable."
A Sociological Yearbook of Religion in Britain 7 (1974): 1-12.

The author proposes three models for a development of common
enterprise in areas of shared concern between theologians and
sociologists.

1.   A sociology of theological positions involving the examination
of theologians and the effect upon them of social realities.

2.   A sociology of the theological situation with the emphasis
here upon the discipline rather than the exponents.

3.   Theological positions as a sociological variable, looking
for example at the social functions of a particular theology.

These provide for theology and theologians to be taken seriously
by sociologists and Gill attempts to do so forthwith by case
studies of Bishop Robinson's controversial *Honest to God* and
the scheme for unity between the Church of England and the
Methodist Church.

0865 Goddijn, H.P.M. and Goddijn, Walter. *Sociologie van Kerk en
Godsdienst.* Utrecht: Aula, 1966.

The brothers Goddijn address fundamental questions on the nature
of the sociology of religion before pursuing more specific problems
which have both sociological and theological dimensions.   These
include vocation to the ministry, institutional religion, the
relationship of theology to the social sciences, religious
pluralism and ecumenism.

0866   Homan, Roger. "Sociology and the Questionable Truth."   In
No Alternative: The Prayer Book Controversy, edited by David
Martin and Peter Mullen, pp.183-190. Oxford: Blackwell, 1981.

   This article is an assessment of the legitimacy of sociological
   methods with particular reference to their deployment
   concerning liturgical reform in the Church of England.   The
   paper engages problems in opinion polling and argues that
   research can be scientific and its results valid even where
   the investigators have prior expectations and expressed
   commitments.   Attention is drawn to a tendency among religious
   professionals to discredit sociology and to regard
   propositions as verifiable only from a position of theological
   insight: it is argued in response that the sociological
   analysis of liturgical change is a legitimate enterprise and
   that opinion polling is invariably a more scientific instrument
   than personal testimony.   See also Homan (0867).

0867 Homan, Roger. "Theology and Sociology: A Plea for Sociological
Freedom." *Theology* 84 (1981): 428-439.

   The paper reviews a generally suspicious disposition of churchmen
   to sociologists but derives some hope of a co-operative relationship from the writings of theologians including Karl Rahner
   and Hans Küng.   The sociologist, it is suggested, has a
   responsibility both to monitor a range of social transactions
   within the Church and to demystify when sacred definitions of
   such transactions have been proposed.   This responsibility is
   effectively discharged only when sociologists themselves are
   allowed to prescribe the research agenda.   See also Homan
   (0866).

0868   Jackson, M.J. *The Sociology of Religion: Theory and
Practice*. London: Batsford, 1974.

   In outward form and structure, this book has the appearance of a
   conventional introduction to the sociological study of religion
   and to some extent it fulfils that purpose; it treats of methods,
   church attendances, secularization and other items on the
   standard agenda.   But the author's desk is quite clearly in a
   vicarage rather than a college.   He always points out the
   limitations of sociological method and insight and is compelled
   by the standpoint associated with Boulard: sociology must serve
   religious endeavor rather than control it.   In Canon Jackson's
   concluding words, "The sociology of religion in the service of the
   church is an instrument, but only one instrument, to make clear
   the paths of the Lord."

0869   Kelley, Dean M. *Why Conservative Churches Are Growing: A
Study in Sociology of Religion*. New York: Harper and Row, 1972.

   Throughout the period 1800-1960 the major American churches and
   denominations increased in size, but in the 1960s at least ten
   of them began to diminish.   Kelley measures and explores this
   decline and at the same time observes numerical growth in the
   conservative churches and the weakness of ecumenical religion

for which he offers little encouragement.   His evidence is
sociological but his conclusions against liberalism are from the
standpoint of "those who are serious about their faith".
Following groundswell reaction there appeared a new fortified
edition in 1977.

0870   Laeyendecker, Leonardo.   "Theologische Veranderingen,
Sociologische Beschouwd." *Sociologische Gids* 15 (1968): 247-259.

Laeyendecker develops a study of the relationship of the infra-
structure of the Dutch Catholic Church to Catholic theology over
the postwar period in which change has been extensive and un-
precedented.   During this period higher education of lay Catholics
has been accompanied by a more critical attitude towards the
Church, its hierarchy and interchange with other religious
traditions.   In the sphere of theology there has been a decline
in the importance of the Virgin Mary and the saints and the
Catholic Church is no longer perceived as peerless.   See also
Laeyendecker (0942).

0871   Löwenthal, Leo.   "Franz von Baader: Ein religiöser Soziologe
der Soziologie." *Internationales Jahrbuch für Religionssoziologie*
2 (1966): 231-250.

The philosophy of Franz von Baader (1765-1842) is presented here
as a religious sociology.   He submitted that "man wanted to be
man without God, but God did not want to be God without men."
Baader's social history begins with the Fall and his theoretical
propositions have to do with the relations of society and
individual.

0872   Lyon, David.   *Christians and Sociology: Towards a Christian
Perspective*.   London: Inter-Varsity Press, 1975.

This is written from the point of view of a Christian who under-
stands the fears of sociology shared by his fellow-believers and
who seeks to allay them by demonstrating the benign potential of
sociological endeavors.   He suggests that the believer should
neither feel his faith to be threatened by sociology nor find it
necessary to compartmentalize it.

0873   Martin, David.   "Rome and the Sociologists." *A Sociological
Yearbook of Religion in Britain* 3 (1970): 1-11.

This paper is a reflection upon an important conference in Rome
on "The Culture of Unbelief" in which contributions to the study
of this theme were made by Robert N.Bellah, Thomas Luckmann,
Thomas O'Dea and others.

0874   Martin, Roderick.   "Sociology and Theology." In *Sociology,
Theology and Conflict*, edited by D.E.H.Whiteley and R.Martin, pp.
14-37.   Oxford: Blackwell, 1969 (0880).

Martin surveys the diverse concerns of sociologists with elements
of the human condition also engaged by theologians.   He traces the
evolution of sociology from its early nineteenth century forms to

the consciously value-free style of contemporary exponents.
Martin sees sociology and theology as explanatory models, both
valid on their own terms and he suggests applications to common
problems such as alienation and original sin.

0875 Mitton, C.L. *The Social Sciences and the Churches*. Edinburgh:
T. & T.Clark, 1972.

This is a widely noticed collection of essays which have the
purpose of commending sociological method to ministers and church
workers.   Many of the contributors are respected sociologists
such as Robert Towler, Bryan S.Turner (0856) and W.S.F.Pickering.
Their essays range over the issues of secularization,
administration, the clergy, church attendance and the sociological
discipline.   They are deliberately presented in an accessible
style.

0876 Peck, William G. *An Outline of Christian Sociology*. London:
James Clarke, 1948.

This is an endeavor in *sociologie religieuse*. The author's
starting point is not the foundation of modern sociology but
Christian theology, and it is in the light of this that social
confusions and social purpose are respectively to be studied and
restated.

0877 Reckitt, Maurice B. *The World and the Faith: Essays of a
Christian Sociologist*. London: Faith Press, 1954.

This is a short collection of essays on nineteenth and twentieth
century English culture by one whose major purpose was to marry
sociology and Christian theology.   The themes of these essays
include the Catholic literati Hilaire Belloc and G.K.Chesterton,
democracy and industry and the sickness of a technocratic society.
There are also studies of mediaeval history with Christianity
being assessed as a civilizing force.

0878 Shepherd, William C. "Religion and the Social Sciences:
Conflict or Reconciliation." *Journal for the Scientific Study of
Religion* 11 (1972): 230-239.

Shepherd cautiously surveys the divide between religion and the
social sciences and does not view with confidence the prospect
of bridging it.   Functionalism is logically and empirically
inadequate although he recognizes the achievements of function-
alists in the theoretical field.   He points to a neglected
psychological dimension in religious belief and suggests that
the approaches of Robert N.Bellah and Thomas Luckmann have the
capacity to engage this.

0879 Westerhoff, John H. "A Changing Focus: Toward an Understanding
of Religious Socialization." *Andover Newton Quarterly* 14 (1973):
118-129.

Religious socialization is one of the most neglected concerns of the sociology of religion and Westerhoff endeavors to illuminate the process by which individuals are inducted in the value systems and behavior norms of a religious society. Socialization is effected by means of participation in rituals, the learning of beliefs and the sharing of myths.   The churches are agencies of socialization and provide the communities with which the learner identifies.

0880   Whiteley, D.E.H. and Martin, R., eds. *Sociology, Theology and Conflict.* Oxford: Blackwell, 1969.

Whiteley and Martin present a diverse collection of papers emanating from a conference held in Oxford in 1968.   The search is for elements in the social sciences which bear upon issues in contemporary Christianity such as, notably, the estrangement of the individual from himself and his fellows.   Cognate themes include power, authority, conflict, original sin and social responsibility.   The volume includes Compton (0860) and Martin (0874).

0881   Whitley, Oliver R. *Religious Behavior: Where Sociology and Religion Meet.* Englewood Cliffs: Prentice-Hall, 1964.

Whitley's contribution to the conflict of sociology and religion is balanced and conciliatory.   He recognizes the limitations of the method and discipline of sociology and he approaches the matter of its desirability as a problem, not as a fact. Procedures and ground rules are indicated before Whitley offers some exemplars of valid sociological study; these include the character of suburban churches in the light of the work of Gibson Winter (0774), the role of the minister and the management of the faithful.

U.   CIVIL RELIGION; POPULAR RELIGION; FOLK RELIGION

0882   Abercrombie, Nicholas; Baker, John; Brett, Sebastian; and Foster, Jane. "Superstition and Religion: The God of the Gaps." *A Sociological Yearbook of Religion in Britain* 3 (1970): 93-129.

This is the report and analysis of a student survey of an eventual sample of 181 persons born in England and Wales concerning a variety of metaphysical beliefs and ideas.   Findings reinforce the view that superstition and allied beliefs in contemporary Britain, a society regarded to be increasingly dominated by rational and scientific criteria, present a problem for sociological interpretation.   A large minority of respondents paid at least lip-service to common superstitions, up to 8 per cent signified conviction, and some 23 per cent declared a belief in astrology.   Among other sociological explanations, the authors suggest that superstitious belief is a product of alienation and is most functional among those who are unable to control their own situation.

0883 Bellah, Robert N. "La Religion Civile en Amerique." *Archives de Sciences Sociales des Religions* 35 (1978): 7-22.

In this influential paper, Bellah argues that alongside the national religion of America - supposing that such a phenomenon exists - there is a religious dimension of a civil kind which is well developed, organized and having such an integrity that it warrants the careful scholarly study that better recognized religious forms also deserve. It is peculiarly American in character and shares with conventional religions such trappings as its own prophets and martyrs, its sacred events and places, its solemn rituals, its own symbols and its own language. See Gehrig (0885) and Hughey (0889) for developments upon Bellah's work.

0884 Clark, David B. *Between Pulpit and Pew: Folk Religion in a North Yorkshire Fishing Village*. Cambridge: Cambridge University Press, 1982.

The village of Staithes on the north-east coast of England is a traditional community with a strong Nonconformist ("chapel") tradition. The passage rituals marking birth and death are among several events in village life that fall either between folklore and institutional religion or else in both camps. The author also examines occupational beliefs and the seasons of the year. See also Clark (0852) and Clark (0917).

0885 Gehrig, Gail. *American Civil Religion: An Assessment*. Storrs: Society for the Scientific Study of Religion, 1981.

American civil religion is variously conceived in the literature as the transcendent religion of the nation (by Robert N.Bellah (0883), for example), as "democratic faith", as folk religion and as religious nationalism. Gail Gehrig's endeavor is the search for a consensus, and this she does around the conception of a religious symbol system which signifies the place of the American citizen in American society and American society in space and time. The volume is useful not least as an overview and evaluation of different approaches to the theoretical conception of civil religion.

0886 Harrell, Stevan. "Modes of Belief in Chinese Folk Religion." *Journal for the Scientific Study of Religion* 16 (1976): 55-65.

This article reports and analyzes an interview survey among residents of a village in northern Taiwan. The analysis points out the problem of distinguishing between believers and non-believers. Instead the author proposes a fourfold typification of intellectual belief, true belief, practical belief and un-belief.

0887 Hertz, Robert. *Sociologie Religieuse et Folklore*. Paris: Presses Universitaires de France, 1970.

Many rituals and symbols are shared and operated by orthodox religion and superstition or folklore. This book is an exploration of these in sociological perspective.   The author treats, for example, of the presentation of death and of the symbolic significance of the right hand.

0888   Hudson, Winthrop S.,ed. *Nationalism and Religion in America: Concepts of American Identity and Mission*.   New York: Harper and Row, 1970.

American national identity is interpreted as a religious inheritance of the Pilgrim Fathers overlain by the experience of the Civil War.   Its characterization is an evocation of the memories of William Bradford, Nathaniel Morton, Cotton Mather and John Cushing.   Such folk heroes are the progenitors of civil religion in modern America, the integrity of which is complicated by the tensions of cultural pluralism.

0889   Hughey, Michael W.   *Civil Religion and Moral Order: Theoretical and Historical Dimensions*.   Westport: Greenwood, 1983.

The characterization of American civil religion is attributable to Bellah (0883) but its conception is, as Hughey shows, within the contribution of Durkheim and Weber.   Hughey goes further than Bellah in studying cases and elaborating the functions of specific core values and civil rituals.   In particular, he instances American food rites and the Memorial Day parade and he studies the evolution of American civil religion from its protestant foundations.   The extensive bibliography is a useful asset in this work.

0890   Isambert, François-André.   *Le Sens du Sacré: Fête et Religion Populaire*.   Paris: Éditions de Minuit, 1982.

Popular religion is considered by some as a significant social fact, by others as a myth; Isambert first addresses this question.   The ontological problem stays with Isambert as he surveys contemporary research on the sacred, explores its conceptions by Durkheim and his followers, examines the place of ritual in society, comments on the cycle of twelve days and discusses the debate on popular religion current in the Roman Catholic Church.   See also Isambert (0076).

0891   Le Bras, Gabriel; Levy-Bruhl, Lucien; Rivet, Paul; and Saintyves, Pierre.   "Pratique Religieuse et Religion Populaire." *Archives de Sciences Sociales des Religions* 43 (1977): 7-22.

Le Bras recalls an interest of forty years standing when he insists on the importance of the study of popular religion and of drawing in this study upon the sociology of folklore.   This presentation draws together also the work of Saintyves with whom he collaborated for some time.

0892   Martin, David.   "Christianity, Civic Religion and Three Counter-cultures." *Human Context* 6 (1974):

Durkheim's classic study is an exploration of the unity of
religion and society.   But in more advanced societies there
is observable a dialectic which transcends this unity and has
Catholic, Protestant and maybe post-Protestant forms.   Civic
religion is expressed both as the unity of cult and culture
and as "a *melange* of superstition, astrology, proverbial
morality and accepted limited personal reciprocities currently
comprising the natural religion of our time." The purpose of
this paper is to articulate and explore the three forms which
the dialectic, as opposed to the normative, can assume.
Reprinted in Martin (0035).

0893 Piwowarski, Wladyslaw. "Industrialization and Popular
Religiosity in Poland." *Sociological Analysis* 37 (1976):
315-320.

The three towns in which the empirical work reported in this
paper was conducted include Nowa Huta, the steelworks outside
Krakow which was founded without a church to demonstrate that
religion was superfluous in socialist society.   Overall some
eighty per cent of the population are found to be believers
but religious ignorance is also reported to be high.   Popular
religion flourishes in spite of industrialization and political
controls but Piwowarski reports some indifference toward the
Church on such issues as marriage.   The association of the
Catholic Church in Poland with Polish nationalism and the
traditional pastoral methods deployed are said to favor the
survival of popular religiosity.

0894 Sandeen, Ernest R. "Fundamentalism and American Identity."
Annals of the American Academy of Political and Social Science
387 (1970): 57-65.

Sandeen addresses the problem of the persistence of an inter-
denominational religious orientation commonly described as
"last-ditch reaction and anachronistic, rural anti-intellectual-
ism".   He analyzes the dimensions of fundamentalism in America
and takes as a particular focus the controversy concerning
evolution.   Fundamentalism is observed in a symbolic relationship with its adversaries.   Fundamentalism is, in Sandeen's
estimation, the authentic conservative tradition and his
article demonstrates that it is not a marginal religious
phenomenon exclusive to the protestant sects but a major force
in mainstream American religion.

0895 Séguy, Jean. "Images et 'Religion Populaire'." *Archives de
Sciences Sociales des Religions* 44 (1977): 25-43.

This is a discussion of the concept of popular religion and an
interpretation of the refusal of images, the social regulation
of them and the ikons of the Orthodox churches.   Séguy here
insists that power relationships are central to the definition
and explanation of popular religious phenomena.

0896   Seneviratne, H.L.   "Continuity of Civil Religion in Sri Lanka."
Religion 14 (1984): 1-14.

The author picks up from Bellah (0883) an interest in the
ambivalence with which political leaders - in Bellah's example,
John F.Kennedy - speak of God by way of casual pious reference
or in hope of legitimation but do not explore the influence
of Christian teachings in the world.   Seneviratne applies this
to the case of Sri Lanka and examines the pageant and so called
"secular rituals" in order to assess the character of civil
religion there.

0897   Southwold, Martin.   "True Buddhism and Village Buddhism in
Sri Lanka." *Religious Organization and Religious Experience,*
edited by J.Davis, pp.137-152. London: Academic Press, 1982 (0013).

The problem addressed, here in the context of Sri Lanka and in
a Buddhist rather than Christian society, is that of popular
religion compared with a form that is purer or more official.
Village Buddhism, for example, is said by some of its critics
to be heavily involved in traffic with gods and other
spiritual beings and this is contrary to pure form.   Village
Buddhist clerics admit to being negligent in the practice of
meditation but find in themselves virtues that compensate;
élite clerics, by contrast, insist upon the prime importance
of meditation and recognize no principle of compensation.

0898   Stauffer, Robert E.   "Civil Religion, Technocracy, and the
Private Sphere: Further Comments on Cultural Integration in
Advanced Societies." *Journal for the Scientific Study of
Religion* 12 (1973): 415-425.

In many analyses civil religion constitutes a broad cultural
legitimation of the systems of advanced societies.   So-called
"privatists" such as Thomas Luckmann and Richard Fenn dismiss
this function and Stauffer's purpose is to bring forward
evidence he believes they overlook; he reaffirms the
significance of civil religion in the scientific analysis of
religion in modern societies.

0899   Tashurizina, Z.A.   "Les Superstitions:Mystification des
Relations Quotidiennes." *Social Compass* 21 (1974): 153-169.

The Christian churches generally disapprove folk myth and
endeavor to replace it with orthodox Christian belief.   The
Russian Orthodox Church and the Baptist Church in the western
world have each campaigned against superstition with limited
effect.   The author of this article documents the survival
of superstition as the failure of the churches to purvey
their official beliefs and suggests that it is futile to
pursue the campaign.   The social demography of superstition
is analyzed; women are more prone to superstitious belief
than men as are less educated groups.

0900   Thomas, Michael C. and Flippen, Charles C.   "American Civil
Religion: An Empirical Study."   *Social Forces*   51 (1972): 218-225.

The work of Thomas and Flippen follows the seminal contribution
to the concept of civil religion and its application in the
United States made by Robert N.Bellah (0883).   They endeavor
to verify Bellah's account by empirical investigation and
analyze a sample of editorials of national newspapers appearing
over the "Honor America Weekend" in July 1970.   They indicate
tendencies peculiar to metropolitan papers and urge further
empirical research to clarify points of potential deviation
from the Bellah thesis.

0901   Towler, Robert, and Chamberlain, Audrey.   "Common Religion."
A Sociological Yearbook of Religion in Britain   6 (1973): 1-28.

Towler and Chamberlain conduct an investigation into the beliefs
held "by the man in the street, as opposed to the man in the
pew," using data collected in the course of a study of attitudes
associated with high fertility.   These affirm the importance
of a religious orientation, even among the lapsed and non-
attending; it is an orientation that bears little reference to
the categories of "official"religion which feature prominantly
in most research designs and is unsystematic in form.

0902   Wilson, John.   *Religion in American Society: The Effective
Presence*.   Englewood Cliffs: Prentice-Hall, 1978.

As well as offering a general sociological perspective on the
place of religion in society, Wilson explores in detail the
religious factor pervading American social life.   He treats
of common religion, civil religion and the implications of
secularization in social and political change and conflict and
in social integration.   Alongside this there is a detailed
examination of institutional forms and the evolution of these,
as from sect to denomination: and Wilson treats of the internalization of the individual through conversion and the
consolidation of commitment.

0903   Wimberley, Ronald C.   "Continuity in the Measurement of Civil
Religion."   *Sociological Analysis*   40 (1979): 59-62.

This is an endeavor to identify reliable indicators of civil
religion: the author relates the bases of a small group of
earlier studies to a series of what Bellah postulates as key
texts of American civil religion.   The markers which feature
in both sets of sources are found to converge.   See also
Wimberley and Christenson (0178), Bellah (0883) and Wimberley
(0904).

0904   Wimberley, Ronald C.   "Civil Religion and the Choice for
President: Nixon in '72."   *Social Forces*   59 (1980): 44-61.

This is an exercise in psephology which assesses the explanatory
power of the concept of civil religion with other more familiar
variables used in the study of voting behavior in presidential

elections.   The notion of civil religion as deployed here
relates to the principle of divine right in asserting the divine
ordination of the nation's affairs and sanctifying the role of
President within them.   Those adhering to such a view were
disposed to elect Nixon in 1972.   The civil religion variable
ranked very highly among other variables such as social background and even, in the cases of some samples, partly
affiliation.   See also Wimberley and Christenson (0178),
Bellah (0883) and Wimberley (0903).

0905 Zulehner, Paul M.   "La 'Religion des Gens': À propos de
Diverses Enquêtes Realisées en Autriche (1970-1980)." *Social
Compass* 29 (1982): 209-221.

Zulehner prefers to operate a concept of "people's religion"
to that of popular religion and this he does within a theoretical
framework provided by Berger and Luckmann and applied by him to
survey data collected in Austria.   He explores the desire to
affiliate as the factor determining the character of the Church
and contrasts this with a Church that adjusts itself in
accordance with the "people's religion".

V.   STUDIES OF RELIGION IN PARTICULAR GEOGRAPHICAL AREAS

0906 Alston, Jon P.   "Review of the Polls: Selected Religious
Beliefs and Attitudes of the French Population." *Journal for the
Scientific Study of Religion* 12 (1973): 349-351.

The author offers a critique of a 1971 survey on the grounds of
the non-differentiation of non-Catholics and the failure to
ask them about frequency of church attendance, in which respect
Catholics were assessed.   But there are still interesting
findings, such as the belief of 22 per cent of French Catholics
that the existence of God is impossible or improbable.   And
only 51 per cent of French Catholics responding defined Jesus
Christ as the Son of God.

0907 Arnold, Pierre.   "Pèlerinages et Processions comme Formes
de Pouvoir Symbolique des Classes Subalternes: Deux Cas Péruviens."
Social Compass 32 (1985): 45-56.

Arnold bases this paper around two examples of pilgrimage in
Peru, a sanctuary in the Andes and an Afro-Peruvian procession.
These are analyzed as manifestations of popular religion in
the context of attacks upon the poorer classes in Peru and
the historic resistance of these represented by religious
practice.

0908 Bakhash, Shaul.   *The Reign of the Ayatollahs: Iran and the
Islamic Revolution*.   London: Tauris, 1984.

Bakhash provides a documentary case study of charismatic leadership in the first five years of post-revolutionary Iran.   The
sensibility of this work is not sociological but the raw

material that it provides is of profound sociological implication.
It explores the religious, economic and social upheaval brought
about since the fall of the Pahlavi dynasty in 1979 and
speculates on international implications.

0909 Black, Alan W. and Glasner, Peter E., eds. *Practice and
Belief: Studies in the Sociology of Australian Religion.* Sydney:
Allen and Unwin, 1983.

This is a collection of a dozen sociological essays on aspects of
the evolution and organization of religion and irreligion in
contemporary Australia.   Subjects treated include country town
religion, church-world relationships and styles of ministry,
the sociology of ecumenism, the Hare Krishna movement, Australian
folk religion and organized irreligion in New South Wales. See
also Mol (0956).

0910 Brown, Sheila. "De l'Adhésion à un Nouveau Système
Religieux à la Transformation d'un Système de Valeurs: Étude d'une
Communauté Rurale Africaine." *Social Compass* 19 (1972): 83-91.

This study is based in a village of South Africa first christian-
ized by missionaries in 1820.   Its concern is the effect upon
rural value systems of the adoption of a new religious system.
The author investigates the reformulation of traditional values
under the impact of Christianity and the replacement of
traditional values by western Christian ones.   The inquiry
was conducted in the age groups 15 to 25 years, 26 to 49, and
50 years and over.   After a century and a half traditional values
linger and the community has only now reached a point of
transition between the two systems, a critical point manifested
in role-conflicts and other contradictions.

0911 Brunt, L. "The 'Kleine Luyden' as a Disturbing Factor in
the Emancipation of the Orthodox Calvinists (Gereformerden) in the
Netherlands." *Sociologia Neerlandica* 8 (1972): 89-102.

The author observes a persistence of stereotypes from the
orthodox Calvinists of the nineteenth century to the extremists
of the present day, and offers a structuralist account of their
emancipation which applies, it is suggested, at least to the
upper échelons of its bourgeoisie.

0912 Bureau, René. "Prophétismes Africains: Le Harrisme en Côte-
d'Ivoire." *Archives de Sciences Sociales des Religions* 41 (1976):
47-53.

An analysis of a modern religious movement in the Ivory Coast
named after the prophet William Harris, a native of Liberia,
who conducted a mission in 1915.   The belief system of this
movement incorporates elements of black and white witchcraft
and offers the hope of achieving the power of the white man's
secrets.

0913 Busia, K.A. *Urban Churches in Britain: A Question of Relevance.*
London: Lutterworth, 1966.

This title appears in the series *World Studies of Churches in
Mission* and the book reports an investigation in a part of
Birmingham, England, which is given the name "Brookton".
The development and sociography of this urban area are amply
documented in the study and denominational organization in
the area is reported in detail.   The research was done by
questionnaires and interviewing and designs appear with
statistical tables in appendices: topics covered include
perceived roles of clergy, the deployment of clergy in hours
per week, distances of the homes of the faithful from their
churches, the demographic composition of groups of converts,
the financial management of churches, Christian teachings
about family life, church membership and its relation to
membership of other voluntary organizations.   In analysis
of results Busia observes the emphasis which clergy give to
salvation as the aim and purpose of their work, points to
the need for more instruction to face the challenges of
contemporary urban life, assesses the church as "community",
explains that the churches are organized for those who enter
their doors but are not equally adjusted to reach outsiders
and discusses issues of church unity.

0914 Caplow, Theodore; Bahr, Howard M.; and Chadwick, Bruce A.
*All Faithful People: Change and Continuity in Middletown
Religion.* Minneapolis: University of Minnesota Press, 1983.

"Middletown" is the pseudonym given to Muncie, Indiana, by
Helen and Robert Lynd in 1924.   It has now three times its
1924 population and there have been various subsequent studies
replicating aspects of the Lynds'.   Caplow and his colleagues
find continuities and change in the religious sphere.
The Methodism which formerly predominated has been succeeded
by new religious movements, Catholic and southern Protestant.
Denomination hostilities have diminished and the boundary
between religious and secular has been blurred, with the
religious organizations becoming gradually more tolerant of
the world.

0915 Carbonaro, Antonio. "Éléments pour une Étude des Mutations
dans les Comportements Électoraux en Italie." *Social Compass*
23 (1976): 263-272.

Party membership and electoral behavior in Italy conform largely
to religious affiliations.   This study relates electoral
tendencies to social class and analyzes changes in electoral
procedures since 1945.

0916 Cipriani, Roberto. "Le Religiosité Populaire en Italie:
Deux Recherches sur la Image et la Politique dans le Sud du
Pays." *Social Compass* 23 (1976): 221-231.

Cipriani provides a study of two cases of popular religion in the south of Italy, the first being magico-sacral in character and the other an example of politico-religious prophecy.   Research was conducted by interviewing, participant observation and the analysis of biographical accounts, with special attention being given to leaders.

0917   Clark, David B.   "Local and Cosmopolitan Aspects of Religious Activity in a Northern Suburb." *A Sociological Yearbook of Religion in Britain*   3 (1970): 45-64.

The author compares two types of Methodist in the suburban district in northern England which he calls "Oakcroft" - those with local and those with cosmopolitan orientations. The author believes that the Oakcroft variety of Methodism resembles the form of church life dominant in a notable majority of Methodist societies and it is local in orientation.   Where those who on all tests emerge as cosmopolitans arrive in one of the two Methodist churches in Oakcroft, they tend to let the locals have their way or else confine their activities to one or two specifically cosmopolitan organizations.   See also Clark (0852) and Clark (0884).

0918   Cousins, Ewert H.   "Les Avatars Contemporains du Sacré aux États-Unis." *Cahiers Internationaux de Symbolisme*   27 (1975): 19-31.

Cousins enthusiastically borrows from Hinduism the concept of *avatar* and applies it allegorically to the conditions of religion in the United States signifying both a demise of traditional religious symbolism and the phenomena associated with secularization and a recovery of symbols and messages from antecedent religious traditions or cultures not formally identified as religious: manifestations of the latter type include the new religious movements of the late 1960s and the use therein of drugs to stimulate religious experience.

0919   Dekmejian, R.Hrair.   "The Anatomy of Islamic Revival: Legitimacy Crisis, Ethnic Conflict and the Search for Islamic Alternatives." *The Middle East Journal*   34, 1 (Winter 1980): 1-12.

A major attribute of the Islamic revival is its social and transnational pervasiveness - through the Arab world, Nigeria, Turkey, Pakistan and Indonesia.   Another is its polycentrism. To a significant extent, the movement back to Islam in modern times appears to be a reaction to the failure of ruling élites in the Islamic countries to establish public order legitimately and within viable political communities.

0920   Deschamps, Christian.   "Les 'Fêtes du Village' en Corée et Leur Signification Sociale." *Social Compass*   25 (1978): 191-208.

This is a documentary study of celebrations in Korean villages which center upon an act of offering.   The author explains these rites in full detail and interprets their sociological significance in terms of the maintenance of village culture and of the cohesiveness of the village community.

0921 Devisch, Renaat and Vervaeck, Bart. "Auto-production, Production et Reproduction: Divination et Politique chez les Yaka du Zaire." *Social Compass* 32 (1985): 111-131.

This paper is concerned with different relationships between power and meaning as exemplified in divination and prophetism. The language of the prophet is offensive and heretic, signifying intrusion, accusation, and the demystification of power relations within the community which the prophet addresses. At the theoretical level, the work of Devisch and Vervaeck commends a revision of existing contributions in this field, notably those of Pierre Bourdieu.

0922 Everitt, Alan. *The Pattern of Rural Dissent in the Nineteenth Century*. Leicester: Leicester University Press, 1972.

An inquiry into the nature of social and religious community with a study of patterns in four English counties, Lincolnshire, Leicestershire, Northamptonshire and Kent. The findings have implications for the utility of generalized conceptions such as "the Nonconformist Conscience" and "the Dissenting Interest".

0923 Faure, Guy-Olivier. "Charisme et Réforme Sociale en Inde." *Social Compass* 29 (1982): 75-92.

Faure makes a study of the charismatic leadership of Harivallabh Parikh in social reform among the Indian peasantry. Parikh was a disciple of Gandhi in his strategy of non-violence. Faure explores his achievements in the light of Weber's elaboration of charisma and uses also the concepts of protest and asceticism.

0924 Garrison, Winfred E. "Characteristics of American Organized Religion." *Annals of the American Academy of Political and Social Sciences* 256 (1948): 14-24.

The paper attributes to the total socio-cultural environment the major influences upon the establishment and development of the American religious formation. Reprinted in Yinger (0070): 433-443.

0925 Gellner, Ernest. "The Unknown Apollo of Biskra: The Social Base of Algerian Puritanism." *Government and Opposition* 9 (1974): 277-310.

The title of this article echoes that of a poem written by André Gide in the late nineteenth century when Biskra was a center of decadence. Gellner treats of the reformist spirit of Islam in north Africa and the burgeoning of a puritan ethic in more recent years.

0926 Goswami, B.B. and Morab, S.G. "Comparative Study of Sacred Complexes in India: A Working Paper." *Journal of Social Research* 13 (1970): 95-108.

The authors offer a useful documentary account of the pattern and distribution of cult centers in India, of sacred rivers and shrines, of rituals, cults, sub-cults and reformist movements. The place of these complexes is assessed in the transmission of Indian religion and with reference to the caste system which provides the structure of religious activity.

0927 Greeley, Andrew M. "Religion in a Secular Society." *Social Research* 41 (1974): 226-240.

Greeley offers a pathology of the state of the sociology of religion in the United States, characterizes its themes and points to its omissions. He complains that the religious alienation of practitioners in sociology from their own traditions affects the quality of the enterprise. Greeley adumbrates some hypotheses and moots an agenda that he hopes will enhance future practice. See also Greeley (0024).

0928 Gustaffson, Berndt. "Staatskirche und Entkirchlichung in Schweden." *Probleme der Religionssoziologie* 6 (1962): 158-165.

The author's focus is upon the established Lutheran churches of Scandinavia which paradoxically have attendances consistently below 5 per cent of their membership. Further, losses to nominal membership are extremely small, sometimes registering less than 1 per cent. Gustaffson's interpretation involves a cluster of factors including the image of the church in the minds of its defectors, secularization in the middle class, the shift from church attendance to private religion, the attractiveness of a "Sermon on the Mount Christianity" which offers moral guidance without ritual participation and the feeling that the churches are useful only in the "overwhelming" times of life. Appears in English as "The Established Church and the Decline in Church Attendance in Sweden" in Birnbaum and Lenzer (0009): 360-365 (abridged). See also Berndt Gustaffson (0929) and Göran Gustaffson (0930).

0929 Gustaffson, Berndt. "The Role of Religion in Modern Sweden." *American Behavioral Scientist* 17 (1974): 827-844.

The article takes account of Swedish religion at three levels: the formal religious presence, folk religion and something somewhat inchoate and having to do with destiny. In the Swedish context religion is analyzed as a reference system, a system of adaptation, and an integrative system. And in strengthening and legitimizing moral and other views widely held, religion in Sweden acts as a system of social control. Though written as a case study of Sweden the article is theoretical in style and has clear applications elsewhere. See also Berndt Gustaffson (0928) and Göran Gustaffson (0930).

0930 Gustaffson, Göran. "Popular Religion in Sweden." *Social Compass* 29 (1982): 103-112.

The article treats of the popularity of Swedish religion with statistics detailing attendance patterns accompanying the demise of the Church of Sweden's official function. See also Berndt Gustaffson (0928) and Berndt Gustaffson (0929).

0931 Harman, Leslie. *The Church in Greater London: A Working Paper*. London: Southwark Diocesan Department of Religious Sociology, 1968.

This study is a case of local enterprise in religious sociology to clarify aims and objectives for the pastoral oversight of an extensive urban area.   The Southwark diocese extends from the city of London southwards to the leafy suburbs of Surrey. It is on the basis of a sociological study of this heterogeneous constituency that a pastoral policy is mooted.

0932 Hewitt, Christopher. "Catholic Grievances, Catholic Nationalism and Violence in Northern Ireland during the Civil Rights Period: A Reconsideration." *British Journal of Sociology* 32 (1981): 362-380.

The period 1968 to 1971 was one of persistent violence in Northern Ireland.   This violence has been most widely explained as the response of Catholics to the discriminations of Protestants.   A second and exclusively Protestant interpret-ation is that the violence reflects traditional nationalism. Hewitt considers Catholic grievances and suggests that discrimination has been overstated.   He finds a closer association between nationalism and the civil rights campaign than has been generally recognized and he submits this to statistical analysis.   For an extension of this analysis see Hewitt (0933) and McAllister (0947).

0933 Hewitt, Christopher. "Catholic Grievances and Violence in Northern Ireland." *British Journal of Sociology* 36 (1985): 102-116.

This follows Hewitt's revisionist interpretation (0932) of the Northern Irish conflict: here he investigates the severity of anti-Catholic discrimination and expands his argument on the causes of violence.   See also McAllister (0947).

0934 Huotari, Voitto. "Finnish Revivalism as an Expression of Popular Piety." *Social Compass* 29 (1982): 113-123.

This treats of revival movements operating within the Lutheran Church in the nineteenth and twentieth centuries and of the Church's assimilation of revivalism.   There is an account of devotional gatherings within the Finnish revivals called "The Societies" and a discussion of the function of revival-ism within the Church, whether as a religious movement, a lay

movement, a protest movement or a traditional movement.
Within society its functions are assessed in terms of status
compensation, political protest and continuity.

0935 Houtart, François.   "Champ Religieux et Champ Politique dans
la Société Singhalaise." *Social Compass* 20 (1973): 105-138.

Houtart refers to the mode of economic production in distinguishing three models of society: agrarian, transitional and
industrial.   His focus is then upon the critical moments in
the evolution of the society of Sri Lanka and these include the
advent of Buddhism, the successive colonizations of the
Portuguese and the British and subsequently independence from
the imperial regime.   The Portuguese occupation is
distinguished by the religious basis of its legitimacy.

0936 Houtart, François. "Les Fonctions Sociales de la Symbolique
Religieuse chez les Bouddhistes à Sri Lanka." *Archives de Sciences
Sociales des Religions* 37 (1974): 23-41.

Houtart studies the relationship between the religious and the
political in rural Sri Lanka, in the towns and their environs.
He notices a transformation of religious symbolism which performs
less of an integrative function and serves correspondingly
increasingly as a form of group expression in a pluralist
society.

0937 Houtart, François. "L'Implantation Portugaise au Kerala
et ses Effets sur l'Organisation Sociale et Religieuse des Syriens
et sur le Système des Castes." *Social Compass* 28 (1981): 201-235.

This is an account of the endeavors toward unity shown by the
Portuguese in Kerala and of their subsequent assimilation of
the social and religious organization of the Syrians.   The
attempt featured the imposition by the Portuguese of the Latin
rite and of a new system of religious hierarchy.   At the same
time there emerged new religious groupings associated with
the Portuguese effort to convert the lower castes to the
Catholic faith.

0938 Houtart, François and Lemercinier, Geneviève. "Modèles
Culturels Socio-religieux des Groupes Élitiques Catholiques à
Sri Lanka." *Social Compass* 20 (1973): 303-320.

The schools question in Sri Lanka has had the effect of
polarizing Christians and Buddhists, an opposition subsequently
rehearsed again in the context of the politics of development.
The principle of westernization is a critical one and the
authors juxtapose westernized and non-westernized Catholic
élite groups.   With the clergy these form three constituencies
surveyed by the authors.   The clergy largely conform to the
attitudes of the westernized élite but the authors note that
each group contains a minority contingent which recognizes in
religion a revolutionary tendency in respect of the social
formation.

0939 Jenkins, Daniel. *The British: Their Identity and Their Religion*.
London: S.C.M. Press, 1975.

The author is a theologian rather than a sociologist and this is
a perceptive work based around his observations and experience;
it is not an attempt to collate survey data but it generates
themes for sociological investigation. The book provides a
commentary upon the established Church of England and the other
religious organizations in England; and there are separate
chapters on the circumstances of Wales and Scotland.

0940 Kamerschen, David R. "Some Socioeconomic Generalizations
Regarding Religion in the United States." *Indian Journal of Social
Research* 13 (1972): 27-36.

Kamerschen's article is useful not for its wealth of statistical
data which are in any case available elsewhere but for the trends
it picks up. Information is collected from polls and national
surveys of various kinds to show changes over a period of fifty
years. At the end of the period, for example, there are more
church members per thousand of population than there were at
the beginning. There is confirmation of the widely supposed
tendency for the major religious traditions to prevail in urban
areas and for minority groups to be established in rural areas.
As is to be expected, the southern states are predominantly
protestant while the Roman Catholic Church is strong in the
northeast. The mean age of Jews is higher than that of
protestants which in turn is higher than that of Catholics.
In rank order of socioeconomic status, Jews come highest, then
Presbyterians, then Methodists, then Catholics. As with much
sociology there is a tendency to confirm commonsense expectations
with sophisticated empirical research.

0941 Kellerman, A.P.R. "Religious Affiliation in South Africa."
Social Compass 19 (1972): 7-20.

This paper details the social composition of the population of
South Africa in terms of racial, cultural, and socioeconomic
variables: its religious composition is presented as denominational affiliation according to race, with comparative data
for 1951 and 1960. Tendencies are then interpreted. Racial,
cultural and linguistic cleavages are shown to prevail in the
pattern of religious affiliation.

0942 Laeyendecker, Leonardo. "Recent Dutch Literature on the
Sociology of Religion." *Sociologia Neerlandica* 8 (1972): 111-117.

In the Netherlands the sociological study of religion addresses
a large number of the problems which engage sociologists in
anglophone countries. Missions to the Dutch colonies such as
Dutch New Guinea and the relationship of Christian to native
religion and economy have been carefully examined. Early
sociological studies of religion were often developed at the
level of the parish but latterly the relationship of Church and
State has been an absorbing interest. The clergy find themselves everywhere in a state of flux if not of crisis, and Dutch

sociologists have been interested in perceptions and changes in
the role in response to secularization.   See also Laeyendecker
(0870).

0943 Lane, Christel. "Some Explanations for the Persistence of
Christian Religion in Soviet Society." *Sociology* 8 (1974):
233-243.

The author explores common explanations for the persistence of
the Christian religion in the hostile conditions of Soviet
society.   First, Soviet sources explain, it is attributable to
ephemeral social inequalities; second, it is explained in terms
of psychological factors; and third, religion is observed to
have adapted in order to secure its own survival.   In a
critical analysis of these possibilities the author suggests
instead that religion offers an ideology of dissidence or
protest and systematizes the thoughts and feelings of those who
cannot subscribe to the dominant ideology.

0944 Levine, Daniel H., ed. *Churches and Politics in Latin America.*
Beverley Hills: Sage, 1980.

The contributors to this volume include scholars and theologians
from North and South America.   They describe the complex
relationship in Latin America between Church and State, the
intense self-examination of Christians there, the development of
new theologies, new religions and social practices and a
heightened sensitivity to social problems.

0945 Ligou, Daniel. "L'Évolution des Cimetières." *Archives de
Sciences Sociales des Religions* 39 (1975): 61-77.

Ligou traces the history of cemeteries in France.   In the early
Christian period town cemeteries were extra-mural and their
association with churches was a later development with
implications for the exclusion from rights of Jews and,
subsequently, Protestants.   In the late eighteenth century
legislation was passed to prevent the burial of the dead within
the walls of the church and the process of secularization of
cemeteries continued in France throughout the nineteenth century.

0946 Lumead, René. "Du Monde Religieux de l'Homme Africain
Aujourd'hui." *Archives de Sciences Sociales des Religions* 41
(1976): 37-45.

A study of the culture shock and destabilization effected by the
penetration of Africa by the attendant religions of colonization,
Christianity and Islam.   Recently the wisdom and education
offered by missionary agencies are succeeded by a new wisdom and
the invention of new reasons for believing.

0947 McAllister, Ian. "The Devil, Miracles and the Afterlife:
The Political Sociology of Religion in Northern Ireland." *British
Journal of Sociology* 33 (1982): 330-347.

While social conflict is commonly perceived as a sectarian antagonism based on archaic differences of principle and the conflicting communities are invariably identified by religious affiliation, the variable of religious commitment has been assumed rather than tested.   The author of this paper uses 1973 survey data to measure patterns of ritual participation, devotion and belief.   It transpires that conformities on these measures coincide with social structural locations and the author suggests that religious commitment has little determinative effect upon the political conflict.   See also Hewitt (0932) and Hewitt (0933).

0948 Macourt, Malcolm. "The Nature of Religion in Ireland."
A Sociological Yearbook of Religion in Britain 7 (1974): 26-45.

The author presents a typology of religious organizations in Ireland with special notes on the Roman Catholic Church and the Church of Ireland, the Presbyterian Church in Ireland and other religious communions.   These are then related to social variables such as the system of stratification without which the student cannot comprehend the religious system.   An appendix offers statistical tables breaking down data for Northern Ireland and the Republic of Ireland.

0949 Maduro, Otto. "Catholic Church, National Security States and Popular Movements in Latin America." *Actes de C.I.S.R.* 17 (1983): 7-17.

The context studied is the changing role of the Church and its relationship to the State.   In the 1950s the familiar pattern in Latin America was a central alliance of Church and State, since when the Church has become more devolved and independent. Maduro analyzes the structure of power involving cohesion, coercion and consensus and examines the material and symbolic dimensions of the power of the Church.   As the Church recedes from a formal position of power, so the "popular Church" accommodates aspirant popular movements.

0950 Marianski, Janusz. "Dynamics of Change in Rural Religiosity: The Case of Poland." *Social Compass* 28 (1981): 63-78.

The focus of this study is the Plok region of Central Poland. Main hypotheses on the dynamics of rural religion are examined and the author offers statistical data on the conformity of respondents to orthodox Catholic principles.   From these there is developed a typology of Catholic religiosity among village inhabitants.   See also Piwowarski (0965).

0951 Martin, Bernice. "Comments on Some Gallup Poll Statistics."
A Sociological Yearbook of Religion in Britain 1 (1968): 146-179.

This is a survey of data randomly collected over a period of ten years by the Gallup organization in Britain.   The accumulated evidence is reported and tabulated under the themes of theological beliefs, church organization and ecumenism, social and moral questions and political views.   It is pointed out

that data of this kind are of limited usefulness to the sociologist
of religion compared with purposive scientific investigations
conducted on the basis of considered hypotheses.

0952   Martin, Hervé and Martin, Louise.   "Croix Rurales et
Sacralisation de l'Espace: Le Cas de la Bretagne du Moyen Age."
Archives de Sciences Sociales des Religions   43 (1977): 23-38.

Mediaeval crosses are a common feature of the countryside of
Brittany and have presented historians with an interpretive
problem.   The authors of this article take up the issue by
suggesting a social function in the proliferation of these
monuments according to designs sanctioned by the Church
authorities.

0953   Matthes, Joachim.   "Religionszugehörigkeit und
Gesellschaftspolitik Über Konfessionalisierungstendenzen in der
Bundesrepublik Deutschland."   *Internationales Jahrbuch für
Religionssoziologie*   1 (1965): 43-66.

This is a detailed demographic study of religion in West Germany
in which the author submits that the religious institutions
represented a stable organizing factor in the radically
destructured society of post-1945.

0954   Mazzacane, Lello.   "Fêtes et Culture Paysanne dans le Sud
de l'Italie."   *Social Compass*   23 (1978): 233-240.

This offers a documentary account and analysis of peasant
festivals in southern Italy.   While some disappear, others enjoy
a revival and the author endeavors to interpret this contra-
diction.   Festivals are related to the compartmentalization of
time between work and leisure and the rites studied are symbolic
celebrations of this economic delineation.   The article is
illustrated with photographs.

0955   Milanesi, Giancarlo.   "Chiesa e Società in Alcune Ricerche
Tedesche Recenti."   *La Critica Sociologica*   28 (1973): 59-75.

The author gives a general account of religion in Germany as
illuminated by recent studies.   The trend toward a civil
religion is discernible but not measurable.   Secularization
affects the German situation as elsewhere and Milanesi observes
the privatization of religion.   Religiosity is seen to vary
according to age, social status and on a regional basis.   The
ascendancy of cultic elements is noticed and its significance
is analyzed *en passant*.

0956   Mol, Hans.   *Religion in Australia: A Sociological Investigation.*
Sydney: Nelson, 1971.

This is a systematic study which draws upon the full range of
concerns and methods deployed by sociologists of religion in
other places.   With numerous statistical tables Australian
religiosity is related to key demographic variables.   Religious
beliefs are related to dispositions and behavior in the moral

fields and there are measures of the religious penetration of
education and the family.   Such a comprehensive work provides
useful and accessible data for comparative study.   See also
Black and Glasner (0909).

0957 Morioka, Kiyomi. "Contemporary Changes in Japanese Religion."
In *Sociology and Religion*, edited by Norman Birnbaum and Gertrude
Lenzer, pp.382-386. Englewood Cliffs: Prentice-Hall, 1969 (0009).

Shintoism and Buddhism appear highly fissiparous in Japan,
accounting for some 330 of its 402 religious groupings in 1962,
and 78 million and 65 million followers respectively.   That
together with Christians and others the number of religious
exceeds the total population of Japan by some 50 per cent casts
some doubt on the statistics, but also points to the peculiar
phenomenon of dual membership, which Morioka examines.   There
is also an early account of post-war offshoots of Buddhism which
in some cases - notably that of the Soka-gakkai - have gained
general notice since this paper was published.

0958 Mueller, Samuel A. and Lane, Angela V. "Tabulations from the
1957 Current Population Survey on Religion: A Contribution to the
Demography of American Religion." *Journal for the Scientific Study
of Religion* 11 (1972): 76-98.

This brings together previously unpublished data from the 1957
Current Population Survey and unifies statistical material on
demographic aspects of American religion.   Data are raw, but
enhanced by some updating from independent sources.

0959 Natts, Hilstan Lett. "Some Structural Problems of Urban
Religion: A Case Study from the City of Durban." *Social Compass*
19 (1972): 63-81.

The author studies the case of English-speaking churches in
the South African city of Durban.   Problems engaged include
the impact on church life and organization of urban development,
initiatives in ecumenical relations and economic factors
bearing upon church activity.

0960 O'Dea, Thomas F. *Sociology and the Study of Religion: Theory,
Research, Interpretation.* New York: Basic Books, 1970.

O'Dea does not attempt to give a comprehensive account of the
sociology of religion but selects areas for substantial
treatment; to that extent the title might be misleading and
the case studies included in this book have not received the
attention they warrant.   The first two sections are given to
studies of American Catholicism and Mormonism respectively.
The Puerto Ricans of New York provide the focus for a study
of social identity and there are examinations on the adequacy
of contemporary religious forms and of religious institutionalization.   The book is basically a sociological essay on
religion in contemporary America.

0961 Omark, Richard.   "The Decline of Russian Religious Power:
Church-State Relations, 1439-1503." *Social Compass* 21 (1974):
207-214.

This paper analyzes the beginning of the end of the Russian
Church in historical terms.   Until the fifteenth century it
enjoyed the privilege of the protection of Mongol authority,
the removal of which by the Grand Duke in Moscow greatly
weakened its political position.   Lands were confiscated and
the Church was subordinated.   It suffered further setbacks
in the eighteenth century.

0962 Ortic, Renato.   "Du Syncrétisme à la Synthèse." *Archives
de Sciences Sociales des Religions* 40 (1975): 89-97.

This is a case study of a Brazilian religion called Umbanda.
This case provides the opportunity to analyze features of
Afro-catholic syncretism and to pursue problems raised by
Roger Bastide in his work on South America.   See also
Willems (0217).

0963 Phillips, Paul T.   *The Sectarian Spirit: Sectarianism,
Society and Politics in Victorian Cotton Towns*.   Toronto: University
of Toronto Press, 1982.

The Victorian period was one of proliferation of religious sects
and the sociology of sect development is necessarily informed
by nineteenth century history.   The sects are essentially
though not exclusively a phenomenon of urbanization and
industrialization and the English cotton towns chosen for this
study were centers of the English Industrial Revolution in
Lancashire - Bolton, Blackburn, Preston and Stockport.
Phillips explores typical associations of political and
religious dissent in these places and observes secularism
alongside sectarianism in the economic context.

0964 Pickering, William S.F.   "The 1851 Religious Census: A
Useless Experiment?" *British Journal of Sociology* 18 (1967):
382-407.

The British religious census conducted on Sunday 30 March 1851
was an ambitious survey of religious attendance throughout
the country.   The returns are preserved and provide useful
data for nineteenth century historians.   But a census on this
scale has never been repeated and it has been suggested that
it was a waste of time.   The facts proven were few; original
objectives were not fulfilled.   However, Pickering suggests,
it was useful if only for demonstrating the complexity of
organization demanded by a survey of this kind, and for indicating regional variations in church attendance, which Pickering
presents in map form.

0965 Piwowarski, Wladyslaw.   "Continuity and Change of Ritual in
Polish Folk Piety." *Social Compass* 29 (1982): 125-134.

After an exploration of the sociocultural context of its subject,
this article offers an analysis of types of religious rituals in
contemporary Poland, including those associated with life-cycles,
the Church's seasons, localities, the home and socio-professional
variables.   Changes in these social situations relate to
changes in respective rituals.   See also Marianski (0950).

0966   Poeisz, Josef J.   "Gruppenisolierung, Kirchlichkeit und
Religiostät: Das niederländische Beispiel."   *Internationales
Jahrbuch für Religionssoziologie*   1 (1965): 113-148.

The author assembles useful empirical data on religiosity in the
Netherlands and is particularly interested in that of the Dutch
Roman Catholics whose group-centrism is found to be more
exaggerated than that of Roman Catholics in other countries.

0967   Pope, Liston.   *Millhands and Preachers: A Study of Gastonia.*
New Haven: Yale University Press, 1942.

A study of the relationship of the churches to the economic
life of Gaston County, North Carolina.   Pope has a special
interest in the roles of the churches and the cotton mills in
each others' development in the late nineteenth and early
twentieth centuries.   This now classic work was undertaken in
a context of industrial action in the late 1920s including the
conviction of communists and their escape to Russia.

0968   Pothen, K.P.   "La Situation Socio-économique des Chrétiens
de Malwa (MP), Inde."   *Social Compass*   18 (1971): 561-574.

The field of inquiry includes the Christian foundations of
nineteenth century India and the work is conducted by interview
and observation of some one hundred families.   Results are
interpreted by statistical analysis.   It was clear that in
the decade preceding the study the influence of Christian
institutions had declined but their future looked secure on
the basis of increasing numbers of members.   In the area under
study Christianity was essentially an urban phenomenon while
in the traditional rural areas the caste-system was stable
and unaffected by conversion to the Christian faith.   The
Church was formerly the principal employer and provider of
education and other services but since Independence its social
role has been variously usurped.

0969   Reinitz, Richard, ed.   *Tensions in American Puritanism.*
New York: Wiley, 1970.

Reinitz here collects a group of papers relating to the Puritan
inheritance of America in historical and sociological
perspective.   These variously concern social control, social
teachings, community maintenance, intellectual currents and
religious organization in Boston and New England.

0970   Remy, Paul and Rouleau, Jean Paul.   "Charismatiques et
Socio-politiques dans l'Église Catholique au Québec." *Social
Compass* 25 (1978): 125-143.

The authors characterize charismatic and socio-political
movements within the Roman Catholic Church in Quebec, Canada.
They identify and explore a relationship between socioeconomic and political changes in Canada since 1960 and
simultaneous transformations of religious faith.   The
movements concerned are taken seriously by the Church which
has responded by attempting to reassert the functional role
of religion in Canadian society.

0971   Robertson, Roland and Campbell, Colin.   "Religion in
Britain: The Need for New Research Strategies." *Social Compass*
19 (1972): 185-197.

The authors complain that in the decade or so preceding their
study the sociology of British religion has been preoccupied
with official forms and only slowly have its students come
to look deeper than the forms on the surface.   They suggest
the need for the development of historical and phenomenal
studies of religious forms and detail four areas of empirical
work that would treat historical process and contribute to the
sociography and historiography of religion.

0972   Sharma, Ursula.   "Public Shrines and Private Interests:
The Symbolism of the Village Temple." *Sociological Bulletin* 23
(1974): 71-92.

The author is intrigued by the paradox that village shrines in
northern India are accorded great symbolic significance but are
little visited by the Hindu faithful - except perhaps the
families associated with their foundation.   She establishes
that these shrines have a symbolic meaning and express collective ideals that are independent of the clientele visiting them.

0973   Shlapentokh, Vladimir.   "The Study of Values as a Social
Phenomenon: The Soviet Case." *Social Forces* 61 (1982): 404-417.

Shlapentokh offers a study of the effect of political change in
the Soviet Union upon the research of values, especially
relating to the conduct of social work.

0974   Sicard, Émile.   "Amérique Latine: L'Église et le Développement
des Pays Latino-Américains, les Classes Sociales, Situation
Présente du Mexique." *Années Sociologique* 21 (1970): 313-332.

Sicard reviews an extensive range of recent literature on the
relation of the Church to the social and class system of Latin
America.   Authors featured include Oscar Delgado, Luis Olivos,
A.Martin Brugarola, L.Molina Pineiro and Ismodes Cairo.   Themes
treated range from the posture of the Roman Catholic Church in
Latin America on economic development to factors operating in
the Mexican Revolution.

0975 Sicking, Thom. *Religion et Développement: Étude Compareé de Deux Villages Libanais*. Beirut: Dar el-Machreq Sarl Éditeurs, 1985.

This comparative study treats of two villages of Bekaa, Lebanon. The one is Maronite and the other Shi'ite. Contrasting styles of development are related to the religious factor.

0976 Slack, Kenneth. *The British Churches Today*. London: S.C.M. Press, 1961.

This is not so much a densely documented and highly statistical survey but an assessment based on prolonged experience and perceptive observation. It is valuable as a handbook for the empirical sociologist as it gives a clear view of intellectual currents, social and religious tensions, the characteristics of constituent communities of the churches of particular ethnic origins and settlement in specified geographical areas. It counsels implicitly against generalization. The book treats in turn of the established Church of England, the Free Churches, the Roman Catholic Church, the Scottish Churches, the Irish Protestant Churches, the churches in Wales, the evangelicals and the ecumenical movement in contemporary Britain. Although the original "Today" was 1961, there was a full revision bringing the book up to date in 1970.

0977 Spilla, Pietrangelo. "La Condizione Giuridica della Religione nell'Unione Sovietica." *Sociologia* 9 (1975): 141-164.

Marxist-Leninist theory in various ways regards religion as redundant in socialist society and therefore anticipates its disappearance in the course of time. However, Soviet practice enshrined in Soviet law imposes certain sanctions and obstacles upon the practitioners of religious faith and these paradoxes are treated in this article. In particular the author views changes in the prohibition of "association" similar to the "combination laws" which operated in the past on English soil.

0978 Suk-Jay, Yim. "Introduction au Mouisme: La Religion Populaire Coréenne." *Social Compass* 25 (1978): 175-189.

The object of study is Mouism, the little known popular religion of Korea. The author is interested in the transmission of Mouism from one generation to another and its place in Korean society alongside Buddhism. The *moudang* which traditionally have been the bearers of Mouism have had their place in society dislocated by the abolition of the Confucian class system and the corresponding changes of religious life are discussed against a pattern of upward mobility.

0979 Tehranian, Majid. "Iran: Communication, Alienation, Revolution." *Intermedia*, March 1979: 6-12.

This is an authentically sociological analysis of the conditions of the Islamic revolution in Iran in 1979. Though not in as many words Tehranian operates a mass society theory and

documents the erosion of intermediate institutions such as the
village, tribe, guilds, voluntary associations, *khaneghah* and
zurkhaneh.   Meanwhile the cult of the State as the embodiment
of all that was good, true and beautiful plagued Iran no less
than other modernizing societies with totalitarian tendencies.

0980 *Television and Religion*. London: University of London Press,
1964.

A report prepared by Social Surveys (Gallup Poll) Ltd on behalf
of the British television company A.B.C., a major broadcaster
of religious programs.   The seventy-seven item questionnaire
used for the survey is reprinted as an appendix: seven hundred
interviews were completed in December 1963 and January 1964 in
each of three broadcasting zones - London, the Midlands and
the North.   Some 413 interviewers were engaged on the survey.
Results are meticulously reported as statistical data covering
a wide range of areas and rendering the survey a classical
source of information on English religious life.   Themes and
problems include the denominational composition of the
population, religious participation, churchgoing, attitudes
by generations, religious beliefs, attitudes to the churches
and to churchgoing, the role and image of the clergy, religion,
sex, birth control and the tolerance of prostitutes, whom
Anglicans were less inclined to condemn than Catholics or
Nonconformists.   There is some market research on religious
broadcasting in general and on the program "Sunday Break" in
particular.

0981 Thapar, Romila. "Asoka and Buddhism." *Past and Present* 18
(1960): 43-51.

The cult of the emperor Asoka is reported as a burgeoning
religious movement in contemporary India.   Asokan symbols are
reported to have been adopted by the Indian government and
much modern political thinking in India is related to Asokan
ideas.   The author endeavors to study separately the man Asoka
and the statesman and to clarify the themes of his imperium that
account for his continuing popularity in the twentieth century.

0982 Tomka, Miklós. "A Balance of Secularization in Hungary."
Social Compass 28 (1981): 25 - 42.

An examination of formal and marginal dimensions of religiosity
in Hungary and of the decline of Church hegemony.   The author
notes changes in denominational structures and compares rural
and urban forms of religiousness.   His conclusion is offered
as a typology in which he identifies modes alongside traditional
religious and non-religious types and notes a proliferation of
variants.

0983 Tomka, Miklós. "Le Rôle des Églises Instituées de Hongrie
dans une Contexte de Changement." *Social Compass* 23 (1981):
93-111.

Hungary presents the case of a country in which the State and popular churches have been displaced and succeeded by a secular ideological system.   Tomka identifies and characterizes three phases: the first half of the twentieth century is typified as State-Church, the period from 1945 to 1950 is a transitional one, and the subsequent period is that of stabilized socialism.

0984 Tönnes, Bernhard.   "Religionen in Albanien: Enver Hoxha und die 'Nationale Eigenart'."   *Ost-europa*   24 (1974): 661-675.

This is a general study of religions in Albania under the Hoxha regime and religious restraint practised as part of a program for "national character".   The main religious groups in Albania are - or "were", as the case may be - Moslem, Catholic and Orthodox.   But any religious presence is perceived as threatening an all-important national political unity and its representatives are persecuted and discredited.   See also Martin (0036).

0985 Tzamimis, Anastase.   "La Sociologie de la Religion en Grèce."   *Social Compass*   22 (1975): 7-17.

Far from being an account of the development of sociology of religion in Greece, this article is an attempt to explain its underdevelopment.   Prominent though religion has been in Greek life, it has not engaged the attention of sociologists who have tended to pursue other specialisms.   What support it has received has largely come from the Church which wanted to use sociology in its opposition to burgeoning anti-Christian ideological movements.

0986 Vrcan, Srdjan.   "Changing Functions of Religion in a Socialist Society: The Case of Catholicism in Yugoslavia."   *Social Compass*   28 (1981): 43-61.

Four periods are surveyed, the last of which begins with the early 1970s.   During this time socialism in Yugoslavia has been challenged by serious problems of its own while Catholicism has undergone changes from within at the global level.

0987 Wiebe, Paul D. and John-Peter, S.   "The Catholic Church and Caste in Rural Tamil Nadu."   *Eastern Anthropologist*   25 (1972): 12.

Wiebe and John-Peter deploy a variety of empirical methods and data searches to investigate in Tamil India the tendency for recruitment to the Christian churches to follow the lines of caste and sub-caste that obtain in the organization of Hindu culture.   What has been elsewhere demonstrated in respect of the recruitment of Protestant missions   (Wiebe, 0770) Wiebe finds also to be true among Roman Catholics.

0988 Woodrum, Eric.   "Towards a Theory of Tension in American Protestantism."   *Sociological Analysis*   39 (1978): 219-227.

The tension between lay and professional domains of power in
American protestantism is explored and theorized in overall
confirmation of the thesis of Max Weber.   Woodrum points to
professional prerogatives in the control of informal power
and the relative independence of the laity from ecclesiastical
organization.   These are principal factors effecting the
resolution of lay-professional conflicts.

0989 Wright, Frank.   "Protestant Ideology and Politics in Ulster."
Archives Européennes de Sociologie 14 (1973): 213-280.

A study of the factors complicating a development of cooperation between Ulster Catholics and Protestants, the latter
fearing incorporation in a Catholic state and legitimizing their
resistance in ideological terms.   There is an alignment of
religious beliefs and political ideologies in the significance
of Irish history: the "Orange" and "loyalist" movement
coincides with Protestant fundamentalism in the religious sphere.
See also the work of Christopher Hewitt (0932-0933).

0990 Yanagawa, Keiichi, and Abe, Yoshiya.   "Cross-cultural
Implications of a Behavioral Response." *Actes de C.I.S.R.*   17
(1983): 299-324.

This paper is an exploration of the religious situation in
Japan with particular reference to the question of secularization, a comparative perspective being provided by reference to
secularization in western societies in which the available
sociological models have evolved.   The Japanese context is
marked by an emphasis upon the dimension of immanence as
opposed to that of transcendence and upon community as the
context of religious practice.

W.   IRRELIGION

0991 Bowes, Alison M.   "Atheism in a Religious Society: The
Culture of Unbelief in an Israeli Kibbutz." *Religious Organization
and Religious Experience,* edited by J.Davis, pp.33-49.   London:
Academic Press, 1982 (0013).

Some kibbutzim are religious, even orthodox, while others
adhere to an atheist ideology.   The author here studies the
historical background of unbelief in the kibbutz federation
Artzi Hashomer Hatzair and atheistic rituals in the regulation
of everyday life, collective and national festivals, *rites de
passage* and ceremonials.   Religious-based models pervade
Jewish unbelief, either because they must be consciously ignored
or else because they are adapted for atheistic purposes.

0992 Campbell, Colin.   *Toward a Sociology of Irreligion.*   London:
Macmillan, 1971.

This is a serious study of the rejection of religion in Britain
and America during the nineteenth and twentieth centuries.
The cases examined include the secularist movements, the ethical
movements, organized positivism, free religion and the
Rationalist Press Association.   The book offers an analysis
of the sources and functions of the irreligious response and
its implications for morality and politics.   The perspective
of a nascent sociology of irreligion is used to challenge
assumptions within the sociology of religion proper.   See also
Campbell (O993).

O993 Campbell, Colin. "Analysing the Rejection of Religion."
Social Compass 24 (1977): 339-346.

While the rejection of religion has important intellectual,
ideological and rationalist dimensions, a comprehensive account
must also heed the social and structuralist context within
which religious beliefs are rejected and that rejection becomes
itself organized and institutionalized.   Campbell distinguishes
reactive irreligion which has Roman Catholicism as its reference
and developmental irreligion which belongs to the era of post-
Reformation Protestantism.   See also Campbell (O992).

O994 Klohr, Olof. "Tendencii Otmirania Religii i Cerkvi v GDR."
Voprosy Filosofii 28 (1974): 147-156.

This is a study of religious activity in the German Democratic
Republic which is intended to demonstrate and confirm the
marxist expectation that after the advent of socialism the
churches will wither away.   Data are presented to show the
escalation of unbelief since 1945: if current trends continue
religious beliefs will disappear within two decades but it is
expected that the decline of religion will be offset by a
stabilization of religious groups.   Religious change in East
Germany differs from secularization in West Germany in quality
as well as in degree and it is supposed that the political and
social formation constitutes the relevant variable.

O995 Ladrière, Paul. "L'Atheisme à Vatican II: De la
Condemnation du Communisme à la Négociation avec l'Humanisme Athée."
Social Compass 24 (1977): 347-391.

This article notes and analyzes a shift of position toward
atheism manifested in the Vatican II document *Gaudium et Spes*.
The change is from politics to anthropology, from outright
condemnation to moderate negotiation.   But anti-communism and
the persistent centrism of the Church survive the change of
stance.

O996 Simon, Gerhard. "The Catholic Church and the Communist
State in the Soviet Union and Eastern Europe." *Religion and
Atheism in the USSR and Eastern Europe*, edited by B.R.Bociurkiward and
J.W.Strong, pp.190-221. London: Macmillan, 1975.

The Soviet Union is an official sponsor of atheism, and religion in any form is officially regarded as otiose in the socialist society.   While the tolerance of certain religious rights is expedient for international approval, legislation favors atheism and makes religious practice subject to sanctions. Christians in a militantly atheistic state face the dilemma of collaboration or martyrdom; but Simon suggests that both of these strategies have the potential of disaster and he advises adoption of a *via media*.   See also the work of Moskalev (O151) and Simon's article in *Ost-europa* (O159).

X.   MISCELLANEOUS

0997   Agassi, Joseph and Jarvie, I.C.   "Magic and Rationality Again."   *British Journal of Sociology*   24 (1973): 236-245.

This is a contribution to a debate on rationality and ritual arising from the work of Beattie.   The authors offer a clarification of terms by distinguishing between rational action, rational thought and thought deemed to be rational. The paper instances the interplay of sociology and philosophy that is often useful in the cause of conceptual clarification.

0998 Beckford, James A. "Religious Organization." *Current Sociology*   21 (1973): 7-166.

Beckford evaluates and subsequently commends the open-systems perspective in the study of religious organizations.   In his finding it gives clarity to the analysis of church, denomination and sect and affords the examination of processes such as recruitment, induction and control.

0999 Berger, Peter L. *The Precarious Vision*. New York: Doubleday, 1961.

A sociologist looks at social factions and Christian faith, in this case with the author's characteristic transcendance of the literature; for Berger is never slavish.   Here he looks at the role of religion in social disaffection and faction. "The Christian faith," he explains, "relates to men stripped of their social roots."

1000 Bourque, Linda Bookover and Back, Kurt W. "Values and Transcendental Experiences." *Social Forces* 47 (1968): 34-38.

The authors investigate two types of ecstatic - transcend- ental experience, the one being essentially aesthetic and the other primarily religious.   They inquire into how common are such experiences, their possible association with certain social and personality variables and the contexts in which they are enjoyed.

1001   Deconchy, Jean-Pierre. *L'Orthodoxie Religieuse: Essai de Logique Psycho-Sociale*. Paris: Éditions Ouvrières, 1971.

   Deconchy provides a meticulous quantitative and analytical study of religious discourse and records and analyzes its vocabulary and its apparent impoverishment. The work is full of statistical data and discourse analysis is used to find indicators of religious conformity. See also Deconchy (0699).

1002   Desroche, Henri. *Sociologie de l'Espérance*. Paris. Calmann-Levy, 1973.

   In sociological perspective, hope is seen as a mirage attracting travellers who never reach it. The travellers studied by Desroche include various Jewish, Moslem and Christian millenarian groups as well as the Fifth Monarchy Men, Mormons, Doukhobors and "Black Messiah" movements in the Third World. Published in English as *The Sociology of Hope*. London: Routledge & Kegan Paul, 1979.

1003   Desroche, Henri. "Socialisme et Sociologie de Christianisme." *Cahiers Internationaux de Sociologie* 21 (1951): 149-167.

   Desroche picks up Wach's concern with the antagonism between the polemic and the apologetic status which might have affected the sociology of religion. While intellectual orientations of students will barely affect interpretations of some reality remote from any of them, these are likely to be intrusive when their subjects are nearer home. This antagonism is explored in respect of socialism and its openness to classification as religious genealogy and of theology and secularization. Appears in English in Birnbaum and Lenzer (0009): 215-225.

1004   Flanagan, Kieran. "The Experience of Innocence as a Social Construction." *Philosophical Studies* 28 (1981): 104-139.

   It is suggested that the great moral paradox of innocence is that the individual distinguished by it lacks the experience that might fortify him. The author discusses four childhood roles in which there are variable social conditions for the identification of innocence. Innocence is realized in a public ritual in which there is a collusion of both actor and audience.

1005   Guizzardi, Gustavo and Page, Enzo. "Religion, Charisma and the Mass-media." *Actes de C.I.S.R.* 17 (1983): 273-283.

   This paper addresses the problem of the possibility of a crisis in religion and approaches a theoretical inquiry not from the starting point of the religious context but from that of development and change in the social system.

1006   Lang, Bernhard, ed. *Anthropological Approaches to the Old Testament*. London: S.P.C.K., 1985.

Social anthropologists study small pre-industrial societies in order to discover how the many aspects of their life form a coherent set of symbols that shape and give expression to their understanding of life.   For the past two centuries, Old Testament scholars have applied insights gained from the study of such societies to the Old Testament, but it is only in the last two decades that they have begun to familiarize themselves with recent developments in social anthropology.   At the same time, social anthropologists have shown interest in the Old Testament as a subject for anthropological investigation, and there has been a developing dialogue between the two disciplines. Bernhard Lang sketches the history of the application of anthropology to the Old Testament.   Essays, by Steiner, Schapera, Rogerson, Overholt, Douglas, Carroll, Leach and Davies, cover the issues of kinship, mythology, Hebrew mentality, sacrifice, prophecy, slavery and exploitation.   See also Richter (1009).

1007 O'Dea, Thomas F.   "Five Dilemmas in the Institutionalization of Religion."   *Social Compass* 7 (1960): 61-67.

O'Dea derives from Durkheim the paradox that institutionalization makes the holy somewhat ordinary: and he adumbrates five dilemmas arising from this - of mixed motivation, of object-ification versus alienation, of elaboration versus effectiveness, of concrete definition versus the substitution of letter for spirit and of conversion versus coercion.

1008 Pettersson, Thorleif.   *The Retention of Religious Experiences*. Uppsala University, 1975.

A scientific investigation of religious experiences as recalled by subjects based around hypotheses derived from Festinger's theory of cognitive dissonance.   The method used is based upon Charles E.Osgood's semantic differential technique and Pettersson thoroughly explores issues of methodology. Conclusions are tentative and highly specific and relate to variations between reports of subjects two days and one week respectively after religious experiences.

1009 Richter, Philip J.   "Recent Sociological Approaches to the Study of the New Testament." *Religion* 14 (1984): 77-90.

The apprehension of the world and religion of the New Testament as a social reality has burgeoned in the last decade.   Such interests have long occupied scholars but in retrospect their work has had its limitations such as sociological naïveté. Richter notices a new seriousness in this survey of recent work.   See also Lang (1006).

1010 Robertson, Roland.   "Religious Movements and Modern Societies: Towards a Progressive Problemshift." *Sociological Analysis* 40 (1979): 297-314.

After Weber and Troeltsch, Robertson is interested in the fundamental distinction of sacred and secular and in the evolution of this distinction in modern societies, particularly that of the United States. His contribution is to the theoretical framework within which religious movements are studied.

1011 Stoudenmire, John. "On the Relationship between Religious Belief and Emotion." *Journal for the Scientific Study of Religion* 10 (1971): 254.

Sixty-four college students with stable patterns of religious belief were wired up to indicate galvanic skin response as a standard measure of emotional change. The questionnaire included a collection of religious statements to which they signified agreement or disagreement. The more powerful disturbances at the emotional level were engendered by statements to which subjects signified strong disagreements.

1012 Tranvouez, Yvon. "La Fondation et les Débuts de *La Vie Intellectuelle* (1928-1929)." *Archives de Sciences Sociales des Religions* 42 (1976): 57-96.

La Vie Intellectuelle was a Catholic journal founded in 1928 by one Father Bernardot. Its sociological significance resides in the role it is reckoned to have played in disposing the Church to a more accepting position vis-à-vis the world. The analysis of Tranvouez includes an examination of the journal's editorial line which is said here to be a reformist one within the capitalist system.

1013 Watt, William Montgomery. *Truth in the Religions: A Sociological and Psychological Approach*. Edinburgh: Edinburgh University Press, 1963.

Beliefs, doctrines and religious practices such as worship are here assessed in their social and historical contexts and as functions of material conditions. So interpreted, the relations between religions are difficult to foster without a corresponding convergence of the societies they serve.

Author Index

This index includes the names of authors discussed in the introductory chapter and those whose works are cited in the bibliographical survey. References to the former are by page number; references to the latter are by entry number and comprise four digits. Where there are references of both kinds, the two are separated by a semi-colon.

Subject Index

Numbers of one or two digits preceding the semicolon refer to pages in the introductory chapter; four-digit numbers refer to annotations in the bibliography.

Title Index

In this index, all annotated items are listed in a single alphabetical sequence. Titles commencing with the definite or indefinite article, in whatever language, are arranged by the second word of the title, except for those beginning with *some/quelques*. Sub-titles are not included, except in order to distinguish works with common titles; for the same purpose, some authors' names are added in parentheses. Numbers of one or two digits refer to pages in the introductory chapter; numbers of four digits are references to entries in the annotated bibliography.

"Abortion Attitudes among Catholic University Students", 0489
"Abraham Hume (1818-1884)", 0079
"Academic Discipline and Faculty Religiosity in Secular and Church-related Colleges", 0300
"Acculturation of Mexican Americans in Public and Parochial Schools", 0596
Actes de Conférence Internationale de Sociologie des Religions, 0091
Act Now, 0583
"Administrative Structures and Political Processes in Protestant Denominations", 0534
"Aetherius Society", 0451
"African Religious Movements - Types and Dynamics", 0309
"After the Alliance", 0047
"Age Differences and Dimensions of Religious Behavior", 0296
"Ages of Faith", 0652
All Faithful People, 0914
"Alliance for Progress", 0046
"Altérité et Identité Vues par le Psycho-sociologue", 0605
"Alternative to Church-Sect", 0316
"Altruism in the Professions", 0688
American Civil Religion: An Assessment, 0885
"American Civil Religion: An Empirical Study", 0900
"American Jewish Denominations", 0499
"American Jewry: Some Social Trends", 0571
"Amérique Latine: L'Église et le Développement des Pays Latino-Américains, les Classes Sociales, Situation Présente du Mexique", 0974
"Amish Agriculture", 0442
Amish Society (Hostetler), 0391
"Amour, Sexualité et Religion", 0242

"Organization and Functioning of the Children of God", 0370
"Organization, Ideology and Recruitment", 0358
"Organization Set and Resources as Determinants of Formalization in Religious Organization", 0471
"Organization Structure of Churches", 0491
"Organizational Aspects of a Jesus Movement Community", 0437
"Organizational Status Attainment of Religious Professionals", 0740
"Organizational Stress and Adaptation to Changing Political Status", 0153
"Organizational Success through Program Failure", 0746
"Orientations, Les Méthodes et la Problématique dans la Sociologie de la Religion en Pologne", 0042
"Orthodox Church and the Charismatic Movement", 0539
"Orthodoxie Enseignée par Renforcement du Réglage de l'Appartenance", 0699
Orthodoxie Religieuse: Essai de Logique Psycho-Sociale, 1001
"Orthodoxy and Economy", 0518
"Other Minorities: Old Order Amish and Hutterites", 0564
Outline of Christian Sociology, 0876
"Ouvriers et l'Église Catholique", 0200
"Participation of Italian Communists in Catholic Rituals", 0802
"Participation, Reform and Ecumenism", 0851
Pattern of Rural Dissent in the Nineteenth Century, 0922
"Patterns of Belief at the Denominational and Congregational Levels", 0478
"Patterns of Catholic Politics", 0175
"Patterns of Occupational Recruitment", 0696
Patterns of Sectarianism, 0344
"Paul Report Examined", 0772
"Paul VI et la Paix", 0468
Peculiar People, 0439
"Pèlerinages et Processions comme Formes de Pouvoir Symbolique des Classes Subalternes", 0907
"Pendulum Swing Theory of Islam", 0120
"Pentecostal Glossolalia", 0383
Pentecostal Movement (Bloch-Hoell), 0322
"Pentecostalist Minister: Role Conflicts and Contradictions of Status", 0771
"Pentecôtisme et Société au Brésil", 0430
People Called Shakers", 0349
"People's Temple and Jonestown", 0422
"Perception et Interprétation Subjective des Causes de la Divison Religieuse", 0538
"Perceptions of Needs of the Aged by Ministers and the Elderly", 0722
Persistence of Religion, 0653
"Persistence of Tradition: Orthodoxy in America", 0613
"Pessimistic Sect's Influence on the Mental Health of its Members", 0412
"Piatdesiat Let Nauchnogo Issledovaniia Religioznogo Sektantstva", 0400
"Plymouth Congregational Church of Louisville, Kentucky", 0549
"Poles: An Exile Community in Britain", 0612
"Polish Schism in the United States of America", 0637
Political Buddhism in Southeast Asia, 0162
"Political Effects of Village Methodism", 0150

"Thérapie et Changement Social dans les Églises Urbaines
d'Afrique du Sud", 0540
"The Three-generations Thesis and the American Jews", 0630
"Tipovi Religioznosti u Seoskim Nascijima Donjeg Pologa", 0299
"Tnevnoc Cult", 0367
To Comfort and to Challenge, 0792
"Toward a Christian Sociological Perspective", 0043
"Toward a Sociological Interpretation of the 'Catholic Pentecostal'
Movement", 0505
Toward a Sociology of Irreligion, 0992
"Toward a Structural Perspective of Modern Religious Movements",
0433
"Toward a Theory of Religious Organizations", 0006
"Toward Jewish Unity", 0854
"Towards a Theory of Tension in American Protestantism", 0988
"Towards Eliminating the Concept of Secularization", 0666
Tracts Against the Times, 0143
Traité de Sociologie du Protestantisme, 0037
"Traitements des Morts dans la Société Socialiste", 0657
"Transformations du Rituel Catholique des Mourants", 0838
"Trend Report of the State of the Sociology of Religion", 0018
"True Buddhism and Village Buddhism in Sri Lanka", 0897
Trumpet of Prophecy, 14; 0356
Truth in the Religions, 1013
"Two Contrasting Types of Sectarian Organization", 0359
"Two Worlds of Clergy and Congregation", 0738
"Typen van Religieus-Kerkelijke Binding", 0820
Types of Religious Experience, 0058
"Typologie des Sectes dans une Perspective Dynamique et
Comparative", 0319
"Typologie Sociologique de l'Ordre Religieux", 0311
Underground Church, 0419
"'Underground' Traditions in the Study of Sectarianism", 0332
"Unknown Apollo of Biskra", 0925
Urban Churches in Britain, 0913
Urban Impact on American Protestantism 1865-1800, 0683
"Urban Problems and Rural Solutions", 0265
"Uticaj Religioznih Seoskih Pozodica U Srbiji na Formiranje
Religioznith Uverenja kod Polomstva", 0775
"Value-Orientations of the Religious Poor", 0258
Values and Organizations, 0816
"Values and Transcendental Experiences", 1000
Values and Violence in Auschwitz, 0272
"Values, Interests and Organizational Change", 0531
"Varieties of the Abandonment of Religious Symbols", 0647
Victorian Clergy, 0715
Vie Juive dans l'Europe Contemporaine, 0555
"Vie Quotidienne, Éthique et Religion", 0256
"Vie Quotidienne, Production de Valeurs et Religion", 0274
"Vie Religieuse et Sécularisation", 0660
Violence and Religious Commitment, 0405
Vocation de la Sociologie Religieuse, 0694
Voice of the Voiceless, 0128
"Walls Within Walls", 0237
"War and Religion in Sociological Perspective", 0291
"Watchtower Movement World-wide", 0361